GEOFF DUKE

GEOFF DUKE

IN PURSUIT
OF PERFECTION

OSPREY

Published in 1988 by Osprey Publishing Limited
59 Grosvenor Street, London W1X 9DA

British Library Cataloguing in Publication Data

Duke, Geoff
    Geoff Duke: in pursuit of perfection.
    1. Racing motorcycles. Racing. Duke, Geoff
    I. Title
    796.7'5'0924
    ISBN 0-85045-838-2

Filmset by Tameside Filmsetting Limited,
Ashton-under-Lyne, Lancashire
Printed by Butler & Tanner Limited,
Frome, Somerset, Great Britain

My grateful thanks must go to the following people:
Charlie Rous, for his help in editing the manuscript;
Harry Johnson, for reminding me of some long-forgotten
episodes in my racing career; Stan Johnson, for providing
invaluable research material; Nick Nicholls and EMAP
Archives, for providing some of the more elusive
photographs; and last, but by no means least, my wife
Daisy, without whose encouragement at the times when
my enthusiasm waned this book would never have been
completed.

Front cover illustration *Riding at full speed at
Bandiana in Australia in 1955*

Back cover illustration (top) *On the winner's rostrum at
Monza in 1953—Commendatore Gilera beams with
pleasure, while I listen closely to chief designer Ing.
Columbo*

Back cover illustration (bottom) *Exiting Governor's
Bridge on my way to first place in the 1951 Junior TT*

CONTENTS

HOW IT ALL BEGAN

THE NORTON YEARS

FROM TWO TO FOUR, AND BACK TO TWO WHEELS

THE GILERA CONNECTION

ON MY OWN

HOW IT ALL BEGAN

A love is born

My interest in motorcycles was first triggered early one Sunday morning back in 1933, when I caught a whiff of that now-rare aroma of Castrol R. I was ten years old and lying in my bed at 60 Duke Street, St Helens, Lancashire, when I heard the steady thump of open exhausts outside, bringing the delicious smell of 'R' in through the open window. The machines were the road bikes of two local enthusiasts; one was a camshaft Velocette and the other a Blackburne-engined Cotton. Little did I imagine then the exciting future in motor sport that lay ahead for me.

During that same year, my brother Eric, almost nine years my senior, purchased his first motorcycle—a new, unit-construction 250 cc New Imperial—for the sum of 33 guineas (£34.65), and thus began my own lifelong love affair with motorcycles.

Visits to Wallasey and Ainsdale for the sand racing and to Parbold for path racing on the pillion seat of Eric's 'New Imp' had me enthralled. Until one day, on the way home from school, I passed a group of people gathered around a crashed motorcycle and its rider who was lying on the pavement. Not having a macabre curiosity, I continued home, little realizing that the injured person was my brother. He had been hit side-on by a Humber car, sustaining 22 fractures to his right foot and ankle.

The surgeon at the hospital requested our parents' permission to amputate Eric's foot. They refused, though, and fortunately so, for the surgeon set about rebuilding the shattered limb, doing a superb job. Even so, it was a very worrying time, for the leg had to overcome gangrene where a spindle, on to which weights were suspended to prevent the leg shortening, had been passed through the ankle.

Needless to say, after that episode the mere mention of motorcycles in the Duke household was forbidden. It was certainly sad for Eric who, until the accident, had been planning to buy a Grand Prix New Imperial to have a crack at road racing. Instead, he turned his attention towards four wheels.

It was around this time, too, that a visit with two friends to a local garage revealed a number of old motorcycles. These had amassed over several years and were machines which had been brought in for repairs, but never collected by the owners.

One of these, lying beneath a heap of worn-out tyres, was a 1923 belt-drive Raleigh. We asked if it was for sale and the answer was yes—we could have it for the sum of 10s. (50p). So, off we went to count our collective savings, returning the next day to buy the machine and wheel it home.

It could not be taken to Duke Street. However, my two friends, Alec and Tom Merrick, the sons of a local doctor, lived not far from my home in a big house with fairly extensive grounds. A detour was necessary to avoid passing 60 Duke Street—in case my mother or father should spot us—but we eventually arrived at the back gate of my friends' home with the silent Raleigh. Once inside, it was safely hidden in one of the garden buildings.

At that stage, neither my parents nor the Merrick family knew of our purchase—but they were presented with a *fait accompli* when the news did eventually become known. Reluctantly, they accepted the situation and permitted us to keep the machine. This was because our original intention had been to use the Raleigh engine to power a four-wheeled device, before discovering that such a project was beyond the range of our schoolboy enthusiasm and capabilities.

So, with the assistance of the doctor's chauffeur, the engine was stripped, cleaned and reassembled. One problem was the absence of a throttle cable, and since a proper replacement was out of reach of our already overstretched financial resources, an alternative method of opening and closing the throttle had to be found.

The absence of a spring supporting the right side of the seat gave me the idea of attaching a piece of string to the underside of the seat, directly above the carburettor. The string was passed through the adjusters and down to the throttle valve, where it was tied with a knot. Throttle control was operated by the rider rising up from the saddle. With the missing spring, the seat went down as you sat on it—and closed the throttle. By standing up, the seat rose, lifted the string and opened the throttle! In addition, there was another problem—the clutch was inoperative, which added to our riding difficulties.

The piece of ground where we intended to ride the machine sloped down away from our 'garage'. There was a wall and a trellis fence on either side, while at the foot of the slope was the garage for the doctor's car.

The procedure was for the rider to paddle the Raleigh down the slope in first gear, using the exhaust valve lifter to release the compression. On arriving at the turning point at the foot of the slope, the valve lifter was released and the rider then stood up on the footrests, allowing the throttle to 'open' and fire the engine. Then, having climbed the slope, the Sturmey Archer-type gearchange was knocked into neutral and the machine coasted back down the slope with the engine still running. It would then be knocked back into first gear to repeat the process.

All of this required an element of fine timing, and as the only 'experienced' motorcyclist (albeit from passengering on brother Eric's pillion), I was given the first 'go'. Much to our delight, after a couple of stalled starts, I was soon circulating with regularity, as did Alec and Tom when they tried.

This wonderful fun continued for some time without mishap, until one day, while practising alone, I inadvertently knocked the gear lever through neutral and into second gear as I arrived at the top of the slope. This caused the machine to leap ahead at great velocity (or so it seemed at the time), but I managed to steer it towards the open gate in the trellis fence. The engine stalled on reaching the lawn on the other side and, apparently unhurt, I was relieved to see no damage had been done. What I could not understand, though, was that the Raleigh's handlebars were wider than the gateway—and yet I had got through! How I managed to do that still remains a mystery. . . .

However, a short time later, I became aware of throbbing in the little finger of my right hand. On looking at it, I saw that the fingernail was hanging by only a thread of flesh, while blood was pouring from the wound. I dropped the Raleigh where it was and rushed to the house, where Mrs Merrick gave me first aid; she detached the nail and bathed and bandaged my finger. Realizing that I dared not put the cause of my injury down to a motorcycle accident, I went home to tell my mother that I had fallen off my 'push-bike'.

As it happened, the accident turned out to be a blessing in disguise. Because our garage circuit was considered to be too dangerous, we were exiled to a farm at Garswood where Farmer Hamilton, who supplied eggs and milk to

As a three-year-old, little thought was given to a possible career in motorcycle racing!

the Merrick household, promised to keep a wary eye on us. Even the five-mile push to the farm failed to dampen our enthusiasm for the old Raleigh, and in any event, when we arrived at Carr Mill Dam, we were able to start the engine and ride along a track for the rest of the way.

Alec, Tom and I spent many enjoyable Saturdays riding our Raleigh up and down the half-mile track which connected the farm with the East Lancashire Road. However, as time went on, and in our search for more speed, we again visited our friendly motorcycle dealer in St Helens and bought a 1928 500 cc side-valve Triumph with chain drive and in running order. Its price was 15s. (75p)!

The advent of this much more powerful machine inevitably introduced a keener competitive atmosphere to our racing scene, and we were soon timing each other over a one-mile, there-and-back course with an old alarm clock! This track was rutted and bumpy like a scrambles course. From the farm it went downhill for about 300 yards and then levelled off before a tight S-bend; it then continued along a straight until reaching the end. Here we would turn, using the adjoining field, before returning to the farm. My record of 95 seconds for the two-way run still stands!

A Dunelt two-stroke with a stepped piston (which frequently seized) and a 750 cc V-twin BSA with sidecar completed our line-up of machines during those early years at the farm. However, the news finally reached my parents that I was riding motorcycles at Hamilton's Farm. They were not happy about it, but, presumably because I had not been hurt, decided to do no more than plead with me to be 'very careful'.

Far more worrying was the fact that my father was troubled with arthritis of the spine, which meant a spell in hospital and forced him to give up his bakery and confectionery business. Then, on doctor's advice, we moved to Blackpool in 1936, subsequently returning to Eccleston, on the outskirts of St Helens, three years later.

The following year, in 1940, I joined the engineering department of the Post Office as a trainee in the automatic telephone exchange at Prescot. This needed transportation to get to and home from work, and when I asked my parents for permission to buy a motorcycle, they agreed, but said: 'Don't expect any financial help for it from us!' They were not being unkind to me; they were convinced that this was the only way to spike my guns. But when my determination, cutting out all spending for pleasure, resulted in producing enough cash to buy, repair, tax and insure a rather decrepit 175 cc Dot, they accepted the situation without further objection.

Army days

It was during my spell at the Prescot telephone exchange that I received my first lesson in the importance of machine preparation and the need for concentration. My Dot machine's rear tyre was totally devoid of tread which, at that time, did not bother me too much—in any case, I could not afford a replacement. However, this would prove to be my undoing.

The approach to the telephone exchange was downhill and I quite enjoyed my rapid left turn into the entrance—especially if anybody was watching! On the morning in question, though, full of the joys of spring—but unaware that overnight work on a drain had deposited a fine coating of sand on the road—I banked over the Dot at the usual angle, only to be dumped unceremoniously in the road, while my precious machine slid on for another 50 yards or so. Embarrassed, but unhurt, I picked myself up and sheepishly looked around for anybody who had seen my downfall. To my relief, nobody was in sight, and fortunately my machine had suffered only a bent footrest. It was a salutary lesson, however.

During 1941, I was transferred to the automatic exchange at St Helens, where I met twin brothers Alan and Don Whitfield, the proud owners of a Manx Norton on which I was occasionally allowed to occupy the rear portion of the racing seat. (Alan was a superb rider and after the war he entered the 1947 Manx Grand Prix—unfortunately he took a spill at Creg-ny-Baa during practice and never actually raced.)

Despite the war, motorcycling occupied most of my thoughts and *all* of my spare cash. So when the opportunity arose to buy a 1934 250 cc Grand Prix New Imperial for just £34, I eagerly accepted the offer of a loan from a friend of my brother, as even this sum was beyond my limited means. The purchase made, the 'New Imp'—which, incidentally, is now an exhibit in the National Motorcycle Museum in Birmingham—was then pushed five miles to Eccleston, where it was totally stripped and rebuilt over a period of months.

Eventually taxed and insured, I set off on my pride and joy in the direction of Ormskirk, enjoying every moment of the ride on the narrow, twisty country roads. The approach to Ormskirk was straight and slightly downhill,

so I was down on the petrol tank and running flat out. I suppose I reached about 90 mph before sitting up and closing the twist-grip . . . but the bike kept on going at undiminished speed! Adding to the situation, there was a T-junction within about 400 yards, preceded by a statue in the centre of the road, followed by a shop with an enormous plate-glass window!

Thinking fast, I snatched at the spark-plug lead, which fortunately parted from the plug terminal and cut the engine, thus enabling me to stop the machine safely. The engine was fitted with a horizontally-mounted carburettor, and I discovered that the ring nut which retained the throttle slide within the carburettor body had come undone, allowing the slide to come almost right out and create a wide-open throttle situation. After that little incident, I always remembered to lock the ring nut with adhesive tape.

It was now 1942, and a total lack of petrol ended my motorcycling. I was also 19 years old, and although liable for military service, my Post Office job, which I really did not enjoy, was classed as a reserved occupation. However, the magazine *Motor Cycling*, through its editor Graham Walker (Murray Walker's father), ran a scheme for voluntary enrolment of dispatch riders into the Royal Corps of Signals, and so I applied.

My application was rejected, though, and I was advised that my only alternative would be to enrol as an instrument mechanic, in the hope of transferring to the motorcycle section. This I did, and after six weeks' preliminary training, I was posted to Catterick where, at the first opportunity, I requested an interview with the Training Officer, who was most amenable. After listening to my plea for a transfer, he expressed his surprise at my wish to become a dispatch rider—considered a very low form of life in the Signals and with a high mortality rate. I finally convinced him that I would not be put off and he then gave me the broadest of hints—if, by chance, I failed to pass my mechanics course, I would probably be demoted to DR. . . .

It worked like a charm, and I was soon one of a squad of 20 riders under the wing of one Sgt. 'Nobby' Clark, and we got on like a house on fire. He was a fine rider, and although one of the few regular army instructors in the unit, he bore no resentment towards the 'civilians' who were gradually taking over as instructors from the regulars.

I passed my course with 96 per cent, and before going off on leave, Sgt. Clark informed me that he had recommended me to be retained as an instructor on my return. Needless to say, I was delighted, but imagine my disappointment when, on returning for duty, I was ordered to report not to Sgt. Clark, but to Sgt. B. H. M. Viney. My disappointment, though, soon disappeared. Sgt. Hugh Viney was the most outstanding rider in the unit. He was a brilliant trials rider and set the standard which I attempted to attain through his example, but never quite did. Nevertheless, for $2\frac{1}{2}$ years, I modelled myself on him—his machine preparation and riding

technique. This experience was to stand me in good stead in later trials riding, and even during my subsequent road-racing career.

To illustrate Viney's brilliance, once every month there was an instructors' trial held on Gandale Moor, close to the camp. The object of this exercise was twofold: to keep the instructors up to scratch, while also demonstrating to the trainees, who acted as marshals and observers, 'just how it should be done'. Whoever won the trial then organized the next one—which meant that Sgt. Viney and Sgt. Bainbridge, a very close rival, invariably arranged alternate trials.

Receiving a 'short back and sides' in the Royal Signals display team

The training officers were also obliged to compete. On one occasion when overnight rain had made conditions particularly tricky, one of the officers arrived at the foot of a difficult hill; after several unsuccessful attempts to reach the 'section begins' card, he gave up the struggle, declaring the section to be 'bloody impossible!' in a loud voice. Organizing on this occasion, Sgt. Viney stood his immaculately-prepared M20 BSA on its stand, ran down the hill and went to a trainee's 16H Norton which had been abandoned as unrideable in the mud where it was stuck. Viney kickstarted the machine and rode up the 'impossible section', feet up. He turned at the top, came back down again and returned the Norton to its place in the mud. Viney then walked back up the hill, restarted his BSA and rode off. Not a word was spoken. This particular trial was won by Sgt. Bainbridge, the only competitor to 'clean' the 'impossible hill'.

Stationed also at Catterick at this time were Charles Markham, a journalist and talented cartoonist, and Harry Johnson, who was to become my lifelong friend and mechanic, looking after my post-war racing machines at most events other than the Grands Prix.

Towards the end of his army service, Sgt. Viney went to a very special unit at Keswick for an instructors' refresher course. There, top-flight pre-war professional competition riders such as Charlie Rogers (Royal Enfield), Bob Ray (Ariel) and Freddie Frith (Norton) were acting as civilian instructors under the guidance of Dick Wilkins, later to be Bob Foster's entrant in the Grands Prix. Dick Wilkins had a Manx Norton at the camp on which Freddie Frith gave the 'students' demonstrations on the narrow, twisty lakeside road—until the powers-that-be got wind of it and stopped this somewhat irregular army practice! During his time at Keswick, Viney was taken to an 'unclimbable' hill by Bob Ray, and after a brief examination on foot, he became the only rider to accomplish a feet-up climb.

I was promoted to Sergeant when Viney was demobbed. The war was over and he joined Associated Motor Cycles (AMC) in South London as leader of the AJS trials team. For my part, I managed to persuade my commanding officer to allow me to take part in a few civilian trials. To help prepare my machine, I wrote to Bert Perrigo, the competition manager of BSA, who kindly provided a 21 in. front wheel and trials tyre, and a 4.00 × 19 in. tyre for the rear wheel, plus sprockets to lower the gearing of my army M20 BSA. This helped tremendously, but the M20 side-valver, weighing some 360 lb, was hardly an ideal trials machine—which I soon discovered when I rode it in the Scott Trial.

Notorious for its bogs, ditches and steep, slippery descents, the Scott, in addition to marks lost on observation, also required riders to go as fast as possible, with the fastest rider creating 'standard time'. Slower riders were deducted a mark for every minute they took beyond this standard time. Thus, it was vital to press on

as fast as possible. Competitors were started at one-minute intervals, and Jack Booker on a 125 cc Royal Enfield went off ahead of me.

I caught and passed Jack before reaching the worst moorland area—where I dropped into the first mud-filled ditch on the moor. Jack negotiated this without trouble on his lightweight machine, giving me a cheery wave as he went by. After struggling to free my heavy machine, I caught and repassed Jack, only to get stuck in mud yet again and to have Jack pass by again and again—for this was repeated several times. This amused Jack, for he was a vastly experienced trials rider. Even so, I managed to finish the trial, if somewhat weary.

I was demobbed in July 1947 and my final two weeks in the army were spent at the Royal Tournament at Olympia in London. I was with the Royal Signals motorcycle display team and one of my 'tricks' was to enter the arena at high speed and, with the aid of a ramp, jump over the prone bodies of a number of my team-mates. On landing, it was necessary to lay the machine almost on its side and broadside around in the 'tan' speedway fashion to avoid hitting the fence at the end of the arena. We were using Triumph twins specially prepared for these events and the footrests were fitted with rubber sleeves with large bulbous ends. These were only for appearance purposes, and after a week of broadsiding they split and hinged upwards when the machine was laid over in a slide.

However, prior to the last jump of the week, and unbeknown to me, the Triumph factory mechanic, anxious to have his wards in pristine condition for the finale, replaced the footrest rubber. . . . Also, as it was the finale, I wanted to put on my best performance. I made my best-ever jump, laid the machine over into its usual broadside—and the footrest dug into the tan! The machine flipped back upright and I was catapulted into the guard fence. I was unhurt, but extremely embarrassed.

On leaving the army and returning home to St Helens, my first move was to buy a new B32 350 cc BSA trials machine with my army gratuity. As I had already written to Bert Perrigo at BSA to enquire about the possibility of finding me a job at the Small Heath, Birmingham, factory, I started riding in north-west area trials, winning the Cheshire Centre Championship and the Northern Experts Trial. Shortly afterwards, the offer of a job in the experimental engine department with Jack Amott took me to Birmingham, where Bert Perrigo introduced me to BSA's ace trials and scrambles rider Bill Nicholson—who persuaded Mrs Pearson, his landlady, to allow me to share Bill's room in her Charles Road home.

Then came the great news that I was to join Bill and Fred Rist in the factory trials team, which I celebrated by winning the 'Best 350' award in the West of England Trial. The day before that event, Bill and I were given a conducted tour of the trial's hills by BSA's Newton

Winning my first trial (St Helens Auto Club) in 1947 on a BSA

Abbot agent, Freddie Hawken, who became a very firm and valued friend. Following Freddie along the twisty country lanes at a cracking pace, I was most impressed by his consistent line and effortless style through the corners. Little did I realize at the time that I was following a rider who had led the Lightweight Manx Grand Prix on an Excelsior, until he slipped off at Creg-ny-Baa, only to pick himself up, restart and still finish second!

I went on to finish second to Bill Nicholson in the Scott Trial where, while practising, I met Artie Bell, the

number-one rider in Norton's road-racing team. The British Experts Trial in Yorkshire that year was won by L. A. 'Artie' Ratcliffe (Matchless); Bill Nicholson was second and Hugh Viney (AJS) third. I finished ninth, but only six marks separated the third and ninth places.

At about this time, I was contacted by my old army friend and mentor, ex-Sgt. Viney, who wanted to know if I would be interested in joining him at Associated Motor Cycles. I was interested, so Hugh arranged for me to visit the South London factory.

During this visit, I was taken into the racing department where Hugh Viney introduced me to Les Graham, the AJS road-racing team leader. In my conversation with Les, I mentioned my ambition to ride in the 1948 Isle of Man Clubmans TT. Les immediately replied that if I joined AMC, the company directors would not allow me to compete! The reason, he told me, was that the public would believe I had works support and that would have been bad for the company's image. Although I made no comment at the time, I was rather taken aback by the company's attitude. Even so, I virtually agreed to join AMC—but fate was to intervene.

A letter from Artie Bell awaited my return to Birmingham. Artie wrote that he had been impressed with my riding at the Scott Trial, and as Nortons were to produce a new 500 cc trials machine, designed by Artie's Northern Ireland partner Rex McCandless, he, Artie, had spoken of me to Norton's technical director and racing manager, Joe Craig—and that Joe had expressed an interest in meeting me to discuss the possibility of my joining the Norton trials team! I could hardly believe my eyes! An opportunity to join the world's most famous racing marque was beyond my wildest dreams—even though the offer involved only trials.

My old friend Charles Markham had rejoined the Temple Press magazine *Motor Cycling* on leaving the army, but we had kept in touch. Charles, who had raced at Donington before the war, had stated many times to army colleagues that, in his opinion, my future lay in road racing. So I contacted Charles and he made an

appointment with Joe Craig for us to meet at the New Victoria Hotel, where Charles invariably stayed when in Birmingham.

This meeting was a success, and Joe offered me a job at the Norton factory and the chance to ride the 500T in trials. My salary would be decided with managing director Gilbert Smith, at a meeting to be arranged.

Overjoyed, I left the meeting with Charles Markham, and then broached the subject of my visit to AMC and how best to break the news of my 'change of heart' to Hugh Viney—to whom I owed so much. Charles said: 'There is no alternative. You must ring Hugh Viney first thing tomorrow morning and put your cards on the table. Mention your disappointing conversation with Les Graham regarding the possibility of riding in the Clubmans TT, and the opportunity that could stem from joining Nortons, and trust that he will understand.' This I did, but Hugh told me of his displeasure and it was some time before we were back on friendly terms.

At my subsequent meeting with Gilbert Smith, I was offered a job to create a small competition department at the Bracebridge Street factory and to ride for Nortons in trials at a salary of £700 a year, plus expenses. Before departing, I also mentioned to Gilbert Smith my desire to race in the Clubmans TT—and this was greeted with positive enthusiasm!

THE NORTON YEARS

My first race on the Island

It was with a feeling of awe that I approached my first meeting with Joe Craig, when I was interviewed for employment at Nortons in December 1947. Once that occasion was behind me, though, I slowly began to realize that behind his dedicated and sometimes ruthless exterior there was an excellent sense of humour, and he became my mentor in many discussions we had regarding race tactics. After my later inclusion in the road-racing team, I would quite often find him in his office late at night, writing detailed notes about the development of the racing engines. Although not necessarily a 'technical genius', a role attributed to him by people who were not closely associated with the company, Joe nevertheless tried most things to extract power during his long career as a development engineer.

When I first joined Nortons in January 1948, I was given a small area on the first floor as a 'competition shop' where, working alone, I prepared my trials and scrambles machines. I saw little of Joe Craig at this time. To do my limited paperwork, I based myself in the office of Norton's former chief designer, Edgar Franks, who was then concerned with answering Norton owners' complaints and queries. As a new boy in a strange environment, Edgar and his secretary were most kind and helpful to me.

What with working for the most famous road-racing marque in the world, my thoughts soon turned towards road racing and, on the strength of a promise of support from managing director Gilbert Smith, I entered for the 1948 Senior Clubmans TT—but was turned down! The entry had been oversubscribed, and as I had no road-racing experience, my application was rejected.

In addition to this disappointment, I had lots of other problems. My trials riding was only moderately successful as I found the 500T Norton much more of a handful than my previous 350 BSA. The harder I tried, the worse I seemed to get. Nevertheless, this did not prevent me gaining the promise of the loan of a standard 350 cc Manx Norton for the September Junior Manx Grand Prix—where my entry, surely one of the first submitted, was accepted.

Determined to leave nothing to chance, I arrived on the Isle of Man one week before official practice began, having ridden up to Liverpool on my scrambles bike, suitably fitted with road tyres and higher gearing. My racing machine was still on the assembly line at the Bracebridge Street factory at this time and was due to follow me by train from Birmingham, via Norton's Liverpool agent, Victor Horsman, whose Bill Quinn saw it safely on to the ferry.

My first-ever lap around the famous 37.73-mile TT Mountain circuit certainly made me realize the challenge it represented to a newcomer to road racing, having had so little time to learn the sequence of bends around the world's second-most-difficult road-racing circuit. Only the Nürburgring is more demanding.

In attempting to learn the circuit, I decided to go over it in three sections—from the grandstand to Kirkmichael, Kirkmichael to Ramsey, and from there back to the start. Allowing myself two days for each section, I set off on my scrambles machine and stopped at every significant bend to study the general surroundings, walking back and forth along an imaginary racing line. When a meal time came due or as darkness fell, I would complete the lap and then continue from the same place at the next session. Endeavouring to remember every bend from the start line to the finish, by the end of that first week I knew in my mind exactly where I was on the course at any given time.

The 500T Norton trials bike

Prior to the first official practice session, I well remember, even to this day, the lecture delivered by Douglas Hanson, the chief marshal, to all newcomers. A Manx solicitor, he was an imposing figure of a man with a prominent nose, hence his nickname 'Beak Hanson'. He put the fear of God into us regarding the folly of 'trying to go too quick, too soon'. I was most impressed.

On the first morning's practice, I could have easily wept with joy as I motored towards the top of Bray Hill for the first time on closed roads—perhaps I sensed what lay ahead for me in the next 11 years! Throughout that first Manx practice session, I remember concentrating all my effort into finding the racing line through the multitude of bends. I rolled back the throttle on the straights to avoid stressing the new engine, but allowed my speed to build up to take bends and corners at something like racing speed.

After each practice, it was straight back to the garage behind my digs in Empire Terrace. After breakfast, I would return to the machine to find it already spotlessly clean at the hands of a young Manx schoolboy, who became my self-appointed and only assistant throughout practice week.

My old friend Charles Markham visited me occasionally. Towards the end of practising, he told me that he had met Joe Craig leaving the Castle Mona Hotel.

Watching the kerb at Governor's Bridge in practice for the 1948 Junior MGP

Joe, always on the lookout for riding talent, rarely missed visiting the MGP. Charles knew this and asked: 'How's young Duke coming along?' 'He hasn't won a bloody trial yet!' was Craig's sharp reply. More to the point of Markham's question, I had not yet figured anywhere near the MGP practice leaderboard either, so presumably that was another black mark against Duke!

During another of his visits to my garage, I mentioned to Charles that I did not have a pit attendant to help me during the race. 'Leave that to me,' he said, and on the night before the Tuesday Junior race day, he brought along just the right man—Bill Clark, the racing cylinder-head specialist who worked for Eric Langton at Odsal Speedway (Bradford). Bill was on the Island just to see the race, and he very kindly agreed to help me.

We discussed signalling arrangements and decided that as it would be difficult to work out my position in such a large entry, he would simply show me my lap time from the previous lap. I was to stop and refuel—petrol and oil—at the end of the third lap

Race day was wet, and thick mist covered the Mountain. So it was not really surprising that when we arrived at Mylchreest's Garage to collect our machines after the Monday 'weigh-in', the riders were told that the start of the race would be delayed.

The weather did not improve and so the race was postponed until the next day, which dawned bright and clear. As I rode in the 'parade' from the garage to the starting grid, I recall that I was not nervous and had no

Hard against the throttle-stop coming out of Bedstead Corner in the Junior MGP of 1948

'butterflies'—but was, instead, full of exhilaration and eager for the race.

As number 12, when the starter dropped the flag, I set about putting into practice all I had learned during the past two weeks. My fastest lap in practice had not been spectacular—some 33 minutes plus—so by allowing the engine to rev more freely, I was sure to improve.

The first lap went without incident. I was riding comfortably, and towards the end of the second lap I was eager to know my first-lap (standing-start) time. As I passed my pit, out came the board: 29.31 (76.71 mph)! Not at all bad, I thought, completely unaware that I was tying for second place with Phil Heath (AJS), just 17 seconds behind Dennis Parkinson. Dennis was riding Francis Beart's beautifully-prepared lightweight Norton, which, with an enlarged fuel tank, could stop after two laps for a quick top-up and then complete the remaining four laps non-stop.

After the poor weather during practising, when mist on the Mountain slowed rapid progress, I discovered that I had a lot to learn in clear conditions. But encouraged by my pit signal, I pressed on—still unaware that I had gained six seconds over Phil Heath and was now within two seconds of Parkinson, mainly due to his slowing for a pit stop.

Happy with my own progress (though still little realizing my position), I pulled in to refuel after three laps, which included taking on oil. 'You're doing all right,' said Bill Clark, who later told me that he was afraid to say more in case I tried even harder and fell off!

Restarting after 30 seconds—six seconds longer than Parkinson—I rushed down Bray Hill, rounded Quarter Bridge and on to Braddan Bridge where, as I switched from left bank to right, my machine went into a violent slide. Fortunately, I was able to regain control, but a quick look down at the right-hand side of the rear tyre revealed a liberal coating of oil. 'Damn it!' I thought. 'Bill must have overfilled the oil tank, causing oil to blow out of the breather pipe and on to the tyre.' Despite this, I pressed on and had no further anxiety until accelerating hard out of the second-gear corner at Ballacraine. I slid right across the road and all but cannoned into the stone wall!

Though impressed at averting disaster, I nevertheless proceeded at a more restrained pace thereafter. My one hope was that, after shedding the excess oil, the tyre would 'dry out', allowing me to start 'trying' once again.

Indeed, by the time I reached Ramsey this had happened, and I was able to continue with renewed vigour. Then, three-quarters of the way up the Mountain Mile, the engine suddenly seized. I whipped in the clutch lever and coasted to a standstill to find the oil tank completely empty. It had split (not unusual in those days), and I mentally apologized to Bill Clark for ever imagining that such an experienced mechanic would have overfilled the tank.

Trying hard at Union Mills in the 1948 Junior MGP

I left the machine resting against a bank and walked on to the Mountain Box where, after asking me my number (12), the marshal replied: 'Oh, what a pity. You were leading the race!' This news obviously delighted me, but my lead at that stage in the race was of course only temporary, for, discounting the oil-smothered tyre, Parkinson's fourth lap was non-stop whereas mine would have included a 30-second pit stop. Nevertheless, though disappointed at being forced to retire, the reason for which was now known, I had proved to myself that I had TT potential.

Dr S. B. (Steve) Darbishire, second and third on Nortons in the 1935 Junior and Senior MGPs, later told me how he and Joe Craig had watched the race at Union Mills on the first lap of the Junior race and how impressed they were by my 'angle of lean'. So much so, in fact, that they proceeded to Cronk-ny-Mona on the inside of the course and then walked through the fields to Brandish Corner, where they arrived just after my departure. Joe asked the marshal if number 12 had gone by? 'Yes,' was the reply, 'but he won't come around again!' He apparently said that, not because of my retirement, but because, in his opinion, I had overtaken another rider in a most lurid fashion—convincing him that I did not have long to live!

Racing through 1949

Nortons, realizing the 'writing was on the wall' so far as the future competitiveness of their 500 cc single was concerned, entrusted the design of a replacement four-cylinder racing engine to BRM in 1949. This was a decision which, in my opinion, was taken in the mistaken belief that BRM were better equipped for the task. In any event, the design and drawing-office staff at Bracebridge Street were already hard-pressed coping with bread-and-butter projects.

This meant that Joe Craig was released from his responsibilities as team manager for the 1949 season to enable him to liaise with BRM on the four-cylinder project. So, for 1949, the Norton team was to be managed by Steve Lancefield in Joe's absence.

As usual, the North-West 200 in Northern Ireland, held in May, was used as the proving ground for the TT machines. Artie Bell and Johnny Lockett were entered in the 500 cc race, with Harold Daniell as Norton's sole factory entry in the 350 cc race.

I entered my 1948 MGP machine in the 350 race and, with my machine, travelled by train to Liverpool, walking the bike to the Belfast boat for the night crossing. On arriving the following morning, the Norton agent kindly provided transport to get me and my machine to Portstewart. The works mechanics and machines were already installed in a private garage close to the circuit, but Steve Lancefield had not as yet appeared on the scene.

Towards the end of the first practice session, my engine suddenly lost power. A small stone had been sucked into the carburettor and damaged the inlet valve seat. As I possessed only a limited tool kit, the factory mechanics, all friends of mine, allowed me to use a corner of the garage where I could remove the cylinder head and repair the damaged valve seat with the aid of their more comprehensive tools. While in the process of doing this, I went off for lunch—only to return and find my Norton with all its bits and pieces out on the pavement! The mechanics told me that Mr Lancefield had arrived and, on seeing my machine in the corner, had simply uttered one word: 'Out!'

Fortunately, the weather was fine, so I was able to continue my work outside with occasional unofficial words of encouragement and advice from the works mechanics. The damaged valve seat really needed recutting, but as there was no suitable equipment available, I had no option but to do the job with elbow grease and grinding paste. It was a lengthy task and was still far from perfect when I finished. Nevertheless, I assembled the engine, and as there was no more practising for 350s, I prepared the machine for the race.

The entry list of 76 for the 350 cc race was formidable, because in addition to Harold Daniell on the factory Norton, the runners included the Velocette pair of Ken Bills and Freddie Frith—who was riding a machine he had ridden to and from the 'Continental Circus' meeting at the *Circuit de Floreffe*! Reg Armstrong and Bill Doran on works AJS machines completed the factory line-up.

I was in the middle of the starting grid for the massed start, and at the end of the opening lap was lying sixth, tucked in behind the ample rear of Ken Bills in a tight group headed by Daniell, Frith, Doran and Armstrong, in that order.

From the second lap, there was no chance of my machine holding the leading trio, who constantly swapped places until Doran dropped out with gearbox

Posing on the 350 Norton for the photographer at Thruxton in 1949 with Harry Johnson—Francis Beart can be seen in the background

trouble with just one lap to go. But I was having the time of my life, particularly along the twisty coast road between Portrush and Portstewart where I occasionally managed to get past Ken Bills. As luck would have it, though, I lost my 'tow' when I needed to stop for fuel— the works bikes were all fitted with long-range tanks and so were going through non-stop.

On the 16th lap, however, Ken Bills was involved in a multiple pile-up while attempting to overtake a group of slower riders, and this left me in a safe third place. The 17th lap should have ended the race, but so close was the battle between Daniell and Frith that the man with the chequered flag, perhaps in his excitement, allowed everybody to steam into an extra lap!

Even so, none of the leading positions changed during that extra tour, which saw Daniell and Frith cross the line together. A blanket would have covered them, but Harold was just ahead and, being on the outside, was

Out on my own in third place at Henry's Corner during the 1949 350 cc North-West 200

almost decapitated by the now over-eager flag man!

We then moved to the Isle of Man for the Clubmans TT, which was one of the most worrying races of my career—but not because it was one of my first events or that it was around the TT circuit. My worry was with the machine I was riding—an 'International' Norton. Although distantly related to the production racing 'Manx' Norton in having an overhead-camshaft engine with an alloy cylinder head and barrel, that is really where all similarity between an 'International' and a 'Manx' model ended.

The Inter was both heavy and equipped with near-useless brakes. In addition, the Clubmans race regulations stipulated that the engine would be kickstarted at the fall of the starter's flag. At that time, I weighed a mere ten stone and lacked the necessary 'beef' to guarantee spinning the engine over compression and on to the firing stroke. This was just not good enough, particularly as my most serious rival was that great all-rounder and highly-experienced rider Alan Jefferies, mounted on a very quick Triumph Tiger 100 twin which

required little pressure on its kickstarter to swing it into life.

In order to overcome this difficulty, I decided to lengthen the kickstarter lever of my Norton a couple of inches by cutting and welding in a piece of steel tubing. The greater swing this provided was sufficient to carry the piston over compression and solved my problem. I also considered fitting a folding cross-piece, similar to that used on trials machines, to avoid the possibility of being thrown off if the projecting kickstarter hit a kerb at the apex of a corner, but I decided against that idea.

The brakes were a major worry, and in an attempt to make the best of a poor job, the front brake drum was carefully built into the wheel with equal tension on the spokes. This was to prevent the drum distorting. The wheels were then turned in a lathe and the drums trued. Finally, the brake shoes were fitted with racing lining material—then actuated, and locked in a position that spread the brake shoes to a fraction more than the

internal diameter of each drum, the linings were turned to provide an accurate, circular fit. All this effort did provide a slight improvement in braking, but the real problem was the small size and lack of rigidity of the brake drums.

Another anxiety was the question of engine reliability. The International engine was known to suffer excessive cam wear when run for prolonged periods at high speed, which obviously affected performance and could easily occur during a TT race. This was a lubrication problem which had recently been cured by providing a central oil feed to the cambox, although there was still some doubt at that time whether this modification was permissible, for the ACU's regulations for the Clubmans TT were strict and modifications had to be homologated well in advance of the event.

However, because I worked at Nortons, it was

Being rather careful in the wet! Here I am going into Quarter Bridge Corner in practice for the 1949 Senior Clubmans TT

The 1949 Senior Clubmans Norton

TCX6   G. .... WINNER JEN. CLUBMANS T.T. 1949

Left *Peeling off for Quarter Bridge in the 1949 Senior Clubmans TT, where I finished in first place*

Above *Here I am pushing off on 'scratch' alongside Manliff Barrington's Beart Norton in the Skerries 100 in 1949*

Below *Caught not looking where I was going! Riding hard, with my chin on the tank, during the 1949 Skerries 100 in Ireland, prior to my exit through the hawthorn hedge!*

forbidden for my engine to be modified, but when I presented the machine, the chief scrutineer, Vic Anstice, looked over the machine and said: 'What, no central oil feed to the cambox?' Apparently, the modification *was* acceptable, and I could hardly wait to push my machine to the Norton service depot in Fort Street to have the work carried out.

The race was over three laps of the Mountain course and was fairly uneventful, apart from one 'moment' when I found myself down the very steep camber of the road on the approach to Governor's Bridge on lap two—and, of course, the poor brakes! At the drop of the flag, my lengthened kickstarter fired the engine at the second attempt, and then, under perfect racing conditions, I won the race from Alan Jefferies at a record average speed of 82.97 mph—with a lap record of 83.71 mph. This was 1 mph faster than that achieved in 1948 by George Brown on a 998 cc Vincent-HRD.

In July, a month after the Clubmans TT, I entered the Skerries 100 in the south of Ireland, riding the 350 Manx Norton I had raced in the 1948 MGP.

In the race I had a battle royal with Manliff Barrington on Francis Beart's lightweight Norton, and was leading until disaster struck! Going through a fast S-bend which had a grass verge on the left and a high hawthorn hedge on the right-hand side of the road, I caught my left

Left *The proud winner of the 1949 Senior Clubmans TT smiles for the camera, while Steve Darbishire (right of the picture) and Francis Beart, wearing dark glasses, look on*

Above left *At Keppel Gate on the Isle of Man during the Junior MGP of 1949, where I finished second*

Above *Crossing the finishing line in second place to Cromie McCandless in the 1949 Junior MGP*

footrest on an obstruction in the grass. This lifted the machine upright and I was catapulted off and through the top of the hedge. Meanwhile, my riderless machine carried on through the hedge as well!

Sustaining a broken leg and lots of razor-sharp thorns which had pierced my leathers and embedded in my very bruised back, I ended up in a Dublin hospital for a week—although, I must say, there was some compensation for my mishap in the caring attention I received from a rather pretty young nurse. . . .

The plaster on my broken left leg was removed only a few days before practising began for the Manx Grand Prix in September. I felt fine and was raring to go, although push-starting was rather difficult.

Practice on my repaired 350 was uneventful, but my first outing on the 500—which had only been completed after I left Birmingham for the Island—was disconcerting, to say the least. It was quite a handful, and when braking hard for Sulby Bridge, the machine weaved so badly I thought it would throw me off! Fortunately, it did not—but so much for the 'unapproachable roadholding'. I thought to myself: 'If this is what riding a 500 Manx Norton is like, they can have it back!'

However, closer examination revealed twice the

Left *Catching flies at Kate's Cottage in the 1949 Junior MGP!*

correct amount of oil in one front fork leg, and none in the other. I suppose a tea-break at the factory must have intervened after the required amount of oil had been poured into one leg; the worker had probably forgotten which side he had filled and, without checking, had poured a second dose into the same leg, leaving the other side empty. After draining and refilling both sides correctly, though, the handling expected from a Norton was once again restored.

The most serious opposition in the 350 cc race was likely to be from W. A. C. 'Cromie' McCandless on Beart's Norton. He had drawn number 33 and I was 97. My late starting number was an advantage for signalling one's position during the race, but it could present a difficult and sometimes dangerous situation when overtaking slower riders—which I was to discover to my cost.

Cromie broke the post-war lap record on the first lap, which I then bettered to take the lead. He then broke it again the second time around and I improved on that by a further eight seconds. But as the fuel load went down, Cromie went faster and faster as the race progressed, and with a larger-than-standard fuel tank, requiring him to take on less fuel at his pit stop, this was a further bonus for him.

After four laps, only 17 seconds separated us. But then, on lap five, as I approached Ramsey Hairpin behind a

The scene after the 1949 Junior MGP, with Charlie Edwards, a Norton works mechanic on holiday on the Island, asking 'What did you drop it for?' What could I say?

group of riders, the last of the bunch, namely Ted Pink on one of the new 7R AJS bikes, braked hard as I rushed up from behind. To avoid a collision, I had to take to the unmade footpath on the right-hand side of the road. This put me in real trouble and, unable to stop on the loose surface, I had to lay my Norton down, bending the left footrest and rear brake pedal, and stalling the engine in the process.

Luckily, I was able to restart without assistance by rolling my machine down a narrow path leading off the road. But then, due to the narrow steering lock, I had great difficulty in turning it around. Eventually, however, I was able to rejoin the race, albeit minus the benefit of the rear brake, only to have the clutch seize coming out of Governor's Bridge!

With only one lap to go, there was little point in stopping at the pits for repairs, as I realized that although my chance to win the race was lost, time spent trying to free the clutch and fix the brake might well sacrifice second place as well. In the end, Cromie McCandless completed his last lap in 27 min 7.4 sec—a lap record of 83.5 mph—thus winning the race by 1 min 15.6 sec.

Senior race day was fine with less wind than earlier. McCandless was drawn number 2, Dennis Parkinson (Norton) was number 12, and I was 23. At the end of the first lap, I led the race from Cromie by 23 seconds, having gone round in 26 min 16 sec (86.2 mph). This was just two seconds outside the all-time Senior MGP record.

On lap two, Cromie made his stop to refuel, taking 24 seconds, having completed the lap in 26 minutes exactly (87.089 mph) to establish a new lap record. However, I

did not slow down to stop and refuel, so my second lap was seven seconds faster at 87.48 mph—which remained unbeaten to the end of the race.

My third lap also took precisely 26 minutes when I stopped for fuel, but the delay of 35 seconds cost me 11 seconds, while Cromie, with time to get back into his stride after the earlier pit stop, was now really flying. The end of lap four saw my lead cut to just four seconds.

The end of the fifth lap saw Cromie in the lead by ten seconds, but at the Bungalow on the last time around, I was apparently back in the lead by four seconds, though unaware of the situation as my signalling arrangements had gone awry. Fate had taken a hand in the proceedings, yet again. On the downhill approach to Hillberry, the small amount of fuel remaining in Cromie's tank had swilled forward and left the feed to the carburettor dry. Realizing what had happened, Cromie had to stop and run his machine's front wheel up the bank to refill the float chamber.

The result of the race was now no longer in doubt. At the finish, I was 43 seconds ahead at an average speed of 86.063 mph—only 0.865 mph outside the 1949 Senior TT average of 86.928 mph.

Left *Diving into bumpy Hillberry Corner on 'full-chat' in the 1949 Senior MGP*

Above *A joyous occasion in the finishing enclosure after the 1949 Senior MGP with Dr Steve Darbishire, 'Max' Maxstead of Smiths Motor Accessories, and Francis Beart, plus Cromie McCandless who finished second*

Below left *Leaving nothing to chance, I crossed the finishing line at full speed in the 1949 Senior MGP*

Below *Enthusiastic youngsters studying trophies and my MGP-winning machine at an Earls Court show*

World records at Montlhéry

Although I worked for Nortons, it was only after winning the Manx Grand Prix in 1949 that I was invited to join the official road-racing team for 1950. However, my first official outing as a member of the Norton works team was towards the end of 1949, when we went to the high-speed banked track at Montlhéry, just outside Paris, to attack some world records. The object of these record rides was to gain publicity just prior to the Motorcycle Show at Earls Court, in November.

At that time, the Norton team, with the machines, used to travel around the Continent by rail, utilizing their local agent's road transport on arrival at the nearest railway station to the race circuit. On this occasion, however, it was decided that Artie Bell and I would take two machines, plus spares and equipment, over to France in my Ford V8 van. Joe Craig and the mechanics travelled by train and boat, while the third rider, Eric Oliver, met us in Paris at the premises of the Norton agent, Monsieur Garreau, where final preparation of the machines was to be carried out.

Garreau was an odd character and, as we recalled so soon after the war, the mirror-image of the French traitor Pierre Laval. During the entire period we were in France, Garreau wore the same shirt, and instead of polishing his boots, he sprayed them with cellulose!

Garreau was indeed extremely scruffy, but immediately on our arrival in Paris, he took Joe, Artie and myself to a very fine restaurant where he was greeted like royalty. On being presented with the bill after enjoying a magnificent meal, Garreau produced an enormous roll of banknotes—which may have had some bearing on his apparent popularity and the fact that he was reputed to be a leading black-marketeer in wartime Paris.

Later that same evening, he took us to a small bar next door to the famed *Folies Bergère* where he introduced us to 'Madame', the owner. She was delighted about our arrival and, with great enthusiasm, showed us a French newspaper which carried a story referring to our proposed record attempts. She then introduced us to two most gorgeous girls. They were sisters and had just finished their performance in the chorus line at the *Folies*. Reluctantly, we were unable to get to know them very

well, for the next day we were due to begin business at Montlhéry and Joe would not allow us to stay out late. . . .

Around the banked track it was soon discovered that, despite his greater height and weight, Artie was consistently 0.4 seconds faster than me. We eventually realized that the advantage came from his better-fitting two-piece leather racing suit, and as the Norton machine had no streamlining whatsoever, it proved how critical a

Below The early two-piece leathers in action in 1949

Inset My original two-piece leathers, with numerous buttons, before I got the idea of a one-piece suit

smooth frontal area can be. A few lengths of sticky tape to fold back the excess material in the arms and legs of my leathers immediately solved the problem, and from then on our full-throttle lap times were virtually identical.

This gave me much food for thought—if the fit of a leather racing suit could be so critical on a high-speed track, it must be equally vital in Grand Prix racing . . . but more on that later.

Having established that we had the necessary urge to break a number of world records, we then had to sit back and wait for suitable weather conditions. We were staying in a small 'pub' in the village, and as the most junior member of the team, I was allocated the smallest

bedroom which had no window. It only had a narrow ventilation shaft which disappeared into the roof.

After two days of incessant rain—which ruled out any thought of record breaking—we were all feeling very miserable. Joe sensed this and, handing Artie a few francs, told us to have a night out in Paris. We needed no encouragement and quickly took off in my van for that superb city and, in particular, that small bar alongside the *Folies Bergère*!

Most delightfully, 'Madame' produced a couple of tickets for the show. And what a fabulous show it was, too. We also spotted the two sisters we had met previously and, as before, they joined us in the bar after the show. The girls were wonderful company, and they offered to take us on a tour of the lesser-known parts of Paris, which was great. We finished up in the market area of the city drinking, or should I say 'eating', superb French onion soup.

We then took the girls home to the apartment which they shared. On entering, both Artie and I instantly recognized a figure in a framed photograph as being a very famous British wartime leader in full dress uniform! And on that photograph was handwritten a most endearing dedication: 'To Madeleine. . . .' We were later shown a telegram sent by the gentleman in the picture who, now dead, was a prominent naval member of the Royal family. It gave the date and time of his arrival in Paris. We were, therefore, really in high society, or rather Artie was, as it was he who laid claim to the lovely Madeleine! As for me, her sister Nanou had a cold and went to bed, while I sat alongside and tried to make conversation in my very limited French.

Dawn arrived with a clear blue sky and brilliant sunshine—perfect riding conditions for record breaking. So when Artie reappeared, we hastened to get to Montlhéry, only to have the van fail to start. The problem was fuel shortage—the fuel gauge did not work in any case, but we carried a jerry can of petrol for this eventuality. Artie pulled the can out of the van and immediately dropped it with a loud clang! He was a little below par, to say the least, so I took over the refuelling and we then set off for the racing circuit, where a rather impatient Joe Craig awaited us.

Artie's powers of recovery were remarkable as the records began to fall, and all the more so when considering that only a few hours earlier he had been responding in record-breaking form to Madeleine's ecstatic cries of: '*Encore, ARRRTEEE!*'

Highly pleased with a bag of 21 world records, we then returned via our different ways to the UK. Joe and the mechanics travelled by train, while Artie and I headed for Calais with the bikes in the van. On arriving at Dover, we drove off the cross-channel ferry into the customs shed, where we saw a single-seater racing car tucked in a corner. This seemed rather strange—until we learned that it had been impounded the previous day when

several thousand Swiss watches were discovered in the fuel tank!

Amid this atmosphere, our arrival in a dark-blue unmarked van with Artie wearing a magnificent fur coat, and with two rather strange-looking motorcycles in the back, created perhaps more than usual interest, so it was not surprising that we were asked to wait. A legion of white-overalled customs officers then descended upon us, 'requesting' permission to 'examine' the van, which they did with extreme efficiency—we were detained for about two hours while the van was all but taken apart! They found a new pair of racing boots which Monsieur Garreau had given me—and which I had not declared. However, they waived charging me any duty. Clearly, they were looking for far more serious things, but to no avail.

In view of the lengthy delay, we were glad to get away at last from Dover for Birmingham. But our problems were not over. Just a few miles down the road, the rear axle of the Ford failed as we approached Hythe. This meant that we had to be towed into a garage for repairs, and it was then necessary to find accommodation for the night. A bill for £24 for the repair does not seem much now but in 1949 that was quite a lot of money—and both Artie and I did not have that much between us! So, before we were allowed to leave, a telephone call to the Norton factory was necessary to guarantee payment. And, would you believe, a few days later, after we got back to Bracebridge Street, I was presented with the account for £24 by the company secretary! After some heated discussion, during which I pointed out that the axle failure could have been due to the heavy load, the secretary offered to pay half the amount. Somewhat disgruntled, I went to see the managing director, Gilbert Smith, and pointed out that Nortons had had the use of my van free of charge, paying only for the petrol and the ferry crossing. Eventually, he did agree that Nortons should pay for the repairs.

To return briefly to the question of Artie's better-fitting leather racing suit which had set me thinking—if the fit of one's leathers made such a difference to lap times around Montlhéry, then it must also be the same in road racing. Also, I realized that the double thickness of material, where the jacket overlapped the trousers at the waist, could become restrictive and uncomfortable when lying in the prone position to reduce wind resistance. In addition, there was little need for pockets and excessive padding. The answer was a lightweight, one-piece, close-fitting suit.

I put this idea to the manufacturers of my 'traditional' two-piece racing suit, who said they would make what I wanted if I could provide a pattern. So, my next approach was to Frank Barker, my local St Helens tailor, who agreed to make the necessary pattern. But this interested him so much that, having made the pattern, Frank then said he would like to have a go at making up the suit.

Above *Frank Barker, the maker of my one-piece leathers, standing with me outside his tailor's shop*

I had already decided that a one-piece separate lining would provide even greater freedom of movement and comfort, and this was made for me by a firm of ballet-clothing specialists in London. It also brought a few ribald remarks from my team-mates! Frank Barker concentrated on the leatherwork and, for a tailor used to working with cloth and without any special equipment, he did a magnificent job for me. The finished suit weighed less than 5 lb and was ready for the 1950 TT.

A further development came from examining a picture of me rounding Kate's Cottage during the 1950 Senior TT. This showed the effect of wind pressure 'flattening' my pull-on racing boots. Frank, therefore, made me a pair of close-fitting, zip-up boots using the same lightweight leather as the suit.

From that time onwards, the traditional two-piece racing suit and heavy boots became obsolete and Frank Barker was inundated with orders. So much so, that his original tailoring business all but ceased.

Right *Well wound up around Bedstead Corner in the 1950 Senior TT. Note the wind-pressure-flattened boots, which were later replaced by a close-fitting variety to reduce wind resistance*

Tyre problems and the 1950 season

To be included in the Norton team in 1950 on an equal footing with Bell, Lockett and Daniell was really something, but to be fortunate enough to start my professional career on the 'new-look' McCandless Norton was a heaven-sent opportunity.

My first ride on the prototype was in the Isle of Man in January 1950, when Artie Bell and I 'illegally' rushed it round Kate's Cottage, and later through the Quarry Bends. I soon realized that this machine set an entirely new standard in roadholding.

Two weeks later, Rex McCandless, Joe Craig, Artie Bell and myself were at the famous Montlhéry road circuit in France, where the new model could be tested under very arduous conditions. The circuit was approximately five miles to a lap (we did not use the banked track at all), with a rather bumpy surface and lots of twists and turns, entailing the use of bottom gear and the clutch on six occasions, plus a total of 42 gearchanges per lap! In spite of this, Artie lapped at over 76 mph, with the 1949 'pool' (72 octane) engine fitted—faster, we were told, than anybody had lapped before, even on alcohol fuel.

We completed about 400 miles, during which Joe Craig had us vying with one another by recording every lap time. Unfortunately, a broken primary chain, which damaged the sprockets, caused us to return home.

Once one or two teething troubles were ironed out, we carried out further tests at the Motor Industry Research Association (MIRA) proving ground near Nuneaton, which was invaluable, for the outer circuit of a little over three miles could be lapped at speeds well above 90 mph. Harold Daniell, Johnny Lockett, Rex and I covered a further 600 miles there—on his arrival, Harold had looked at the machine, with its relatively high seat and tail, and had turned to Joe to ask: 'Where's the step-ladder?'

Finally satisfied, the 'Professor' (Artie's nickname for Joe Craig) decided to build a completely new machine incorporating all the new ideas which he and Rex had evolved from the various tests carried out. From this conception came the first of the 1950 TT machines—the models which would sweep the board in the Leinster 200,

North-West 200 and the TT. Harold Daniell was to have had the honour of being the first to ride the new racer in a race at Blandford in April, but was unable to do so due to an unfortunate spill at an earlier meeting at Silverstone, where he and I had a great set-to on Manx Nortons until, in an overtaking manoeuvre, Harold grounded his megaphone and slid off, cracking a bone in his hand. I had already entered the event with my Manx machines, so Joe asked me to ride the works model in place of my own 500.

The opposition, in the shape of Ted Frend on the twin AJS, did not materialize due to a slight misfire which eventually led to the Ajay's retirement from the 500 cc final. This was very disappointing from our point of view, but at least we were able to demonstrate the superb handling qualities of the new Norton by breaking George Brown's 1000 cc record. I was unable to ride in the handicap event (the last event of the day) because I had to be in Scotland the next morning to weigh in for the Scottish Six Days Trial. Not knowing the true

Above *Out on my own in the 500 race after Harold Daniell fell off, cracking a bone in his hand, at Silverstone in April 1950. Note the massive crowd*

Right *Feet up, so far! On Town Hall Brae in the Scottish Six Days Trial of 1950*

Below *A superb dice with the 'Master' Harold Daniell leading at Silverstone Saturday in April 1950—both of us were riding Manx Nortons*

TN 17   THE NORTON "A" TEAM.   JUNIOR T.T. 1950

circumstances, one well-known newspaper's motoring correspondent stated in his column the next day that G. E. Duke, after the 500 cc final (30 miles), was too tired to ride in the handicap event!

Then came the North-West 200. Poor Harold was still out of action, so Artie Bell and Johnny Lockett rode the 500s. These two had quite a battle way out in front, finishing in that order, while Australian Harry Hinton, who borrowed my Manx machine, finished a comfortable third.

For the 350 cc race, I had a lone 350 Norton which, in perfect conditions on practice morning, lapped at over 86 mph—faster than the previous year's 500 cc lap record! However, race-day conditions were not so good, for a hot sun had caused the tar to melt and there was a strong head wind on the long straight between Coleraine and Portrush.

I made my usual bad start (due to lack of boot grip, I later discovered), but managed to take the lead from Wheeler on his very rapid Velocette about two miles out of Portstewart on the first lap. Artie had previously

The Norton 'A' team, consisting of Bell, Lockett and myself, lined up in the garden of the Castle Mona Hotel for the 1950 Junior TT

warned me that the tar was very liquid approaching the sharp, left-hand bend at Coleraine. However, it turned out to be much worse than I had imagined, as the 'skating rink' extended for 300 yards before the bend. On the approach I applied the front brake gently, only to lock the front wheel. I released it immediately. By this time, though, the bend had loomed up and all the marshals were running for their lives. I decided I could not possibly take the bend, so I did a quick lap around a lamp-post placed in the middle of the road, mentally docking myself three marks for footing! The rest of the race was fairly uneventful, and my 350 eventually carried me home the winner at a record average speed, with the lap record thrown in as well.

Nortons had entered two teams for the 1950 Junior (350 cc) and Senior (500 cc) Isle of Man TT races and, to my surprise and delight, I was elevated to the first team with Artie Bell and Johnny Lockett. Harold Daniell would lead the second team, with the two Australians Harry Hinton and George Morrison riding their standard Manx machines. Although then 41 years old and perhaps a shade too heavy to get the best from a 350, Harold, the lap record holder at 91 mph from 1938, was still a power to be reckoned with on a 500 machine.

Whether by accident or deliberate intent on the part of Joe Craig, it appeared that Artie had the best 350 cc engine, while I had the fastest 500. Under the guidance of the 'Professor', we concentrated our efforts during practising on these particular machines.

It was during the Wednesday morning practice that I cracked the first over-90 mph lap since pre-war. It was on this, my third lap, that I succeeded in taking Hillberry flat out in top gear, only to change down through loss of revs on the following rise. After that, I realized that time could be saved by taking Hillberry, and beyond, full-bore in third.

During that same practice session, Artie put in a meteoric 85.93 mph lap, which unofficially shattered the 350 cc lap record of 85.30 mph set by Stanley Woods on a Velocette in 1938. Thus, the scene was set.

The weather on Junior race day was near perfect and

At the 1950 Junior TT with Bill Clark, the Norton factory mechanic who was my pit attendant at my first race, the 1948 MGP

Bob Foster, the only previous Junior winner, started favourite on number 8. There were precisely 100 starters—40 mounted on AJSs, 32 on Velocettes and 25 riding Nortons, the remainder being two BSAs and one Guzzi. Foster's factory Velocette was fitted with a monster eight-gallon fuel tank to allow a seven-lap, non-stop run. Artie was number 64 and I was 79. This was a positive disadvantage and unquestionably dangerous, as we had to overtake much slower riders, many of whom could provide the unexpected by suddenly changing line or speed at a crucial moment.

I was subsequently instrumental in persuading the ACU to bring in a grading system which put acknowledged top-flight riders into the first 20 places on the starting grid. This was a move which I am sure relieved both the 'overtaker' and the 'overtaken'.

As number 79 in 1950, though, I must have been overcome by the occasion, for when the starter dropped the flag, I ran but dropped the clutch too quickly. Without sufficient muscle to carry the piston over compression, it kicked back, so I had to pull back and start again.

To my astonishment, my signal at the end of lap one, indicating my position at Ramsey Hairpin, showed me to be in second place—two seconds down on Les Graham's AJS. The surprise was that Artie was six seconds behind me, while Foster, hampered by eight gallons of fuel, was fourth and 13 seconds behind Bell.

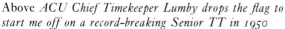

Above _ACU Chief Timekeeper Lumby drops the flag to start me off on a record-breaking Senior TT in 1950_

Top left _Approaching Union Mills with the rear wheel off the ground during the 1950 Junior TT_

Left _A relaxed but thoughtful Harold Daniell just prior to the start of the 1950 Senior TT. He earned pole position on account of his win in 1949_

Above _Approaching the bottom of Bray Hill flat out in top gear and with chin on tank in the 1950 Senior TT_

However, as the Velo shed its weight, so it speeded up, and 'Fearless' Foster was the first to break the lap record with 26 min 16 sec. Bob's effort was not repeated, though. The cam spindle of his rear brake sheared and retired him from the race at Quarter Bridge. I set exactly the same time as Foster, but Artie, now with the bit between his teeth, whistled round in 25 min 56 sec, an average speed of 86.49 mph.

A superb refuelling performance by my 'regular' TT pit attendant, Dr Darbishire, in only 18 seconds, gained me two seconds on Bell and ten seconds on Graham. But there was no holding Artie's Norton, which increased its lead all the while to win by 77 seconds at a record 86.33 mph.

I had just one incident—more amusing than serious—going through the S-bend by the Shell filling station at Glen Helen on the second lap. I went into quite a hectic slide and regained control just in time to see a number of spectators, who were sitting on a stone wall, do a rapid flip backwards—presumably into the river below!

Incidentally, it was during his speech at the prize-giving after this race that Harold Daniell, who annexed

third place from Les Graham on the last lap, praised the comfort of his machine and said it was 'just like riding on a featherbed'. Thus, the name stuck.

The Senior TT was another superb day—and for me there was a more competitive mount than Monday's 350. After the Junior race, Artie revealed that his rev-counter had been showing 7600 rpm on the Sulby Straight, against the 7200 maximum of the other team members' machines. No wonder he had cleared off!

In the Senior race, Harold Daniell, the 1949 winner and drawn number 1, set off like a rocket. He completed the first lap 29 seconds behind me, with Artie and Johnny Lockett tying for third place, a further eight seconds behind. But on his second lap, poor Harold's clutch began to slip and he gradually lost ground to the rest of the Norton team and Les Graham's 'porcupine' AJS.

My race was uneventful almost beyond belief. The opening lap of 91.38 mph was inside Daniell's 1938 record but did not count, because at that time the starting line was 70 yards further down the road than the line used for timing purposes. However, my second lap did the trick at 93.01 mph, and my lead over Artie, who annexed second place on lap two, increased on each successive lap.

At the refuelling pit stop, I took on the minimum amount of petrol to finish—but this was almost my undoing. My next flying lap was the fifth, which established a lap record of 93.33 mph. From then on, I began to change up at lower revs, which probably saved

Above *The 'Artie Bell line' around Governor's Bridge in the 1950 Senior TT*

Above right *A memorable occasion—my first TT win! Crossing the finishing line just ahead of Artie Bell in the 1950 Senior. Note the huge crowd!*

the day for me, because as I rounded the '33rd' for the last time, on the seventh lap, the engine missed a beat. Fuel starvation?

At Governor's Bridge I was on Artie's tail and we crossed the finishing line together. My greatest ambition had been achieved—I had won the Senior TT. When the usual check was made of the first three machines to finish, though, my petrol tank was completely dry!

After such a highly successful Isle of Man TT, the Norton team travelled to Spa for the Belgian Grand Prix—and the first outing for the 'Featherbed' in a continental race. We were confident that the superb handling of the McCandless-designed frame would really pay off on the fast sweeping curves of the picturesque Francorchamps circuit in the Ardennes, even against the far more powerful four-cylinder Gilera machines.

The 28 bhp engine in our 350 was, however, no match for the combined efforts of Bob Foster and his works Velocette. This was confirmed during practising and in the actual race. Even Artie Bell's TT-winning 350—with the unaccounted-for extra 400 rpm—failed to match the speed of the Velocette, and I had to be content with third place.

Later that day, while on the starting line for the 500 cc race, I was approached by Les Graham and then Artie, who both warned me to stay clear of the Italian rider

Carlo Bandirola. He was reputed to do funny things, like shutting off his Gilera four in the middle of fast bends!

Suitably impressed, I made a comparatively leisurely start and arrived at the beginning of the long Masta Straight in seventh position—behind Graham and Bell who were swapping places at every opportunity with the Gilera squad of Pagani, Bandirola and Masetti, plus Artesiani on an MV. Then, to my surprise, I was drawn along in the vacuum created by this mass of machinery and found myself on Masetti's tail when we arrived at Stavelot, where I had little difficulty passing him around the outside of this ultra-fast sweep. On the following climb, Artie Bell steamed by and the order at the end of the first lap was: Bandirola, Bell, then me, with Graham snapping at my heels.

For the second time on the Masta Straight, greater speed again gave the Gileras command, with Les and Artie hard in their slipstream. Incredibly, after their dire warning to me before the start of the race, they both

Right *The winning Norton team, with myself, Artie Bell and Johnny Lockett finishing first, second and third in the 1950 Senior race respectively. Managing director Gilbert Smith and Joe Craig are standing between the riders*

THE WINNING NORTON TEAM SENIOR T.T. 1950
LOCKETT 3RD. DUKE WINNER. BELL 2ND

scooped up 'Bandi' around the fast Stavelot Curve at the foot of the uphill climb to Francorchamps' famous hairpin.

With his four-cylinder power, Bandirola promptly repassed them again on the next straight and all three then dived together into the quick, double left-hander near the top of the hill. Les was sitting on Bandirola's back wheel, with Artie a couple of yards behind and to Les' right. I was behind them—watching and wondering—positioned to Artie's left.

Suddenly, Bandirola shut off his throttle. Les Graham had to brake violently and, locking the front wheel, his AJS twin went down, man and machine sliding off to the right. This left Artie Bell with no option. He had to try and get around the fallen 'porcupine' by taking to the rough on the right-hand side of the road—but he had no chance. Graham was left lying in the road, but his machine continued sliding along and, inevitably, was hit by Artie's Norton—who disappeared with both bikes in a cloud of dust beneath an elevated observation post which collapsed. Probably realizing what had happened, Bandirola glanced back, and then pressed on!

Furious at what I had seen, and convinced at that moment that Bandirola was totally responsible for causing the appalling accident, I set about catching him, being aided in this pursuit by the slipstream of the other two Gileras, which breezed past my Norton on lap three. We all caught and passed Bandirola during the fifth lap, his machine having begun to give out tell-tale puffs of blue smoke from its exhausts.

I then determined to set about the other two—Pagani and Masetti—slipstreaming them along the straights and then using the superior handling of the Norton to pass them on the inside, or outside, at every opportunity. I forced them to rev their four-cylinder engines more and more, until they too began to puff out smoke. And with that, I knew I had dented their performance and was able to pull away at last.

After dropping them from my slipstream, so vital with naked machines, I established a 45-second lead until, on lap 13 of the 14-lap race, disaster struck! There was a loud bang and I felt something hit my backside, followed by 'juddering' from the rear wheel. A large section of the tread had detached itself from the casing of the rear tyre.

I toured back to the pits to learn that Harold Daniell

Typical Duke treatment for Francorchamps Hairpin at the Belgian GP in 1950

Flat out in top gear at the Belgian GP in 1950, before my retirement due to tyre problems

and Johnny Lockett had both retired with the same problem. I also learned that poor Artie was badly injured and in hospital as a result of his accident. Artie was later flown home to the London Clinic, but, even with the best treatment possible, he lost the use of his right arm and was never to race again. As it happened, Artie was to live on until 5 August 1972, whereas Les Graham, comparatively unhurt in the Belgian disaster, would be killed on an MV four in a crash on Bray Hill during the second lap of the 1953 Senior TT. . . .

There was, of course, a great to-do about our total tyre failure and the late Dickie Davis, Dunlop's legendary racing manager, eventually explained that the problem had been traced to a fault in a joint of the tread rubber. He said that new tyres, with special attention paid to these joints, would be flown to Holland the following week for the Dutch TT. Dickie gave me his personal assurance that there would be no more trouble—and I believed him, despite the fact that, not being directly involved as a technician, he should not have made such a personal guarantee.

Practice at the Dutch, on the old road circuit, was

uneventful and there was no sign of any recurrence of the tyre trouble. On race day, Bob Foster cleared off as usual on his Velocette in the 350 race and I eventually gained second place after slipstreaming Bill Lomas on another Hall Green Velocette.

The 500 race took on the familiar pattern of Masetti's Gilera four accelerating from the start, with me on my single-cylinder Norton in his slipstream, and Les Graham on the 'porcupine' AJS twin just behind. But it would prove to be a very short race for me. On only the second lap, while being 'towed' along by Masetti at 200–300 rpm over the Norton's normal maximum in top gear, and having just left a long avenue of trees lining both sides of the road, there was another ominous 'bang'. The rear wheel locked, the bike went out of control and literally stood up on its front wheel! Fortunately, I was thrown on to the grass verge at the left side of the road, but the bike went end over end down the road and was a total write-off.

No bones were broken and my only visible injury was a cut on my back. I must have pulled every muscle in my body, though, because the following morning I could hardly drag myself out of bed. The aches and pains were unbelievable, and with the Swiss Grand Prix at Geneva only two weeks later, we had real problems. There was no way I intended risking being thrown down the road like that once more and I vowed never to race again on Dunlop tyres—and I never did.

However, with no other alternative at the time, we settled for using 'standard' Pirelli racing tyres. These had a very hard tread compound, for minimal wear, no doubt, and were immediately dubbed as 'wooden tyres' by Johnny Lockett.

While our mechanics struggled to repair the ravages of the previous two races, team manager Joe Craig, Harold Daniell, Lockett and I motored to Monza in Harold's Standard Vanguard estate car. The object of our trip was to assess whether or not it would be worth our while entering the 'Lion's Den'—the Italian Grand Prix—that September.

It was my first-ever visit to Italy and came as quite a contrast after tidy and unravaged-by-war Switzerland; once we crossed the border, everything looked so pitifully run-down. We duly arrived at Monza and booked in at the Marchesi, an old hotel by the entrance gate to Monza Park. At that point also, Harold went straight to bed with an upset stomach.

Most interestingly, the only other visitors staying at the hotel were the original BRM team of Raymond Mays and Peter Berthon, the designer, and a squad of mechanics, one of whom was doing the test-driving of the then very new 16-cylinder, supercharged Grand Prix racing car. Indeed, dropping unexpectedly in on the BRM team like that provided considerable interest for us, but it was to become an extreme embarrassment. On the circuit and when it was firing on all 16 cylinders, which was not often, the engine sounded superb. But while we were there, rarely more than one flying lap was completed before it went off-song. Goodness knows what

The BRM on test at Monza in 1950, with a youthful Stirling Moss looking on

the eagerly-watching Italians, spying for Ferrari or whoever, must have thought. . . . And on reflection, this should have sown a seed of doubt in Joe Craig's mind—for he had only recently then entrusted the design and development of Norton's own four-cylinder 500 cc racing engine to BRM!

However, more concerned then with our own reason for visiting Monza, we did a few laps of the circuit in Harold's Vanguard, before Joe and I walked around to get the feel of the unfamiliar place. We decided that as we still had a fighting chance of winning the 500 cc World Championship, we would return for the Grand Prix that coming September.

Meanwhile, back in Geneva for the Swiss Grand Prix, race day was very wet. The circuit consisted of fairly long straights up and down both sides of a dual carriageway. There was a hairpin at one end and a few other slowish corners, while the surface was mainly concrete.

Shortly after the start of the 350 race, there was a multiple pile-up triggered off by a mighty slide on the part of the race leader, Les Graham. Incredibly, Les managed to stay on his 7R AJS and stormed away into a massive lead.

Back in the resulting mêlée, I managed to scramble over the pavement without falling. Bob Foster did fall off, but quickly restarted. Although I could make no impression in catching Les, about halfway through the race Bob passed me down one of the straights and only just failed to catch Graham before the finish.

The 500 race was yet another Graham benefit. He always raced well in the wet and Leslie was certainly on top form that day, beating the Gileras of Masetti and Bandirola, while I could do no better than hang on to fourth place.

Back in England, Joe Craig set to work to find more power, while I went to Blandford to try and restore my lost confidence. . . .

The next important race of the season was the Ulster Grand Prix. As I had no knowledge of the Ulster course and it was necessary to grab as many points as possible for the World Championship (which now seemed out of reach), I decided to spend a couple of days on the course before practising started, borrowing a trials machine off Cromie McCandless for the job.

Full of confidence after my success at Blandford on August Bank Holiday Monday, I set sail on my first practice lap and arrived at Muckamore in what seemed like no time at all. I duly motored down the Clady Straight and met the first jump (downhill approach) at about 6400 rpm in top gear, not thinking that it was necessary to ease off for this. However, I took off and seemed to go up and up, very nearly turning the plot right over backwards at a mere 116 mph. Another lesson learned!

I did about eight or ten laps in practice. The motor was going so well that I decided not to 'wear the plot out' by

The first appearance of a Bracebridge Street-built featherbed Norton at Blandford in 1950, where I came first

doing any more laps once I had earned a favourable place on the starting grid.

The Ulster Grand Prix must go down on record as my easiest race in 1950. It was decided that I should refuel as early as possible, that is, at the end of the fifth lap. The edge that I now had on Les Graham's AJS, with regard to both acceleration and maximum speed, plus the super handling of the Norton, enabled me to build up a substantial lead in the first five laps. However, I had just finished taking on fuel, when Graham flashed past the pits with Johnny Lockett hard on his tail.

Trying all I knew, I regained the lead at Muckamore on the same lap, and then gradually drew away. Towards the end of the race, though, rain fell on different parts of the course. Some excitement occurred when, arriving at the two concrete-surfaced bends before Nutts Corner, with about two laps to go, the road conditions suddenly changed from dry to wet. As I had already banked my Norton over for the bend, there was nothing I could do but wait and see. On crossing the tarred joint in the middle of the road, the bike suddenly went into a full-lock broadside which did not terminate until I was almost on the grass. To add to my troubles, somebody fell off in front of me at Nutts Corner! However, I managed to avoid him and continued on my way, somewhat subdued.

All was well from then onwards, and with Masetti unable to finish higher than sixth place, I again had a fighting chance of collecting the 500 cc World Championship.

Everything now depended on the race at Monza—the *Grand Prix des Nations*. Joe Craig, for his part, put all he knew into providing engines capable of winning. To win the Championship, it was necessary for me to win at Monza and for Masetti to finish no higher than third place. Rather a tall order, to say the least!

We travelled by road to Italy, the journey taking rather longer than anticipated, owing to a spot of bother with the van trailer at the Italian frontier. However, we eventually arrived at the Hotel Marchesi, where we had stayed on our previous visit a few weeks earlier.

Having got there two days before the start of official practising, we decided to make full use of the comparative peace and quiet by putting in as much practice as possible. This enabled us to confine our 'official' practice to just a few qualifying laps, and gave us the chance to study the opposition in action. Dickie Dale and I spent considerable time watching at the first bend after the start—a very fast right-hander which kept on going round with a couple of bumps on it. One full-blooded attempt by Ted Frend on an AJS produced a glorious broadside, which induced Dickie to dive behind the nearest tree. No doubt I would have been with him, but I happened to be looking at my stop-watch at the time. Incidentally, of the Italians, Artesiani was by far the most impressive round this curve. Perhaps I should say here that I found it just possible to take this flat out (6800 rpm on a 4.2:1 top gear—about 125 mph), but it was necessary to sit up a little at this speed, as I was working to inches, not feet, as regards line. This resulted

Meticulous preparation for the Grand Prix des Nations, *at Monza in 1950*

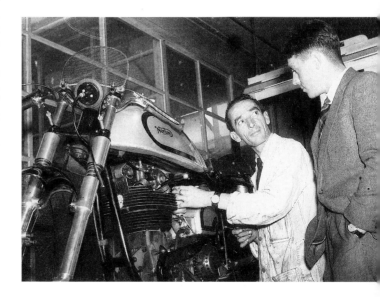

Above *Les Graham shakes me by the hand after I had beaten him to first place in the 350 cc race at Monza*

in a drop of 300 rpm coming out of the bend.

I did about five laps of 'official' practice, three with Masetti on my tail. I reduced my best lap time to 2 min 17 sec in an attempt to shake him off, but without success, so even recording the fastest practice lap did not encourage me very much. To add to our troubles, the Italian food was not agreeing with us. Harold had a day in bed with tummy trouble, and both Johnny and Dickie were feeling off-colour. With so much at stake, I was reduced to bread rolls the day before the race, as a safeguard.

The great day duly arrived, hot and sunny. I had previously arranged with the 'Professor' to treat the 350 cc race as practice for the 'big one', so I had no intention of trying to win. It was thought at the time that Harry Hinton was our man for the job, as his motor was going very well and he had recorded some very fast practice laps.

In the scuffle at the start, some bright spark ran over my foot, which did not make pushing the model any easier. However, at the end of the second lap I was in the lead, thanks to a tow off first one, then another, of the leading six. Just to give an idea of the pace of the race, I might add that at the end of lap three I was lying fifth. This chopping and changing carried on for some time. Graham was the major menace. Every time I snatched the lead, Harry Hinton would come steaming by, towing Les Graham, Dickie Dale and Johnny Lockett behind him. Twice when Les took the lead from me, I got a tow

Right *Facing the wrong way—for the camera—before the race at Monza in 1950*

On the cobbles at Monza in 1950

off him, pulled alongside, and then eased off to stop him taking advantage of _my_ slipstream. I hoped at the same time that Hinton with the 'quick' machine would take full advantage of this and draw away from the group, but with Johnny and Dickie hanging on, he was unable to do this.

With about three laps to go, Johnny disappeared from the scene, while Dickie, who was slipstreaming him at the same time, lost contact with the rest of us. Things were getting serious, and I could see Les being able to work a fast one on Harry and me. So, taking the lead at the start of the last lap, I made an all-out effort. At the start of the long flat-out section of the course, I had a 30- or 40-yard lead. With Les creeping up on me, my position was saved partially by an increase in revs from a tow off Ernie Thomas, whom I was lapping, but mainly by the sporting action of that great Australian rider Harry Hinton. Realizing that to pass Graham would mean towing him back up to me, Harry stayed behind, sacrificing his chance of winning and actually losing second place by less than a yard.

With several hours to wait before the 500 cc race, I went back to the hotel for a sleep. However, I returned just in time to see Eric Oliver round off the race of his career by winning the sidecar class, against what I considered to be far greater opposition than I would have to contend with in the 500 cc solo event which followed. His success against such terrific odds gave me considerable encouragement.

I made a fair start in the 500 race, taking the lead from Bandirola's Gilera at the end of the second lap. To my surprise, I was still in the lead at the end of lap three, but as I had feared, Masetti was a mere two seconds behind on his Gilera. He was obviously playing a waiting game. There he stayed for several laps—and then, on the long straight down to the two bends before the finish of the lap, just for a change, he steamed by as though I was standing still. I always realized that the Gileras were fast, but had never seen anything quite like that one! Mr Taruffi had obviously made a special effort. I regained the lead at the bend after the start, only to lose it again on the straight a few laps later.

I reasoned that the Italian was merely checking to make sure he could pass me before the end of the lap and cross the finishing line in front. So I decided to take a chance and try to regain the lead in between the last two bends, which were very close together. I succeeded, which may have helped to shatter Masetti's schemes. Once more, at about three-quarters distance, he drew up alongside, but was sitting up! (I almost had my head under the handlebars at the time!) However, he dropped back again and from then onwards I knew he was fading.

Well down to it past the start at Monza on the 500 featherbed Norton in 1950

My lead was increased lap by lap, until I received the chequered flag almost a minute in front. It was then that I learned that the race had been stopped with one lap still to go! I cannot describe my joy and pride in winning this race. It was ample recompense for missing by one mark what a few weeks before had seemed completely out of my reach—the World Championship.

Looking back at the 1950 season, I was more than satisfied with my first year as a member of the Norton works team, although the year was marred by Artie Bell's terrible accident at the Belgian Grand Prix and the tyre problems which had prevented me from winning the 500 cc World Championship by a mere one point, at the first attempt. A rather uncompetitive 350 also meant runner-up position to the all-conquering combination of Bob Foster and Velocette in that World Championship class, but, to some extent relieved of the pressures which had dogged my trials riding now that I was a fully-fledged member of the road-racing team, I was delighted to win the National Victory Trial in Shropshire.

Happily, the question mark hanging over our choice of tyres was also resolved. Although I was primarily a racing rider, development had always interested me and I was often called into Joe Craig's office to be included in technical discussions. It was at such a conference that I learned of Joe's visit to the Avon India Rubber Company's factory in Melksham, Wiltshire, at the invitation of managing director O. F. Swanborough. The object of the visit was for Joe to witness comparative tests between the then-existing Avon racing tyres—made in those days predominantly for the 1000 cc Vincent HRD Black Lightning—and the racing tyres of two rival manufacturers.

Joe reported to the conference that it was plainly evident that the Avon tyre was outstanding in its performance on the test rig. He said the point which had impressed him most of all was that where the rival tyres were run at a simulated speed of 120 mph, the Avon was run at 122 mph. And where the rivals ran for ten minutes, the Avon was run for 11 minutes. No mention of this extra loading was made by the Avon technicians—Craig had timed the tests for himself.

Nothing more was said at the time, and later that week I accompanied Norton's managing director, Gilbert Smith, and Joe Craig to a meeting with Dunlop's senior director, Mr Price, and their technical director, Mr King. I was never sure if I was asked to be present at the meeting in the hope that I could be persuaded into racing on Dunlop tyres again—subject to the tread-throwing problem being cured, of course—or if I was at the meeting to provide the excuse, if any was needed, for a decision already taken by the Norton management. (At that time, unknown to me, they had already decided to sign a contract with Avon for the supply of tyres for both racing and production machines.)

However, at that memorable meeting, I recall Gilbert Smith and Joe Craig both being very forceful, and with the memory of being flung off in the Dutch TT still fresh in my mind, I also said my piece. Mr Price was most apologetic, but Mr King tried to explain, admitting that, after 'someone' had complained about the rate of wear with Dunlop racing tyres, the tread depth had been increased without carrying out a test programme. They did not carry out a safety test, he said, because: 'We thought we had a lot in hand.'

At that point, Gilbert Smith produced an Avon racing tyre and requested that it be tested alongside the Dunlop equivalent. He said he wanted photographs taken of the two tyres during the test. Incredibly, Mr King then astonished everyone by stating that Dunlops were not concerned with comparing rival products. I thought Gilbert Smith was going to explode! However, Mr Price quickly grasped the situation and said that the test would be carried out, and with that the meeting at Fort Dunlop ended.

A few days later, I was called to Gilbert Smith's office at Bracebridge Street. He told me that Dunlops had completed the comparison test and agreed that the Avon tyre had proved best. With that, and anxious not to lose Norton's business, they had promised to carry out an extensive development programme to come up with a reliable racing tyre. On the strength of that promise, Gilbert Smith then asked me if I was prepared to change my stance. My emphatic answer was 'No!', reinforced as it was by the attitude of Dunlop's own Mr King, who had not exactly filled me with confidence during our earlier meeting. Thus, the change to Avon tyres was confirmed.

World Champions of 1951

Bearing in mind that I was already 25 years old when I started racing in 1948, I still believe that 1951 was my peak year as a rider—assisted in no small part by the arrival at Bracebridge Street of a gentleman by the name of Leo Kuzmicki.

Leo had served with the Free Polish Forces during World War 2 and, not wishing to return to his native land, had been given a job at Norton's Bracebridge Street factory as a general dogsbody, which included sweeping the factory floor. It was while he was carrying out this menial task that racing mechanic Charlie Edwards inquisitively discovered that Leo had been a lecturer on internal combustion engines at Warsaw University before the war. Charlie could not wait to impart this news to racing boss Joe Craig, who, after relieving Leo of his broom for an interview, gave him a new job in the racing department the following morning!

Leo Kuzmicki was a brilliant engineer, but in my opinion he was never given the credit he was due by Norton Motors—altogether, he was a quietly spoken, very approachable, brilliant man.

Although I had finished the 1950 season as runner-up to Bob Foster in the 350 cc World Championship, the works Norton was no match for the works Velocette. This was because the all-aluminium cylinder head of the Velocette, with its cast-in valve seats, was more efficient than the Norton design, which at that time was a bronze skull cast into an aluminium shell. The better disposal of heat enabled the Velocette engine to run on a higher compression ratio than the Norton engine, without suffering detonation caused by the low-octane (80) petrol used in racing at that time. Thus, it was this little problem that Joe Craig handed over to his new-found expert, Leo, while he, Craig, concentrated on extracting more power from the 500 cc engine.

Leo Kuzmicki greatly valued Joe's vast experience, and would discuss with Joe any engine modification he proposed to make; quite often Joe would be able to offer specific advice from his own previous experiments which, in some instances, he had carried out years before. Leo never ceased to be amazed by this wealth of knowledge. For my part, I found Joe Craig to be an attentive listener whenever I suggested modifications or ideas which I had come up with as a result of our various test sessions, practices or actual races.

However, Joe was generally unsympathetic towards any member of the team who threw one of his precious works Norton machines down on the road. He also did not take kindly to any rider who he felt was not performing up to his expectations in a race. On one such occasion, after the French Grand Prix at Albi in 1951, I remember Johnny Lockett complaining that during the race, while he was in seventh place, Joe deliberately turned away from him when he passed the Norton signalling point.

Contrary to what one might expect from such an engineer and an ex-racing rider of considerable fame and talent, Joe was a hair-raising driver, causing Artie Bell, whenever he could not avoid travelling with Joe as the driver, to sit in the rear seat. In Artie's own words, this was in order to be: 'As far away from the accident as possible!'

Joe never took kindly to Norton's decision to stop works bike development and to race pre-production machines, for he always took great delight in putting it across the Italian multis with his 'out-dated single'—but only if he could prepare the best possible machinery of its kind for the starting line. It was, in fact, the pointlessness of racing virtually production Manx Nortons against the Italian works multis that eventually decided Joe to seek the quiet of retirement. He went to live in Holland, having then recently married a Dutch lady . . . but after only a few brief months, Joe was tragically killed in a car accident while on his way to the 1957 Dutch Show from a holiday in Austria.

To return to 1951, my job at Nortons at this time was concerned with building off-road competition machines in a 12 × 12 ft competition department, plus fettling my short-circuit racing machinery, so I often worked late into the night. Leo also seemed to do most of his best thinking after hours and he often wandered into my 'comp shop' with a piston, cam or cylinder head in his hands, and would explain to me the reasons for the modifications he was making.

Painstakingly methodical and strictly taking only one thing at a time, Leo showed me a flat-topped piston with which he replaced the previous massively-domed design. He also explained to me the theory of 'squish', which seemed so unconventional at the time. The net result of all this 'burning of midnight oil' was a phenomenal 30 per cent increase in power—from 28 bhp at 7200 rpm to 36 bhp at 8000 rpm. And that was on fuel with a lower octane rating than present-day two-star!

It was with this knowledge, and armed with the first machine to be fitted with the new 350 cc engine, that I was sent to Northern Ireland for the North-West 200 held on the very fast Portstewart–Coleraine–Portrush circuit—Joe Craig's favourite proving ground prior to the Isle of Man TT.

Practice was uneventful, but I was full of anticipation for the race because the engine was unbelievably smooth and, at 8000 rpm, appeared to be travelling at '500' speed along the straights.

In the race, although there was little serious opposition, the lap record tumbled and I built up a commanding lead. Then suddenly, shortly beyond Shell Bridge at the start of the full-bore Coleraine–Portrush section, the engine cut out completely and I coasted to a standstill. The problem seemed to be ignition failure, and when it was later discovered that the spark gap of the mica-insulated KLG sparking plug had widened considerably, this was wrongly blamed for the failure—although it was proved to have contributed to the fault.

Back at Bracebridge Street the engine stripped to perfection—but the plug problem was worrying. KLG had supported Norton's racing efforts for many years, but they had no suitable alternative to offer. Reliability, though, was paramount, so we switched to Lodge for the Swiss Grand Prix at Berne, which was held just before the Isle of Man TT that year—and which necessitated a flight direct to the Island immediately after the racing, but that is another story. . . .

Anyway, at the Swiss, race day dawned wet, and the otherwise-superb Berne circuit, with its mixture of smooth tarmac and cobbles, often under trees, was notoriously slippery.

In the 350 cc race, riding with the required wet-weather caution, but aided and abetted by that wonderfully tractable squish-head engine, I built up a comfortable lead—only to have the engine cut out on the sixth lap when victory appeared to be in the bag. This time there was no fault at the sparking-plug gap. We discovered that due to the higher compression ratio and revs of the engine, arcing was occurring inside the magneto, leading to its eventual failure. Although the spark plug had been a contributory factor at the North-West 200, the ignition failure in fact stemmed from the magneto.

With rain still falling, the 500 cc race confirmed our worst suspicions. Nobody, if they are honest, delights in racing in the wet. But given time to explore the conditions of the road surface, I could usually cope. My start in the race, however, was mediocre, and at the end of the first lap Fergus Anderson, renowned for his wet-weather riding, led on the wide-angle V-twin Moto Guzzi. In second place was George Cordey, while I was some way behind in third place.

By the end of the second lap I had closed the gap with Cordey, and on the third I passed both Cordey and Anderson to take the lead. Then, on approaching the pits during the fourth lap, my magneto failed and I coasted in to retire—having set the fastest lap of the race the third time round. This was a speed of 89.4 mph, against Anderson's race-winning average of 80.1 mph! However, in fairness, it must be said that there was little need for Fergus to press on once I had left the scene.

Thankful that confirmation of our ignition problem had come before the Isle of Man TT—even though practice on the Island had by then started—we left the Swiss circuit for Berne airport, somewhat subdued. The airport was, in fact, a large grass field, and we were met at the small terminal building by a dapper Swissair pilot who had arrived from Zurich in a DC-3 Dakota aircraft, in freight-carrying mode, that had already been refuelled.

We were later joined by the AJS team, plus Fergus Anderson, Tommy Wood and others, to make a total of 12 passengers and 13 machines. There was some debate as to the best load configuration, but it was eventually decided to load the machines crosswise, with the passengers on bench seats along either side of the fuselage.

The pilot spoke perfect English and was extremely efficient. The machines and all luggage and equipment were weighed before being stowed, but it was soon apparent that the load was more than he had anticipated, for as the last few machines went aboard, so too a similar weight of fuel was pumped out.

As an ex-RAF fighter pilot, Les Graham of AJS, together with Tommy Wood, gave us a running commentary on the proceedings—which hardly filled the rest of us with confidence! With all aboard, the pilot announced that we would need to land at Brussels airport to take on more fuel, and where also the runway was long enough for the aircraft to take off with a full load. But that was not possible at Berne, so the pilot took a Jeep for a run along the length of the airfield and, on returning, simply said: 'That should be OK!'

It was raining and quite misty when we taxied out to the end of the field, and the DC-3 was then backed up as far as the perimeter fence. The twin engines were revved right up and, on full power, we began the take-off run. We seemed to gather speed very slowly on the soggy grass and I felt we would never get off the ground . . . but we did, and with no apparent panic (as far as the pilot was concerned) we cleared the far boundary fence by just three or four feet—certainly no more. Once that was achieved and we were in the air, things settled down a little. But Joe Craig, who never enjoyed flying anyway, spoke not a word during the entire flight.

On our descent into Brussels, I was invited to sit in the co-pilot's seat for the landing, which was made with perfect precision. And then, after refuelling, I was the 'co-pilot' once again; this remains a wonderful memory, for our flight path took us across London, which was ablaze with lights for the Festival of Britain celebrations that year.

Our Swiss pilot, quite alone and without a proper co-pilot or navigator, headed for the Isle of Man where, as we approached at about midnight, the cloud thickened. This did not seem to bother him, though, despite the fact that he had never before landed at Ronaldsway. He brought his plane down steadily through the low cloud to make yet another perfect landing—accompanied by sighs of relief from all concerned. With his feet safely back on the ground, Joe Craig regained his voice and asked the pilot where he would be staying for the night. 'I'm not staying,' he replied. 'When the aircraft has been unloaded, I shall fly home to Zurich!'

With the ignition problems behind us, thanks to our North-West 200 and Swiss Grand Prix outings, Nortons approached the 1951 Junior TT with confidence. My 350 cc engine was incredibly smooth and free-revving, and this combination, along with perfect weather conditions, almost produced a disaster on my first practice lap! It happened as I approached the long, rock-faced, right-hand sweep before Laurel Bank. I was so exhilarated by the occasion that I failed to realize, until almost too late, that I was approaching this deceptive bend at a speed more akin to that of the previous year's 500. I had no option but to lay my machine over to the point where both wheels began to break away and, still on the overrun, negotiate the following left-hander totally off line!

The TT course, although not quite as difficult to learn as Germany's Nürburgring, is unique. There are so many blind, or near-blind, bends which are _just_ full-bore, and after a year's absence one was always 'impressed' by the first couple of practice laps—especially on the 500 which, inevitably, was a bit quicker than the previous year's model.

The law looks on as I enter Parliament Square, Ramsey, on my way to winning the 1951 Junior TT

Above *Airborne at Ballagaraghan, now flattened out, in the 1951 Junior TT*

Above right *Leaving Governor's Bridge in a hurry, during the 1951 Junior TT*

Monday's Junior TT was run in ideal conditions and established the pattern which was to apply, almost without hindrance, for me throughout that season. Riding with number 48, I led from start to finish, breaking the lap record from the standing start (the starting line was now back up the road and coincided with the finishing line) at 89.75 mph, followed by a second lap, the fastest, at 91.38 mph—and coincidentally the same as my first lap on the 500 in the 1950 Senior race!

Australian Harry Hinton held second place for two laps until he fell at Laurel Bank, leaving Lockett in a safe second spot until the end. Jack Brett, who took over Dickie Dale's ride on a works Norton at the last minute, finished third (Dale had been taken ill during practising).

In almost windless conditions, my 350 was slightly undergeared and I needed to roll back the throttle at several places around the course. Despite this, after establishing my lead, I changed up at about 6800–7000 rpm—about 500 revs below normal. The quite remarkable tractability of the engine enabled me to round all the really slow corners, except Governor's Bridge, without slipping the clutch. I had discovered during practice that a progressive opening of the throttle produced better acceleration, even coming out of Ramsey Hairpin, than the power-consuming practice of slipping the clutch to keep the revs within the powerband.

Perhaps the most noteworthy happening to emerge from this race, though, was the outstanding performance set by Rhodesian newcomer Ray Amm, who finished ninth. His consistency was remarkable in that, apart from the standing start and refuelling laps, his times were 26:23, 26:21, 26:23, 26:24 and 26:21.8. Ray subsequently became Norton's leading rider and quite a sharp thorn in my side. The writing was on the wall. . . .

In the Senior TT, with a fastest lap of 93.52 mph under my belt, I had reason to be confident, but Les Graham, although mounted on the then-still-unproven four-cylinder MV, was quite capable of rising to any occasion if his mount was competitive.

As the 1950 winner, I had the benefit of starting at number 1, while Graham was way back on number 90. Personally, I preferred the freedom of a clear road ahead of me, unlike some riders who seemed to require the close proximity of others to give their best. However, I found no difficulty in racing against the clock, and it was from 1951 onwards that I consciously started making a big effort on the opening lap of each TT I contested with a capable machine, with the intention of demoralizing the opposition.

Right *Receiving the chequered flag at the end of a record-breaking Junior TT in 1951*

I was therefore quite shattered on arriving at Ramsey Hairpin, on lap two, to be shown a board marked '3 –1', indicating that I was in third place, one second behind the second-place man! As I then proceeded over the Mountain like the proverbial 'scalded cat', my brain was working overtime. Les Graham had started almost 15 seconds after me, so Steve Darbishire would have been unable to signal me from the pits at the end of the first lap, as Graham had not then gone by my signaller at Ramsey. Les must be flying, I thought. But who was in second place? Was it Bill Doran (AJS) or Jack Brett?

In fact, I had been shown the signal prepared for Brett—who had come into the Norton team in place of Dickie Dale who was ill with pleurisy. The actual situation was that I was leading the race after the first lap by 41 seconds from Lockett and Doran, who were tying for second place; Graham was lying sixth. To my relief I was given the correct information as I next passed the pits, but with the added haste of my second lap, 23 min 47 sec, it gave me a new lap record of 95.72 mph. Had I ridden the complete lap with the same urgency as I did

The 1951 Senior TT—I used a handkerchief as a means of avoiding a sore throat caused by my habit of riding with my mouth open!

from Ramsey, I feel sure I would have topped the 96 mph mark.

Jack Brett fell at the Gooseneck on lap two, and I was 78 seconds ahead of team-mate Lockett, who was slowly pulling away from Doran. Graham retired at the end of lap two with valve-gear problems. That enabled me to ease up—which was probably just as well, because by then an over-abundance of oil had found its way on to the rear tyre from the chain oilers and had begun to cause the occasional slide. By lap seven, there was so much oil escaping that I was having difficulty in keeping my feet on the footrests. However, Lockett retired at Ramsey with a broken chain on the final lap, which brought Doran into second place—4 min 22.4 sec behind me.

For myself, I was elated. I had joined that select band of TT riders—Stanley Woods, Jimmy Guthrie and Tim Hunt—who had achieved Junior and Senior TT doubles on Nortons. What a tribute to such superb machines.

After my double success at the Isle of Man TT, it was back to the Continent for the Belgian Grand Prix at Spa-Francorchamps. I was confident of a competitive ride in the 350 cc race around the ultra-fast 8.8-mile circuit, but was anxious to discover just how much more power had been extracted from the Italian 500 cc Gilera, Guzzi and MV multi-cylinder opposition. I did not have to wait long for the answer. Several riders bettered my 1950 lap record during practice by up to ten seconds, but the fastest was Doran with 4 min 53 sec at 107.7 mph (an 11-second improvement) on the AJS 'porcupine' twin.

On the evening before the race, I went for a walk with Joe Craig to discuss my riding tactics for the 500 race. Fortunately for us, the fuel for the races supplied by Gulf was officially of 80 octane rating, but it was in fact considerably higher than this, which enabled us to raise the compression ratio on our 500 cc engines. This produced a marked improvement in the performance of our singles, but was of little benefit to the multis.

I told Joe that if I could make a super start, aided by the downhill road which virtually eliminated the usual initial acceleration advantage of the multis over a single, and if I could hold the lead to La Source Hairpin close to the end of the first lap, I reckoned I would be in with a chance. It was essential to the success of my plan that I not be overtaken during the first lap by any of the more powerful opposition, because if that happened, I would be reduced to slipstreaming them along the straights and would be unable to have a clear run at the fast sweeping bends where the superb roadholding of the Norton came into its own. We decided that, at least during the early part of the race, if my plan worked, signals would not be necessary, as I would be able to see my pursuers by looking back along the road after rounding the hairpin.

It was on the way back to our hotel from that walk that Joe Craig, while talking generally of racing, paid me a great compliment. He told me that during his many years' involvement in road racing, in his opinion, only two riders had been 'naturals'—Tim Hunt, who had ridden Nortons during the early 1930s, and me!

The following day, the 350 race worked to perfection. I made a cracking start and led all the way to the finish at a record 100.52 mph, with a lap record of 101.3 mph. My team-mate Johnny Lockett came second and Bill Lomas (Velocette) was third.

Only one MV four, ridden by Carlo Bandirola, came to the start for the 500 race, but otherwise all was set for a classic battle with 31 starters competing from ten nations. Despite my big effort, Gilera's Umberto Masetti, the 1950 winner, beat me off the line from his solitary position at the front of the grid. Even so, I rode around the outside of him at the first bend, Eau Rouge. Trying all I could, I arrived at La Source ahead of Geminiani (Guzzi)—I saw him entering the hairpin as I departed.

Manx photographer Bill Salmond, Len Parry, Ken Kavanagh, Reg Armstrong and I pose with my Senior TT machine in 1951

So far, so good, I thought. Behind the Guzzi rider was Nello Pagani (Gilera four) and Bill Doran (AJS twin).

At the end of the second lap, Geminiani was about 100 yards further back from the hairpin as I left to complete the circuit in 4 min 56 sec (106.64 mph). Third, fourth and fifth places were occupied by the Gilera trio of Masetti, Pagani and Alfredo Milani at this time.

I was riding right on the limit, with both wheels drifting at long full-bore bends like Stavelot, but was in my element. Even so, on the fifth lap, Geminiani closed the gap slightly with a new lap record of 4 min 54.8 sec. Then, on the eighth lap, I managed 4 min 52.8 sec (107.8 mph). By lap 12, Milani had overtaken Geminiani with Reg Armstrong (AJS), Pagani and Lockett following, in that order, to the end of the race.

Looking back, the 1951 500 cc Belgian Grand Prix, then the world's fastest road race, must go down in my book as the hardest race of my career. And as I stood on the winner's rostrum, listening to our national anthem, it was also my proudest moment.

Above *Joe Craig, myself, Johnny Lockett and Jack Brett photographed with my A90 Austin Convertible at the Dutch TT in 1951*

One week later came the Dutch TT on the 10.2-mile Van Drenthe circuit at Assen in the north of Holland. This was a very different race altogether. Consisting mainly of long straights and slow corners, it was likely to be a Gilera benefit. However, uncertain weather prevailed throughout the previous week and Friday's practice was in the wet.

As the Dutch circuit was noted for its slippery surface, some of it being cobblestone, I decided to try shallow saw cuts in the treads of both tyres on my 350 in an attempt to improve grip. In the wet practising, this did indeed prove to be advantageous.

On Saturday's race day, ominous black clouds threatened rain, although the roads were actually drying. Then, within 30 minutes of the start of the 350 cc race, out came the sun, which caused worry about increased tyre wear if the race was to be run on totally dry roads. It was decided to change the rear tyre for one with no saw cuts. The front tyre was not changed, though, as undue wear was not a likely problem. Also, as time was short, I decided to retain the front tyre used during practising.

A high wind blowing from the south-west promised higher speeds along the start/finish straight as 35

Left *A discussion at Hooghalen during practice for the Dutch TT between myself, Lockett and Brett, with Joe Craig studying his notes*

Above _Looking a little dejected, being escorted back to the start after crashing at 115 mph when leading the 350 race at Assen, Holland, in 1951_

machines were lined up for the start in front of around 200,000 spectators. As the light glowed green, Norton team-mate Jack Brett and I were first away, side by side, but I led into the first bend and built up an eight-second lead over Bill Doran's AJS, Brett having fallen. Lockett and Armstrong were third and fourth.

With the help of the following wind, my 350 was really flying on the approach to the flat-out S-bend after the start. Too late, I realized at near 500 cc speed that I should have peeled off earlier into the 'S'—I was then forced to bank over at a much greater angle than usual to keep on the racing line.

The front tyre suddenly lost all grip and down I went! The cut tread had reduced the tyre's rigidity and it folded over. My machine was extensively damaged, and as for myself, one elbow had lost a considerable amount of skin and flesh, but I was able to walk back to the paddock for medical attention.

Meanwhile, Doran raced on to score a fine win, while Brett fell off for the second time; Armstrong (AJS), who had been battling with Lockett for most of the race, also fell off, bringing Lockett down with him. So, on that occasion, the entire Norton factory team bit the dust!

In the 500 cc race, there were three official entries from AJS, Gilera and Norton, with four from Guzzi and four from MV Agusta. The field was 32 strong for the 18-lap, 185-mile race.

I was on the second row of the grid, with Masetti (Gilera), Pagani (Gilera), Geminiani (Guzzi) and Doran (AJS) ahead of me. By anticipating the green starting light, though, I managed to lead into the first corner. However, Fergus Anderson (Guzzi) led at the end of the opening lap, having breezed by me down the straight to Hooghalen.

At the end of the second lap, I had regained the lead but only a few yards separated the first six machines of myself, Anderson, Pagani, Masetti, Milani and Bruno Ruffo (Guzzi). Masetti overhauled both Anderson and Pagani during the third lap, and in so doing set the best lap time for the race—6 min 20 sec (97.28 mph).

After two more laps, both Masetti and Pagani steamed ahead of me down the long straight to Oude Tol, with Anderson fourth. Meanwhile, I took every opportunity to overtake the Gilera riders on corners, provided I was close enough to do so after slipstreaming them down the straights.

On lap ten Anderson dropped his Guzzi at Bartelds

Below _Leading the Gilera four-cylinder machines of Masetti and Pagani at the S-bend where earlier I had crashed my 350 in the 1951 Dutch TT_

Right *Crossing the finishing line at Assen—first in the 500 cc race*

Bocht, but by lap 13 I had opened up a 100-yard lead over Pagani, with Masetti lying further astern. Both Gilera machines were puffing out tell-tale blue smoke after being driven so hard and on lap 14 they retired, leaving Milani to uphold Gilera prestige a mere ten seconds behind me. With this third successive win, my 500 cc World Championship hopes were now very high.

With little respite, the following week found us at the *Circuit Raymond Sommer* on the outskirts of Albi, south-west France. But where Britain had dominated in Belgium and Holland, it was Italy who gained honours in France.

The triangular 5.5-mile circuit had two very fast tree-lined stretches, while the third leg of the course embodied a downhill S-bend where general traffic had worn through the road surface. The exit from the slow hairpin in the village of St Juéry was also extremely slippery, while the finishing line was on the first half of a tight double bend.

Sultry heat during practice, plus a thunderstorm on Saturday night followed by rain on race day, dampened

Below *Early, happier times at the Dutch TT after winning the 500 race in 1951. Joe Craig has obviously forgiven me for throwing away one of his 350s a couple of hours beforehand!*

Right *Crossing the finishing line at Assen—first in the 500 cc race*

Above *With Stirling Moss at the Sportsman of the Year presentation, held at the Savoy Hotel in London*

front wheel going ahead just after we crossed the line.

Following subsequent wins in both the 350 and 500 cc classes of the Ulster Grand Prix, on the Clady circuit, I became the first rider to achieve a double world title in the same year, while Norton gained the Manufacturers' World Championships. However, in the last event of the world title series, the Italian Grand Prix at Monza, although I won the 350 race comfortably, the 500 was a different case altogether. Milani cleared off at the start and I could do no better than finish fourth behind the similar four-cylinder Gileras of Masetti and Pagani. It was becoming very evident that a British multi-cylinder challenger was needed.

My feelings at the end of such a year as 1951 can be summed up in one word—ecstatic. I had scored a unique 350 and 500 cc double in the World Championships, was voted 'Sportsman of the Year', and had been awarded the RAC's coveted Segrave Trophy. A personal satisfaction for me, though, was that I had scored an Isle of Man TT double, which had only been achieved by three 'greats'— Tim Hunt, Jimmy Guthrie and Stanley Woods.

Below *Saying my piece after receiving the 1951 Sportsman of the Year award*

most riders' spirits. Also, the Norton mechanics had been at full stretch coping with damaged cylinder heads and pistons burnt by the 'official' but nevertheless low octane fuel provided for the meeting. The compression ratio of the 350 and 500 cc single-cylinder Nortons had to be lowered, which took the edge off performance, but the twin- and four-cylinder machines of AJS, Gilera and Guzzi were virtually unaffected.

It was raining steadily at the start of the 350 cc race, but I soon settled down and within three laps had a 15-second advantage over my own team-mate, Jack Brett. Then, when the rain ceased and the road dried, my lap speed increased until I held a clear minute lead at the chequered flag, adding maximum points and a third win towards the 350 cc World Championship.

The 500 cc race, though, was a different matter. Milani and Pagani cleared off on their Gilera fours, although Doran (AJS) was to beat Pagani for second place and finish only eight seconds behind Milani at the finish. A maximum effort on my part to beat fourth-placeman Masetti across the finishing line came to nought, with my

FROM TWO TO FOUR,
AND BACK TO TWO WHEELS

A busy weekend

In 1952, I left the Norton factory to become a partner in a motorcycle business in St Helens. However, I made an arrangement with the factory to ride for them in all the classic races—but with freedom to enter other events of my own choice.

This worked well in general, but in February of that year *Motor Cycling* discovered that I had agreed to ride at San Remo on the day after 'Silverstone Saturday', which that journal sponsored. And Gilbert Smith had promised that the Norton team, including myself, would compete at Silverstone! I was prepared to fit in with any scheme that could be devised to enable me to race at both events—but there was the added complication of qualifying with practice laps at both meetings.

None of the scheduled flights could whisk me back and forth in time, but it was discovered that Fleet Street used a British European Airways freight plane every Saturday night to get newspapers to the South of France. Fortunately, BEA agreed to take two passengers—myself and Bob Holliday of *Motor Cycling*—on their flight to Nice.

Practice for the San Remo meeting was scheduled for Friday and Saturday afternoons, with Silverstone's also on Friday. To cope at the Italian end, Count 'Johnny' Lurani was consulted, and at his request the *Moto Club San Remo* agreed to change Friday's practising to the morning.

This would enable me, together with my late wife Pat and Harry Johnson, my old army friend from Catterick who was also to look after my Norton, to drive in a borrowed Austin A40 and trailer to San Remo, qualify for the race and then drive to Nice to catch the afternoon plane to London's Northolt airport, arriving at Silverstone later that evening—albeit, too late for practice. Fortunately, the Silverstone regulations permitted a practising period on Saturday morning. This was intended for riders who, with good reason, could not practise on Friday. The race stewards accepted me in this category.

With the San Remo practice completed, I left for England and arrived at The Sun Inn, Brackley, on schedule. The hitch came, unexpectedly, when trying to cover the few miles to Silverstone the following morning. I had to be at the circuit by 8 am for my practice. But with the roads jammed with traffic, the car taking me to the circuit was hopelessly held up and it seemed that I would not reach the circuit in sufficient time to qualify. Luckily, a mobile policeman on a Triumph Speed Twin saw my predicament and offered to take me and my luggage perched on the rear mudguard of his machine. It was uncomfortable, but all went well and the effort was rewarded by wins in both the Junior (350 cc) and Senior (500 cc) championship races.

Escorted once again by the same police officer, we then set off in Bob Holliday's car for Bob's North London home where a hot bath and a meal welcomed me. Awake again at 2 am in order to be at Northolt by 2.45 am, at 0400 hours BST we were airborne for Nice.

Taking delivery of the caravan in 1952 which always threatened to take charge of my J2 van when going downhill

Left *Riding the 350 around Woodcote at Silverstone*

A Fiat Topolino awaited us, and with Bob and the luggage crammed into the back of what is really only a two-seater, we set off on the 40 or so miles to San Remo, with our driver providing an excellent impersonation of Fangio. We arrived shaken, but still in one piece.

I managed to get a couple of hours' rest before the race in which, fortunately, I did not have too much serious opposition. Towards the end, I was almost dozing off, when suddenly I realized that a single-cylinder Gilera Saturno was breathing down my neck. The shock had me bouncing off a straw bale and bending a footrest. Luckily, I was able to collect my senses together in time to make it first to the finishing line—from where I went straight to bed!

Right *And they say motor racing is dangerous! Spectators line the roadside during the 500 race at Codogno, Italy, in 1952—this race was held the weekend after my travels between Silverstone and San Remo!*

Below *Urging the 500 Norton along at Silverstone*

An introduction to car racing

On the day I was presented with the Sportsman of the Year trophy in 1951 at the Savoy Hotel in London, Lord Brabazon asked me if I had ever thought of racing on four wheels. I answered that I had not, but that I did enjoy driving fast cars. Lord Brabazon then suggested that if I was interested (and I was), he could arrange a test for me with Aston Martin. I was subsequently contacted by John Wyer, Aston Martin's racing manager.

I feel the best way to describe what followed is to quote John's own words in the book *Racing With The David Brown Aston Martins*.

'In 1952 we acquired two drivers of very great potential, Geoff Duke and Peter Collins. I had already met Geoff at MIRA, when he was testing a Norton for Joe Craig, and that was the first time I had seen him ride. It really was an astonishing performance—I had never seen anything like it in my life and was enormously impressed.

'Then Lord Brabazon mentioned to David Brown that

Bob Walsham of Avons feels the tyre while I chat with officials at Easter Goodwood in 1952

Duke (who had won both the 350 and 500 cc World Championships in 1951) was interested in trying a car. He just wanted to find out if he was any good.

'I was in touch with Geoffrey and offered him a car which he came to drive at MIRA, having done a lot of testing there.

'We used the perimeter circuit (this was before the high-speed banking had been built) and he really was sensational right from the start. He asked me not to time him to begin with, as he just wanted to get the feel of the car; but I did so for my own interest and in the first spell he was only a second slower than the best time we had ever done.

'The car was one of the lightweight DB2s and he came in to say that it was very different from anything he was accustomed to, but that he felt he could get the hang of it, given time.

'So he went out again and in his second session went faster than any of our drivers had ever gone on that circuit—and this was the first time he had ever driven a car in anger!

'I promptly signed him up. Because of his motorcycle

Pensive before the start at Easter Goodwood in 1952— my first race with Aston Martin

commitments, he only drove for us four times that year (including that sensational drive at Berne) before he crashed during a motorcycle race in Germany and broke his ankle. We signed him again for 1953, but he was not happy in the team and went back to motorcycles full-time after only two races, at Sebring and Silverstone.'

John Wyer concluded: 'I know that my opinion of Duke's abilities as a driver differs from that of most contemporary observers and the generally accepted judgement is that he was a very great motorcyclist who failed to make the transition to cars.

'I maintain that I had more opportunity to evaluate him than anybody else and I am convinced that he had great potential.

'Temperamentally, he had difficulty in settling down in the team and certainly the established drivers did nothing to make it easier for him. Not unnaturally, they resented the fact that he got more publicity than they did. But I will always regard Geoff Duke's early retirement as a loss to motor racing.'

My first race with an Aston Martin was at the BARC Easter meeting at Goodwood in April 1952, where I came second in the prototype DB3. This was just prior to our departure by road for the motorcycle races at San Remo, described earlier.

Left *The bonnet adrift in my first race with Aston Martin at Goodwood; I finished second to Stirling Moss*

Below left *Through the chicane in front of a crowded grandstand, again at Goodwood in 1952*

Then in May, at Silverstone, I crashed when an MG, which I was about to lap, broke a con rod and dropped all its oil at Stowe Corner. I spun off the track and into the catch fence, but was able to restart and continue in the race. On the next lap, though, I had just set up the car for Abbey Curve—which was flat out in a DB3—when the car went straight on! I thought the steering had failed as a result of the earlier spin-off, but, as it turned out, something had failed within the steering box. The marshals standing in the adjoining wheat field had to scatter as I did my impression of a high-speed combine

Right *Quiet reflection before the start at Silverstone*

Below *After the spin, but before the Silverstone harvest*

harvester, filling the radiator grille with straw before the car came to a halt.

My next race was at Berne, where I had my most enjoyable race with Aston Martin. Berne was my kind of circuit and I knew it very well. It was the only Grand Prix where they held car and motorcycle races at the same event, and in previous years, after finishing my motorcycle practising on the Norton, I would always go to the S-bend at the top of the hill just to watch Fangio—the absolute maestro. So when Aston Martin asked me if I would like to drive at Berne, I was delighted. I was also pleased that the car was a DB2 because it handled like a motorcycle—it went where it was pointed and stayed on line.

Reg Parnell and I both had lightweight DB2s, while the main opposition consisted of four Mercedes-Benz

In the pits for a check-up during practice for the 1952 Empire Trophy, Isle of Man. The wires were starting to come adrift

Right Diving into the Manx Arms at Onchan on the Island in the 1952 Empire Trophy Race

300 SLs and two works Lancias. There were two practice sessions, but in the first one my car did not go at all well. So for the second outing John Wyer suggested that I should drive Parnell's car, which I did. And what a difference! I recorded the fifth-fastest time, behind the four Mercs. But as I had used Reg's car, this put him on the second row of the grid while I was at the back!

There was an amusing incident after this particular session. At the end of motorcycle practice, Joe Craig watched the car practice at the first bend after the start—a quickish right-hander. Now, Joe was an excellent judge of both riding and driving ability, so I had asked him to tell me later what he had thought of my driving. When I asked him for his opinion, he said: 'Very good. But in the second session, *Parnell* was really flying through there.'

In the race itself, as I was on the back row of the grid, I did not get a very good start. But as my car was going very well, I picked up a few places on the first lap, including passing one of the Lancias. Then, on the 13th lap just before the top of the hill, Rudolph Caracciola's Merc left the road, hitting a tree head-on which then fell across the road! His three Merc team-mates were ahead of him, so they escaped. But we had to 'queue up' while the tree was removed. The Mercedes trio had completed almost another lap by the time we got on the move again, but I eventually got into fourth place, although I was lapped by the more powerful German cars after my car went on to five cylinders for the last two laps.

My last race of 1952 was the British Empire Trophy Race held on the Isle of Man. I drove a DB3 which, although more powerful, did not handle like the DB2. I made quite a good start, but spent the first couple of laps trying to find somewhere to overtake Duncan Hamilton's Jaguar. Once I managed to do that, though, I had a comfortable lead, and if I had maintained my average speed I would also have won on handicap.

But that was not to be. Coming down the hill towards the Manx Arms, my engine cut out; a wire at the back of the dashboard had become detached—a recurrence of a similar failure during practice. I managed to do a temporary repair and limped back to the pits to get it properly fixed. Then, a couple of laps later, the crankshaft of my engine broke!

Back at the pits, David Brown apologized. He told me that the engine had already done a terrific amount of running on the test-bench. He explained that the factory had primarily looked upon the Manx race as good practice for me, not as a serious outing—had they realized that I might drive so well, they would have given me a decent engine!

Right In the lead, after quite a dice with Duncan Hamilton's Jaguar in the 1952 Empire Trophy

Motorcycles to Aston Martins

At the same time as I was venturing into the world of car racing, my motorcycling career with Nortons was continuing at a pace. Our first Grand Prix in 1952 was the Swiss, at Berne, and for the second year in succession this first real test of the latest Nortons revealed problems which could otherwise have spelled disaster in the TT. The 500 cc engine had been given a new cam which allowed the exhaust valve to return more rapidly to its seat—too rapidly as it turned out, for towards the end of practice, the head broke off the exhaust valve in the engine of Dave Bennett's machine; Dave was a newcomer to the Norton team, making his first appearance in a continental race and showing exceptional promise.

Opposition in the 350 cc race came from two of the new AJS triple ohc models in the hands of Bill Doran and Rod Coleman, as well as a third works AJS—a single-camshaft edition—to be ridden by Jack Brett. There was also the very new three-cylinder DKW from Germany with Siegfried Wünsche aboard; in all, there were 28 starters. I led throughout the 21 laps of the 4.5-mile Bremgarten circuit, tailed at the beginning by Reg Armstrong, but after two laps Coleman displaced him, with Brett fourth, and so it stayed to the end.

During practice for the 500 cc race, some damage was done to the cylinder heads of the Nortons due to the 'official' fuel, which was not the specified 80-octane clear. This, plus the new exhaust cam, was what had caused the valve head to break off in Dave Bennett's engine. The engine was therefore rebuilt for the race, complete with new cylinder head and valves—which, in all probability, turned out to be a tragic turn of fate.

The 500 cc race was a much more competitive event than the 350, with three works Nortons (myself, Armstrong and Bennett), three AJSs (Doran, Coleman and Brett), three Gileras (Alfredo Milani, Masetti and Liberati), and two MV Agustas (Graham and Bandirola), plus 14 others to make up a field of 25. Brett, Armstrong and I were first off the line, but at the end of the first lap Graham was chasing me; Brett was third, Coleman fourth, Armstrong fifth, Masetti sixth, and Doran, riding the latest shorter-wheelbase AJS, was seventh. Graham's new five-speed MV was showing remarkable speed—

after five laps the gap was only nine seconds. But, at the end of lap eight, Graham stopped at the pits to retire. Armstrong also retired, owing to persistent cutting-out of his engine. Masetti and Milani both called at the pits, and Coleman lost a whole lap when he had to change a spark plug. What changes of fortune!

Then, as I crossed the finishing line to complete my 19th lap, disaster struck! The exhaust valve dropped in, producing a horrible clanking sound. This left Brett in the lead, but then, on lap 21, he too stopped to remove a loose front mudguard! The advantage passed to Doran, with Dave Bennett five seconds in arrears, and Brett now four seconds behind Bennett.

On lap 24 Brett led Bennett, with Doran, who was having trouble with his gearchange, lying third—but very few yards separated all three. Then on lap 27, with only one lap to go, there came a tragic end to a promising career when Dave Bennett went off the road and suffered injuries from which he died.

In the closing stages of that race, I had been standing in the pits worrying about the possible outcome of Dave's lone battle with two far more experienced riders—and my worst fears sadly came to pass. What a cruel twist of fate. If Dave's engine had lasted through the practice, the valve breakage would almost certainly have occurred during the race and thereby saved his life.

Following the Swiss, the motorcycling circus moved to the Isle of Man. I could not claim that the 1952 Junior TT was one of my momentous victories, for, apart from persistent cramp in my right leg, the ride went without incident. My first lap took 25 min 5 sec (90.27 mph)—nine seconds faster than the opening lap of 1951. That established a lead of 37 seconds over Rod Coleman (AJS), although only four seconds separated Coleman from Ray Amm (Norton), Jack Brett (AJS) and Reg Armstrong (Norton).

The second lap was my fastest in 24 min 53 sec (91.0 mph), but it was still six seconds outside the previous year's record. Even so, I was able to ease up from then onwards in response to signals, and the race average of 90.29 mph was surprisingly a new race record—my fourth in consecutive TTs. Reg Armstrong

finished second, Coleman was third after Amm fell at Braddan Bridge on lap three, and Brett retired with engine trouble at the Stonebreakers Hut on lap four.

My Junior TT success on the Monday four days earlier, plus the knowledge that our exhaust cam trouble of Switzerland had been solved, should have filled me with confidence for the Senior TT. Victory in the race would give me a Senior hat trick—something that even the great Stanley Woods had missed. But something told me that I would not pull it off—and after my hunch proved correct, Steve Darbishire told me that he, too, had had the same premonition.

The beginning of the end came just after reaching Union Mills on the first lap, when the engine began misfiring. It was intermittent, but when it did occur, maximum revs dropped from 7000 to 5800 in top gear.

Parliament Square in the 1952 Senior TT, prior to my retirement with clutch trouble

The primary chain seen dropping on to the road as Reg Armstrong wins the 1952 Senior TT

The most likely cause of this was a particle of dirt in the jet well of the carburettor, because the trouble was at its worst after a spell of high load and revs, but then cleared itself when I throttled back.

To make up for the maximum speed I was losing, I had to 'scratch' around the twisty sections, and although the misfire persisted throughout the second, third and fourth laps, my lead over Les Graham's MV four steadily increased. Much of this advantage was caused by Les who overshot his pit when stopping to refuel, costing him some 55 seconds and probably the race.

Despite my engine's misfiring, I should have been comfortably placed, but at Governor's Bridge, near the end of the fourth lap, I pulled in the clutch as usual to keep up the revs and the lever suddenly went slack in my grip. That, I knew, was it! I would soon be out of the race.

I stopped at the pits where Steve Darbishire adjusted the clutch cable to take up the slack. It worked momentarily, but after a few test pulls, the cable again went slack. The cage spacing the rollers which formed the clutch bearing had broken up, causing the rollers and the clutch sprocket to tilt. Previously, these rollers had been fitted without the tin cage, which was perfectly reliable. But some bright spark in the drawing office at Bracebridge Street had decided that was not good enough and had specified that the bearing cage, a standard fitting on standard road machines, should also be fitted to the Manx racers! Needless to say, this 'improvement' was dropped after this one demonstration of its possibilities.

Above *The Norton team lined up at Hooghalen on the old Dutch TT circuit in 1952. From left to right: Jill Amm, Ray Amm, myself, Joe Craig, Reg Armstrong and Ken Kavanagh*

Below *Enjoying a chat and a cigarette with the lads at Assen in 1952! Reg Armstrong and Ray Amm are the smokers, while Ken Kavanagh and I merely observe*

Meanwhile, back at the pits, I knew that if I could persuade the engine to restart, I could continue in the race. However, I decided against this for two reasons: firstly, apart from the personal risk to myself, I would have had no means of disengaging the engine from the rear wheel if anything went wrong, thus being a danger to other riders; and secondly, my primary chain was slack and dry of oil, which meant that it was unlikely to last three more laps.

After my retirement, which elevated Les Graham to first place, a battle royal developed between himself and Reg Armstrong (Norton). But by Ramsey on the fifth lap, Armstrong was at Graham's rear wheel, and by the end of that lap he had gone ahead and was only 12 seconds adrift on corrected time. After six laps, Armstrong now led Graham by four seconds. The MV rider was in some sort of trouble—he had missed a gearchange when his foot slipped, due to oil on the gearchange pedal, and touched valves causing a loss of revs.

So for Reg Armstrong and Norton it was all over, bar the shouting—but there was one more incredible moment to come. As Reg closed his throttle on crossing the finishing line, the primary chain of his Norton snapped and dropped on to the road!

A short time later, after being narrowly beaten by Masetti on a 500 Gilera four at the Dutch TT and in the Belgian Grand Prix, I was asked by the organizers at the

All lined up with Bill Doran (AJS) and a works Moto Guzzi for the Belgian GP in 1952

Schotten circuit in Germany to ride the works 350 Norton there on 13 July 1952.

This long, tree-lined road circuit had an indifferent surface, with quite a lot of concrete that had cracks filled with tar. Not at my best after two very demanding Grand Prix races, my problems were compounded when, after very few practice laps, a wasp got into the arm of my leathers and gave me a very nasty sting. The swelling from this prevented me from further practising, but as Ray Amm, my main competition, was riding a production Manx Norton, my limited knowledge of the circuit was not too serious.

However, in the race and with one lap to go, Charlie Edwards, Norton's mechanic, gave me a signal to slow down as I was then two minutes ahead of Ray Amm. In such circumstances, my usual response was only to reduce the stress on the engine by changing up earlier. This was a cardinal rule of mine to avoid any possibility of relaxing and losing concentration which could cause me to make a mistake.

On this occasion, however, still a trifle jaded after the cut-and-thrust battles with Masetti in Holland and Belgium, I relaxed, lost concentration and peeled off at the first of two very fast left-handers flat out in top—instead of flat out in third! The second bend being the faster, the moment I banked over I realized my error, closed the throttle and banked over still more until both wheels began sliding. I almost got away with it, but each tree on the outside of the bend had a straw bale propped against it and I caught one of these with a footrest and my foot. This caused my machine to slew and, fortunately for me, to dive between two trees into a ditch. At that moment I lost consciousness, but came around a few minutes later to find myself surrounded by spectators and with a doctor giving me an injection.

I was in great pain, having dislocated my right ankle, broken the top joint of my left big toe, and had a long gash down the front of my left leg. At the small country hospital where I was taken, the resident surgeon, who must have been approaching 80 years old, did a wonderful job on my ankle and I cannot speak too highly of the care and attention I received during my stay.

However, quite apart from the pain of my injuries, it seemed that every time I dozed off to sleep, I had a rerun of the accident in such vivid detail that it became quite harrowing. I have always believed that it is only those accidents that can be attributed to personal error which, along with natural ageing, ultimately cause a racing rider

The first bend after the start at Schotten, Germany, in 1952. The picture gives a first-class impression of the road surface at the circuit where I had my only serious accident in motorcycling

Leading on the 350 Norton at Schotten in 1952, before the crash!

to lose his competitive edge. I can honestly state that my crash at Schotten was the only occasion during my entire racing career where an accident was due to my error. It was certainly the one and only time I ever allowed my concentration to lapse.

There then followed 13 weeks in plaster below my right knee, and during that time I suffered a great deal of pain which required pain-killing drugs and sleeping pills. I am sure my doctor felt that I was being a bit of a 'softy', but on going to Southport Hospital to have the plaster removed, all was revealed. . . . An X-ray was called for, and as the young lady X-ray operator was not exactly sure of just what was required, she took a number of shots from my knee downwards. Imagine my surprise when the specialist later told me that the fibula in my right leg had been broken and had knitted together on its own, trapping a nerve in the process—hence my pain! After the plaster was removed, my ankle was virtually solid, so in addition to regular physiotherapy at the hospital, I did a great deal of walking across the sand dunes behind our house at Southport which soon loosened things up.

In September, I had a telephone call from Austin Munks, pre-war winner of two Manx Grand Prix races in 1933 and 1936. Austin told me he was on quite friendly

Right *Fun with Peter Collins in the Aston Martin Race Department*

terms with 'Mr Gilera' and wondered if I would be interested in riding for the Gilera factory in 1953—if he could arrange it. I said I was undecided as to what to do, as there was also the opportunity of becoming an official member of the Aston Martin team. However, we agreed that there would be no harm in testing Gilera's reaction to the possibility of my being 'available' for the next season.

There was a quick affirmative response to this by letter from Mr Gilera—but in the meantime, I had a visit from Gilbert Smith of Nortons to enquire if I would resume riding for them in 1953. I questioned him about the state of development of the new water-cooled, four-cylinder engine, as this exciting prospect had been dangled before us like a carrot in the past. On this occasion, though, Gilbert admitted that there was no possibility of the Norton four being ready for racing in 1953. I told him that I would have happily been involved in the development, albeit slow, of an engine with a winning future . . . but not with the single which, so far as I was concerned, only had a past.

I also told him that, in my opinion, my desperate attempts to beat the Gilera fours in Holland and Belgium were partly responsible for the Schotten crash. He refused to accept this and suggested that my problem stemmed more from having attended too many motorcycle club dinners and dances during the previous winter! Indeed, I did attend such functions, but only because I believed it to be part of my commitment to the Norton factory.

With nothing more to be said, Gilbert Smith departed in a rather unforgiving frame of mind regarding me, which was, though I little realized it at the time, to have a profound influence on my future.

I was then far from sure about my true feelings towards continuing my racing career on two wheels. I was certainly reluctant to go foreign at that stage, and with no likelihood of the Norton four appearing, I decided to accept John Wyer's offer of a place in the Aston Martin team for 1953.

My first race outing was to be in a 12-hour event at Sebring, co-driving with Peter Collins in a DB3. The cars were shipped to New York and then taken on to Sebring by transporter, with Peter Collins in accompaniment. Meanwhile, John Wyer, Reg Parnell, George Abecassis and I met at London airport for a flight to New York via Boston. Our TWA flight arrived from Frankfurt in foul weather and when we later met the American captain of the aircraft in the VIP lounge, the feeling was rather proud when he said that he would not have landed at any other airport in the world in such bad conditions.

Giving a lift to Peter Collins, before Sebring in 1953

The weather grew worse and although we boarded the plane, a Super Constellation, it did not take off, and while still sitting on the tarmac we were even served a meal. Further delayed, we returned to the terminal building, and it was not until the following morning that we finally took off for Boston, where the aircraft was refuelled before flying on to New York.

We then had another worry. Half an hour out from New York, we encountered very low cloud and some shaky turbulence. The aircraft flew into it with flaps down, which did not please Reg Parnell who spent the whole time peering out of a window, trying to catch a glimpse of the Empire State building. Eventually, however, we made a perfect landing and were later told by a customs officer that ours was the only aircraft to have landed at Idlewild that day. It was particularly reassuring to be told that our pilot just happened to be TWA's top man.

But back to racing. . . . Sebring in fact turned out to be my most disappointing race with Aston Martin. I found the circuit dull and uninteresting—added to which, ultra-long-distance events were not really my cup of tea. But what with sharing the DB3 with that very fine driver Peter Collins, plus being the new boy in the team, I was naturally anxious to do well.

In the race, Peter drove the first stint and built up a commanding lead which I managed to maintain until, in my anxiety not to let the side down by losing time, I dived inside an MG on a medium-speed right-hand bend, only to discover that the much slower car was holding an inside line, while the Aston was in fact drifting. A collision was unavoidable and my car spun, ultimately to clout a course marker that was a large oil drum filled solid with cement. Realizing that I had done something drastic to the rear suspension, I limped the car back to the pits, where the damage was found to be so extensive that we were forced to retire.

Conducting an interview with Raymond Baxter

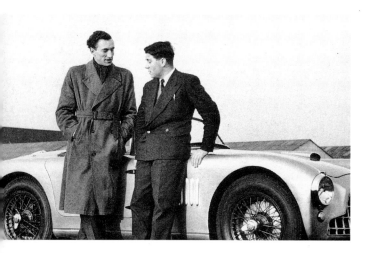

On reflection, I suppose I should have waited until after rounding the bend to do my overtaking, which in my much faster car would have been easy. But on two wheels, I was used to diving into a gap when it presented itself—and I had not expected the MG to have used so little road.

I gathered, too, that Peter Collins made some scathing remarks to John Wyer regarding my 'status' as a driver. Certainly, so far as I was concerned, the already charged atmosphere soon became unbearable and I began seriously to question whether I had made the right decision in changing from two wheels to four.

In this frame of mind, I returned home to Southport where, a couple of days later, I received a telephone call from Graham Walker, then editor of *Motor Cycling*, the sponsors of Silverstone Saturday. Graham was anxious for me to ride at the Silverstone meeting and he promised that Nortons would provide me with a works 350 and 500. Remembering the outcome of my earlier meeting with Gilbert Smith, the Norton offer surprised me— even so, Graham assured me that the arrangement for me to have a brace of works machines had been agreed.

I was delighted and duly arrived at Silverstone for the first practice session, where I awaited the arrival of the Norton racing van. However, when it did eventually arrive, there was only one machine on board—a brand-new 350 cc standard Manx model. There was no explanation for this substitution of a production bike for the promised works machinery, but I was told that a 500 cc Manx model was being assembled at Bracebridge Street and would arrive later.

I was far from happy because I realized that a pair of new and unraced standard machines would not be competitive. Nevertheless, I did not wish to let Graham down, so I put on my leathers and went out on the 350. It was correctly geared for Silverstone, but would only reach 6800 rpm down Hangar Straight, some 400 rpm below normal peak revs for these machines. The engine was checked over, but nothing was wrong—as I suspected, it was too new, still tight and needed bedding in. My only hope was that it would improve and reach normal performance during the race.

The 500 cc model eventually arrived at Silverstone on race morning and Graham Walker offered to arrange for me to have one practice lap on it before the race. I declined—sticking my neck out had never been my forte, and I had no intention of doing so on that not-so-memorable occasion.

Still keeping my end of the bargain, though, I did race the 350, and although seventh place was just about my worst result ever, I enjoyed it so much that I realized two wheels were the life for me. The race was both uneventful

Right Pride before the fall—here photographed at the Florida International 12 Hour Grand Prix of Endurance, at Sebring

and uninspiring, but adding to my pleasure, Tom Joy, Avon Tyres' technical manager—and a wizard with a stop-watch—told me afterwards that he had been timing riders around Stowe Corner and I had been consistently 0.4 seconds faster than anyone else.

Some weeks later, I was told the story of the missing works machinery which had been promised to me. Ken Kavanagh, the Australian rider who had taken over from me as the premier rider in the Norton works team following my crash at Schotten, had heard on the grapevine that Joe Craig had instructed the racing department to prepare two machines for me to race at Silverstone. Incensed by this news, he apparently stormed into the managing director's office and threatened to tear up his contract if 'Duke' got works bikes for Silverstone! So much for the promise made to Graham Walker. . . .

Towards the end of that month, April 1953, I received another telephone call from Graham Walker to my surprise, asking if I would ride works Nortons in the Isle of Man TT. After the previous problem, this astonished me—but I *was* interested. Of course, none of the factors which had caused me to turn down Gilbert Smith's offer of a contract for 1953 had changed. But as I did still believe at that time that a works Norton could yet win on the TT circuit, if not on the Continent, I told Graham that I was willing—but only in the TT and only, in view of what had happened regarding Silverstone, if Gilbert Smith asked me personally.

Graham came back to me with the request that I visit Gilbert Smith at his Henley-in-Arden home, where he was ill and confined to bed. I was due to race a DB3 Aston Martin at Silverstone on 9 May and said I would call in to see Gilbert on my way to the circuit for practising on 7 May. On arrival, his wife took me up to the bedroom where Gilbert greeted me pleasantly enough. I asked about his state of health and we continued to chat for about half an hour on a great many diverse subjects—but not TT racing. In fact, the subject of my riding for Nortons in the TT was not mentioned at all, and totally bewildered, I eventually left for Silverstone, wishing him a speedy recovery as I departed.

The following day, during a break in practice at Silverstone, I walked across to Abbey Corner for a closer

look, where I was approached by a marshal whom I recognized. He greeted me and asked if I had seen that day's *Birmingham Mail*. I had not, so he produced a copy of the newspaper which carried a story referring to a statement made by 'Gilbert Smith, managing director of Norton Motors'. The story claimed that I had pleaded to be given the opportunity of riding works Nortons again and that, in response to this, Gilbert Smith had said: 'There is no place for Duke in the Norton team!'

I could hardly believe my eyes. It was patently obvious that Gilbert Smith had never intended to offer me machines for the TT—or anywhere else for that matter— and although my visit to his home had failed to provide the ammunition he required, since I had not asked him for the TT machines, he must have telephoned the

My first test session with Gilera at Monza, with Commendatore Guiseppe Gilera and Alfredo Milani

Right *Pushing off for the first time with the Gilera at Monza in May 1953*

Birmingham newspaper with his statement the moment after I left his bedside!

The following day, the clutch of my Aston Martin packed in after only 15 laps of the sports car race, and so I set off home, thinking very deeply about my future. I do some of my best thinking while I am driving or riding, and by the time I reached Wellington, in Shropshire, I had decided what to do. I stopped at the first telephone box and rang Austin Munks to ask him whether he thought Gilera would still be interested in me riding for them. Austin felt certain that Gilera would still be keen, and promised to contact the factory in Italy the next day.

During the following morning, Austin rang me at home to confirm that Gilera were indeed interested and would get in touch with me direct. That same afternoon,

I received a telegram which read: 'Delighted to have you. Please come to Arcore to try machine as soon as possible, Giuseppe Gilera.' The next day I was on a plane bound for Milan, where I met Piero Taruffi in person for the first time, and began an association with Gilera that was to become a wonderful experience for me.

My first test ride at Monza was a brief affair. However, apart from a tendency to find 'neutrals' instead of gears, the smoothness and power of the four-cylinder engine was a dream on the ultra-fast surface of the *autodromo*. A stroke of luck was that we had experienced the same gearchange problem at Nortons when the old Sturmey Archer-type gearbox was replaced with the Burman style used in the featherbed racers. I suggested to the Gilera engineers that their machine might respond to the same cure, which I was willing to explain, but they were reluctant, saying: '*Our* riders have never complained about the gearchange.'

The problem stemmed from two factors: first, the tendency for the inertia of the gearchange selector mechanism to 'throw' beyond the gear required and into the following neutral; and second, a short, heavy spring activating the camplate plunger which, because of its strength, would progressively shorten until it no longer located the plunger in the camplate. The first problem could be solved by restricting the stroke of the selector mechanism, so that the inertia carried the camplate plunger into the next gear position and held it firm without going beyond and into a false neutral; the second problem could be solved by providing a longer housing and a longer, softer spring to activate the camplate plunger.

If they were not actually resentful, the Gilera engineers were certainly reluctant to respond to my explanations of the trouble, but after some discussion, where I made it perfectly clear that, as far as I was concerned, it was necessary to make the modifications, they finally agreed. Apparently, it was not possible to change the length and strength of the camplate plunger spring, but by some means or other they reduced the stroke of the selector mechanism. This modification was ready for me to test on the track the following morning and, hey presto, no more missed gears!

Alfredo Milani was then sent out on the same machine. After a few laps, he stopped and was closely questioned. My knowledge of Italian at that time was precisely nil, but I gathered that he had to confirm that the gearchange was much better. From that moment on, I never had any difficulty in finding a receptive ear in the Gilera racing department whenever I wanted to suggest a possible solution to a particular problem.

On returning home, I immediately contacted David Brown, who was most understanding when I told him why I was unhappy in my relationship with the rest of the Aston Martin team. I explained, too, that my brief, if unsuccessful, Norton ride at Silverstone had also served to convince me that my true vocation lay with two wheels and not four. He immediately agreed to release me from the Aston Martin contract and we parted on a friendly basis.

As a postscript to my time spent with Aston Martin, however, there is an interesting story to relate. In the past I had had so much help from both Castrol and Avon Tyres that, quite apart from my belief that both companies were at the time technically ahead of their opposition, I wanted, if possible, to retain my association with both firms for oil and tyres when I joined the Aston Martin team. I knew that Avons had racing-car tyres on the stocks and I was convinced that once I managed to persuade Aston Martin to test them, the tyres would sell themselves by proving to be the best, which was in fact the outcome.

However, there were problems regarding Castrol, for Astons at that time were contracted to Shell. My desire to use Castrol oil in my car resulted in my being summoned to Shell-Mex House in London, where I was met by their motorcycle competitions manager, Jimmy Simpson, who introduced me to a gentleman who was obviously one of Shell's top executives. Indeed, it was not until comparatively recently that I discovered he was in fact Mr Vignoles, their managing director at that time. He explained how Shell were supporting Aston Martin, what a great oil Shell was, and how satisfied Aston Martin were with using it.

After listening to him, I replied that I had been using Castrol oil throughout my motorcycle racing career and wished to continue to do so—which, I suppose, coming from a new boy to motor racing was just too much! Without any preamble, the Shell man said that if I insisted on using Castrol oil, I would never drive for Aston Martin—nor would I get a drive in any other worthwhile British car. 'It's like that, is it?' I said. 'Yes, I'm afraid it is,' he replied, and on that note the meeting ended.

I was shattered. Not so much by what he had said, but by how he had said it. I returned to my hotel, telephoned David Brown of Aston Martin and told him precisely what had happened. He was most upset and called me the next morning to say: 'Geoff, you *will* be using Castrol in our cars.' Apparently, he too had had a meeting with Mr Vignoles and had told him that only he (David Brown) decided who would, or would not, drive for Aston Martin! And there the matter closed.

Money! Money! Money!

When I joined Nortons in January 1948 as a member of the trials team, responsible also for assembling and maintaining the factory machines and to promote Norton at club functions (I attended 55 such occasions during the winter of 1950–51), it had been for a salary of £700 a year. Later, after I had joined the road-racing team, my contract guaranteed minimum earnings of £1500, but it also called for the pooling of all prize money and bonuses from accessory manufacturers—tyres, oil, plugs, chains, etc. This arrangement, if the team had been required to ride to orders, would have been reasonably fair. But that was never the case and therefore worked against me.

For example, in 1951, when there were only two official members of the team, Johnny Lockett and myself, I won both the 350 and 500 cc World Championships. Due mainly to the influx of Italian multi-cylinder machinery, Johnny was not so fortunate and his earnings were minimal by comparison. So, when our earnings were shared, I was effectively subsidizing Norton's racing costs. In addition, any prize money won at the TT (first place was £200) was kept by the factory because, they claimed, of the high cost of competing in the TT.

At the end of 1950 I received an unexpected letter from Piero Taruffi offering me a ride on a Gilera four in 1951. At that time, though, I felt I owed my allegiance to Britain and Norton, and so that first approach from Gilera did not go beyond the initial letter. However, there was also an interesting request for a meeting from Nigel Spring, Freddie Frith's entrant in 1949 when Fred won the 350 cc World Championship on a Velocette. I met Nigel Spring at the end of the 1950 season at Brough airfield and what he told me made most interesting listening. His offer was to be my entrant on a factory-prepared 500 cc AJS 'porcupine' twin. I would be paid a retainer of £3000, plus all prize money and bonuses.

It slowly began to dawn on me that, quite apart from my absolute enthusiasm for road racing which I kept throughout my riding career, if I were successful, I could actually make money from motorcycle racing as well! After meeting Nigel Spring, I could hardly wait for Monday morning and the outcome of my request to see Gilbert Smith, Norton's managing director. He listened attentively to my account of the meeting with Nigel and then surprised me by saying that Nortons did not expect me to ride for them for less than I could get elsewhere. He said that, in fairness to other team members, the basic contract had to remain, but I would receive a retainer of £3000. It later transpired that this would be paid to me by way of a separate contract with Castrol. Apart from my insistence that Nortons give up the benefit of retaining any TT prize money, this arrangement also applied in 1952.

As far as the 1950 TT was concerned, though, my Senior TT win netted me £600, the £200 prize money going to Nortons. However, an interesting comparison was revealed in a chat I had with that great TT ace Alec Bennett, at Thruxton in 1951. A winner of five TT races during the 1920s, Alec told me that his last Senior win on a Norton in 1927 was worth about £3000. He was also paid £100 for setting the fastest lap in practice. I cannot explain this massive variation in TT values, quite apart from the effect of 23 years' inflation, but I assume it came from the massive competition that existed during the 1920s between the manufacturers. It was either that, or Alec was a much better businessman than me!

My arrangement with Gilera in 1953 more than doubled my earnings, and the offer included the use of an apartment close to the factory if my wife and I had chosen to live in Italy. At that time, though, my wife was pregnant, and uncertain of how well we would settle in a foreign land, the free apartment was declined. However, at the end of the 1953 season we took a holiday in Italy which we both thoroughly enjoyed. So we were highly delighted when, during the 1954 TT, Piero Taruffi, speaking excellent English and translating for Commendatore Gilera, offered to buy an apartment in Rapallo (on the Mediterranean coast) for our sole use. It was a gift I most gratefully accepted. And it was not the only example of the generosity of this charming, most caring man—at the end of the 1954 season, and with another 500 cc World Championship in the bag, he presented me with a new Lancia Gran Tourismo car!

Piero Taruffi was, in my opinion, the most outstanding combination of team manager and engineer I have ever

A very generous gift from Commendatore Gilera—my Lancia Gran Tourismo, photographed at Rapallo, Italy

had the good fortune to know. Here was a man, immediately friendly and appreciative, with whom one could discuss—and argue—the relative pros and cons of a machine, knowing that when the final decision was reached, action would be taken. As a result, by 1954, the 500 Gilera was transformed from a quick but almost unmanageable device into a world-beater.

Taruffi was meticulously careful in everything he did. His thoroughness made most rival teams green with envy. His practical experience was invaluable to me as a rider, and although extremely pro-Italian, his help and advice were as readily available to me as to either Milani or Liberati. It was a great blow to me personally when Taruffi's active participation with the Gilera team management ended in 1956—so much of their success had stemmed directly from his pioneering work.

THE GILERA CONNECTION

My first Italian season

The circumstances surrounding my move to Gilera, influenced as they were by the attitude of Norton's managing director, Gilbert Smith, made me more than anxious to win the Senior TT in 1953 for my new team.

My team-mates, Reg Armstrong, Dickie Dale and Alfredo Milani, all had some race experience with the potent four-cylinder machine, and my first practice session around the Island quickly confirmed that I had rather more than just gear-selection problems (as experienced at the Monza test session) to worry about.

The power unit was, of course, superbly smooth, and with 60 bhp on tap there were no worries in that direction. But the roadholding on the bumpy Mountain circuit was something else entirely. Attention to the rear suspension occupied most of our time. We had the choice of two types of shock absorbers: Italian Riv units, which were so hard it was almost like riding on a rigid frame, and German Sturcher units, which were adjustable on bump and rebound. This adjustment feature would have been useful, but the units lost most of their effectiveness when the hydraulic fluid overheated, due, no doubt, to being overstressed by the TT's bumps.

After completing 13 standing-start and stopping laps, I eventually decided to use the Sturcher units set to give a hard ride initially and then, when 'fade' set in, still retain a modicum of damping to retain control. Inevitably, considering the wide sump of the engine and two exhaust pipes either side, these would ground as I negotiated the notoriously bumpy Kate's Cottage, causing the rear wheel to leave the ground (but only if I was really trying, of course).

The weather on race day was superb and record crowds were all around the course, waiting to see if the MV Agustas in the hands of the brilliant Les Graham and

Above right The Junior TT in 1953—relaxing at Keppel Gate while others work! From left to right: Alfredo Milani, Bernasconi (the company secretary), Piero Taruffi and myself

Right Giovanni (seen as a blur!) checks the chain tension prior to departure for a wet practice in the Senior

Awaiting the signal to start early-morning practice for the 1953 Senior TT in the Isle of Man. Note the high position of the engine in the frame

Carlo Bandirola, plus a gaggle of Gileras, could better the factory Nortons of Ray Amm, Ken Kavanagh and Jack Brett, and the AJS twins of Rod Coleman, Bill Doran and Robin Sherry. There was little doubt that our most serious opposition would come from Les Graham on the much-improved MV, despite the fact that it suffered from excessive ground clearance. Also, I was not convinced that the Earles leading-link front fork, which Graham favoured, was really suitable for road racing.

In any event, with Graham's starting number being 18, plus Brett on 20, followed by Armstrong, Dale and Kavanagh, my starting number of 67 meant that I was going to have my work cut out picking off some of the riders in front of me. At least Ray Amm, with number 61, was in a similar situation and within striking distance for me. However, I had no idea of my own potential, not having completed even one flying-start lap during practice.

I decided my best plan of action was to pile on the coals from the start and hopefully demoralize the opposition. Indeed, after the first couple of miles to get the feel of the monster, things were going well for me. That is, until I arrived at Alpine House, a flat-out right-hand sweep on the approach to Ballaugh Bridge. By that time, the rear shock absorbers had lost some efficiency and I was in trouble. During practice, I had worked up to taking the sweep flat out in top gear—approximately 140 mph—but I had not done it with a near-full tank of petrol. As I cranked over into the bend, the Gilera started to weave

and continued to do so until I finally managed to regain control, by which time I was in the left side gutter at the exit of the bend, and sitting bolt upright! I made a mental note, there and then, always in future to practise with a full tank of fuel.

I completed that opening lap with no further excitement and as I passed the pits I was given my position and the time interval, phoned from our signalling station on Sulby Straight, about halfway around the course. I had a 15-second lead at Sulby, presumably ahead of Les Graham. But on the rise beyond the slight right-hander at the foot of Bray Hill, I was confronted by a smouldering machine on the right-hand side of the road, totally unrecognizable as Graham's MV. Indeed, tragically, Les had crashed, being killed instantly.

When I reached Sulby, I was shown my first lap time, 1 +38, and at Ramsey I had caught Ray Amm. With hindsight, I suppose I should have contented myself with sitting behind Ray, but at that stage I did not know that Graham had crashed and that Amm was in second place. In addition, following Amm, who was putting up quite a lurid performance, did nothing for my peace of mind! So I overtook him on the Mountain Mile and went into the third lap with a three-second lead.

Then the dreaded gear-selection problem started again. Occasionally, a rapid change from first to second would select a false neutral, and a further prod on the lever engaged top, which resulted in lost urge as the revs dropped below the power range. This enabled Amm to get into my slipstream, although I was not aware of his close presence at the time, being too busy to look back. Coming out of Ballaugh, it happened once again, and although I managed to engage second gear, Amm was able to take advantage and nip ahead.

There then commenced the most frightening few minutes of my entire racing career, following closely behind Ray Amm with the 'bit between his teeth'. Perhaps the worst moment was when Ray drifted to the outside edge of the road and on to the grass at the three extremely fast left-handers before Windy Corner. Convinced that Ray Amm had had it, I backed off, only to discover that this was all in a normal day's work for the Rhodesian, who stayed upright and pressed on with undiminished fury!

We arrived at the pits in close company, Ray stopping to refuel after having lapped in 23 min 15 sec, at an average of 97.41 mph. It was the fastest lap of the race and a new record, regaining the three-second advantage I had held on lap two. Breathing a sigh of relief when he pulled in (I was not due to stop until the end of lap four), I decided to press on with all haste so that I could refuel the next time around and restart before Ray completed his fourth lap, thus depriving him of the opportunity to slipstream my Gilera.

But that was not to be. Accelerating hard out of the

slow right-hander at Quarter Bridge, I drifted a little wider than normal and my rear wheel hit a patch of molten tar which had oozed from beneath some newly-laid granite chippings. The Gilera went into a full-lock slide and, unaccustomed to a light flywheel, I snapped shut the throttle and the engine stopped. The rear tyre bit, the machine jerked upright and went into a lock-to-lock wobble before we hit the deck. Unharmed, I rushed to pick up the machine, only to discover petrol pouring out from the shaped platform at the bottom of the tank, on which the rider rested his arms while lying prone. The rough road surface had ground through the metal and there was no way that I could get back into the race.

Ray Amm went on to win at a record race speed of 93.85 mph, while Jack Brett was only 12 seconds behind

Accelerating out of Governor's Bridge in the 1953 Isle of Man Senior TT

in second place—it was a good win for Nortons. Reg Armstrong was third on his Gilera. Any celebrations, though, were marred by extreme sadness at the death of Les Graham.

As already mentioned, I first met Les after my interview with Jock West at the AMC factory in south London, prior to my joining Nortons in 1948. Hugh Viney had taken me on a tour of the factory, which included a quick look into the racing department, plus a handshake and a few words with Les, who was already a top-flight racing rider. Later, in 1949, when my future was more or less established (but I was nevertheless still an unknown), I met Les Graham again at a short-circuit meeting at Haddenham, an extremely narrow and twisting circuit around a small airfield in Buckinghamshire. I was riding my 'short-circuit' 350 with its 50/50 petrol-benzole engine, while Les was on a very quick 7R AJS, running on alcohol fuel.

Top *The start of my 350 cc heat at Haddenham in 1949, which I won. Arthur Wheeler is number 1*

Above *My 350 Manx Grand Prix machine at Haddenham in 1949, with a short-circuit fuel tank, which ran on a 50/50 petrol-benzole mixture*

Left *Chasing Les Graham at Haddenham, with World War 2 bombers as a backdrop*

I won my heat and Les won his, so we met in the final. Les made his usual cracking start, but I managed to sit on his tail. This state of affairs lasted for several laps; although I could see no chance of passing, I managed to hang on, and the repeated glances Les made to the rear told me he was aware that I was on his tail. Suddenly, Les overdid it. Without warning, he went off the road and lightly struck some straw bales. Though he hung on and regained the road, I was able to take advantage of this heaven-sent opportunity by slipping ahead and taking a 30-yard lead which he was unable to regain.

As I crossed the finishing line, I remember wondering what would be the reaction of this man Graham to being beaten by a comparative novice. I need not have worried.

As I came to a standstill, Les drew up alongside, thumped me on the back, shook my hand warmly and, beaming all over his face, said: 'Damn good show! Wonderful ride!' Les Graham was a thorough sportsman, every inch, and his death was a great loss to us all.

My first outing on the Continent with Gilera was at the Dutch TT at Assen where the long straights were a real bonus for a machine as powerful as the four-cylinder Gilera. Practice was uneventful, except for when a thoughtless farmer drove a horse and cart across the road in front of Reg Armstrong who was flat out at around 150 mph at the time! Reg survived, but he stopped at the pits at the end of that lap, looking several shades paler!

Race day dawned in unpromising fashion with a strong north wind and low, heavy cloud which threatened rain. The 16-lap 500 cc event, covering 163.8 miles, had 34 starters. The MV fours were absent, but there were six Gileras for Armstrong, Colnago, Dale, Masetti (the 1952 winner), Milani and myself. There were also four works Nortons, three 'porcupine' AJS twins and Walter Zeller on the works petrol-injection BMW. In addition, Fergus Anderson and Enrico Lorenzetti were on fully-enclosed four-cylinder Moto Guzzis, which were making their first appearance in a Grand Prix.

The sun was breaking through as I shared the front row of the grid with two other Gilera riders. But it was Kavanagh's single-cylinder Norton that was first away from the second row, and although I took the lead, I was still being harried by Kavanagh and Ray Amm.

After a disappointing TT, here I am heading for my first Championship win on the Gilera at Assen, Holland, in 1953

I had set up a clear lead by the end of the third lap, though, which I was able to steadily increase until crossing the line at a record average of 99.92 mph. Reg Armstrong came through to take second place—which gave him the lead for the World Championship—but this was after Amm's Norton ran out of fuel during the last lap while lying second.

Delighted with gaining my first World Championship points on a Gilera, the following Sunday took us to the Belgian Grand Prix, run in blazing sunshine on the 8.77-mile Spa-Francorchamps circuit in the Ardennes.

On pole position, I shared the front row of the grid with Ray Amm, Ken Kavanagh and Jack Brett on a third factory Norton. I took the lead from the start, only to have Milani tow the wily Amm and Kavanagh past me on the flat-out climb after Stavelot. Trying very hard, Amm led the first lap with Kavanagh second, Milani third and me, fourth!

Milani regained the lead during the second lap and I moved up to third place, with a new lap record. On lap four, I went by both Kavanagh and Milani to gain the lead, while on the seventh lap, the fastest of the race, I pushed the lap record up to 112.34 mph—but Milani and Amm were not far away and Milani repassed me on lap 12. However, I regained the lead before the end of that lap.

Then suddenly, on the climb towards La Source Hairpin, my engine cut out on one cylinder. I stopped at the pits where my mechanic changed a sparking plug and I resumed the race in fifth place. The engine, though, was still on three cylinders, and as it was pointless to continue, I retired at the pits with one lap to go.

After that result, the press were convinced that I had wrecked my engine in my effort to stay ahead of Milani and Amm. The real reason for retiring, though, was somewhat different—and equally embarrassing for Gilera. The engine's four carburettors were controlled by a tubular shaft mounted on small ball bearings. Each of the throttle slides was connected by a short length of control cable to an arm welded to the shaft. All that had failed was a nipple on the end of one cable, which had been insecurely soldered and had pulled off—thus keeping that one throttle shut.

The German Grand Prix was scheduled to be held at the notorious Schottenring on 23 July. The AJS, Norton, Gilera and Moto Guzzi team men decided unanimously, after inspecting the course before practising started, that it was no place to go 'dicing' for World Championship honours on 350 cc machines, let alone the 500s! The road was under 16 ft wide in places, being both tree-lined and very slippery.

Faced with the withdrawal of works teams in the 350 and 500 cc races, the stewards decided that only the 125 and 250 cc events would qualify for world title points.

The French Grand Prix was staged on the Rouen-Les Essarts circuit. It was held in excellent weather, but Ray

Here I am being closely followed by Ken Kavanagh (Norton) while in pursuit of Reg Armstrong at Rouen in 1953

Amm crashed towards the end of the 350 race after taking the lead from Fergus Anderson (Guzzi). This took some of the pressure off me in the 500 cc race, but Reg Armstrong had a surprise up his sleeve. . . .

Reg—christened 'Armstrong the Undecided' by Signora Taruffi because he continually swapped brakes, shock absorbers, gear ratios and sometimes even a complete machine—was unusually quiet. I suppose I should have suspected something from this, but it was not until the flag dropped and Reg went off into the lead like a scalded cat that the penny dropped.

By the time I had coped with Kavanagh to take second place on lap three, Reg was but a speck in the distance, and it took me seven laps of hard work to catch him going up the hill to Beauval. Here I made a particular effort, and making use of Reg's slipstream, I pulled out to pass him, only to see his machine start to pull away again from mine!

So that was it—I slotted in behind once again. Reg was

really flying and cranking so far over that I could see wisps of dust flung up by the closeness of his footrests to the road. Passing him by normal means was out of the question. In any case, I realized, he would be able to repass me with ease on the straights as his machine was so very fast. I had to choose some unexpected place to overtake, in the hope that he would be shaken into believing that I had lots of reserve power. My only chance was that I might be able to make a break and get away before he realized he had been duped.

The approach to the right-hand hairpin Nouveau Monda was a gentle left sweep, so it was necessary to brake for the hairpin while banked over. Here I made my move. As Reg swung left to line up for the hairpin, I took him on the outside, which placed me on the wrong side of the road for the hairpin. By braking hard, though, I just made it to take the lead. Reg must have been totally unaware of my presence, because my plan to pass him worked perfectly. I got away and in a few laps had opened up a ten-second gap. Meanwhile, Kavanagh had been passed by Milani. Thus, the final result was Gilera one, two and three, while Reg's six World Championship points for second spot put him well ahead on the title table with a score of 20.

The Ulster Grand Prix, run for the first time over the 7.5-mile Dundrod circuit, promised to be a close contest between AJS, Norton and Gilera, the Moto Guzzi and MV Agusta machines having failed to arrive.

I made a rapid start from the flag and went ahead, with Kavanagh in second place. I pulled away by some four seconds on each of the first six laps, before settling down to a comfortable 25-second lead. It was a fast race, though, and at half-distance both Kavanagh and I set a joint lap record of 91.74 mph.

At about that time, too, my clutch began to drag badly. After all three Norton riders had made rapid refuelling stops, I pulled in to replenish my tank after 19 laps—and one minute ahead of Kavanagh. Anticipating trouble with restarting, I selected second gear for the push, but the rear wheel locked. I then tried third gear and, heaving the machine forward, the rear wheel turned and the engine coughed into life—but not before Kavanagh had streaked into the lead.

My problem, caused by a broken clutch plate, upset the gearchanging and the selection of a false neutral sent me sliding into a bank. Following this, the uphill exit from the very tight hairpin also cost me valuable seconds as I coaxed the engine on to four cylinders. Then, on the last lap, as I came upon a gaggle of riders at the hairpin, I all but stalled the engine. All in all, I was fortunate to finish in second place after Kavanagh; Brett was third and Armstrong fourth.

With that result, the 500 cc World Championship points table was taking on an interesting appearance: H. R. Armstrong 23; G. E. Duke 22; K. T. Kavanagh 18; W. R. Amm 14; J. Brett 13; A. Milani 12.

One week later we were at Berne for the Swiss Grand Prix. The 4.5-mile Bremgarten circuit was one of the best in Europe and certainly a riders' course. Gilera fielded six of the 24 machines in the 500 cc race, which also included three works entries from BMW, two factory Nortons and a Horex.

The Gilera squad had lapped most rapidly in practice and claimed four of the five front-row positions. Ken Kavanagh was on the lone Norton alongside Armstrong, Milani, Colnago and myself. In the race, although I made the quickest start, Milani sailed past on the climb up from the lowest point of the course, and he led the opening lap. I was next, then Dickie Dale (Gilera), Jack Brett (Norton), Colnago and Kavanagh, who was followed by Derek Farrant and Rod Coleman on AJS twins. Brett

Concentration in the effort to stay ahead of Alfredo Milani's Gilera at the 1953 Swiss GP at Berne

then retired with a faulty gearchange, while Coleman came up to fourth, with Colnago and Armstrong then lying fifth and sixth.

Already the lap record of 96.68 mph set up by Brett in 1952 was eclipsed—Milani returned 97.64 mph the second time around and I did 98.06 mph on my third lap and 98.4 mph on my sixth, by which time I had closed right up to Milani. On the seventh lap, though, both Coleman (fourth) and Kavanagh (eighth) were credited with remarkably high speeds of 100.92 mph and 99.42 mph respectively. Coleman's time of 2 min 41.2 sec was queried, but later confirmed after consultation between the FIM jury members and timekeepers.

Dale lost his third place when he called at his pit, and on the eighth lap I squeezed past Milani. But try as I might, I could only edge away from him. It was in this race that I realized just how good a rider Alfredo Milani was.

Colnago eventually closed on Coleman and a ding-dong battle developed with first one and then the other in front on succeeding laps until Colnago established a clear lead, with Coleman having to be content with fifth place. At the end of the race, Gilera machines filled the first four places after Kavanagh, who had been scrapping with Zeller (BMW), retired with mechanical trouble on lap 21. My eight points from this victory brought my total up to 30, with Armstrong on 27 for second place.

It was clear, therefore, that the Italian Grand Prix would be critical in deciding the 500 cc World Championship. During the practising period, though, there was disappointment, caused by the non-arrival of both the AJS and Norton factory teams. There was also very nearly a riders' strike, settled only at the eleventh hour, over whether the British riders employed by Italian factories should be paid starting-money by the race promoters. The private riders, although not directly involved, lent their support to the factory men—and this would become crucial two years later when the private entrants requested the support of the factory riders in another argument about pay at the 1955 Dutch TT, but more on that later.

The three days of practising at Monza took place in scorching weather. There was a surfeit of full streamlining, upon which Ray Amm, his shoulder still in plaster after his 350 cc spill at Rouen, gazed wistfully. He was full of regret that he could not have a crack with the Norton 'kneeler'. Also fully streamlined was the in-line, four-cylinder-engined Moto Guzzi, but the fastest time in practice went to Carlo Bandirola on an MV with 2 min 12.1 sec—which was still nearly two seconds slower than the 108.09 mph lap record established by the late Les Graham in 1952.

Although my Gilera engine had been going well during practice, on being stripped down for a checkover back at the nearby Arcore factory, a major fault was found to be developing which meant we needed to build a new motor in a hurry. Chief mechanic Giovanni Fumagalli set about doing this, and during the early hours of the morning of the race Mr Gilera personally ran the engine on the test-bench before it was installed in my machine. I was then called from the nearby St Eustorgio Hotel to test the machine up and down the 12 ft public road outside the factory gates. All was well, so I returned to the hotel for breakfast.

After the warming-up period for the race, Armstrong, Nello Pagani and I were standing at our respective pits while the mechanics changed the spark plugs, when suddenly, there was panic! The start-line marshal had started the race without waiting for us! Fortunately for me, I was the most prepared and was able to join the race as some of the mid-field runners were just getting away. But this was not the case for Reg and Pagani—they were at the rear of the field.

By the end of lap five, I was in the lead with Dickie

Ecstatic, straight after winning the 500 cc class at Monza in 1953

Dale tailing me, then Cecil Sandford (MV), Libero Liberati (Gilera), Fergus Anderson (Guzzi), Giani (MV), Pierre Monneret (Gilera) and Bruno Francisci (MV)—plus Armstrong, despite the delay. At quarter-distance, Dale and I were neck and neck out in front, with Sandford a close third and Anderson fourth. By lap 14, though, I had a ten-second lead over Dale, while Sandford's machine was beginning to fade and Anderson needed to make a brief pit stop.

At the finish it was Duke, Dale, Liberati, Armstrong and Sandford. Dickie Dale set the fastest lap at 2 min 10.4 sec (108.01 mph), but my average speed of 106.84 mph was a new race record.

Although I was now the undisputed 500 cc World Champion, Dickie Dale and I decided to return to

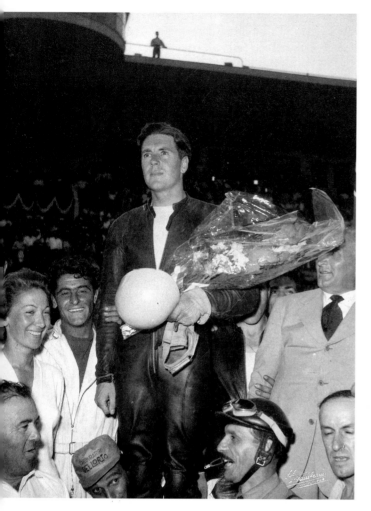

England to attempt Scarborough's narrow and tortuously twisting Oliver's Mount circuit on Gilera fours. After an enjoyable battle with Dickie in the early stages of the race, I recorded the fastest lap and went on to win, with Dickie in second place.

Then, a silly accident during practice put me out of the Hutchinson 100 at Silverstone. While just cruising around the outside of Beckett's Corner on a warm-up lap, I hit a patch of loose gravel and fell, resulting in bruising, facial cuts and slight concussion, leading the doctor to advise that I should not race the following day. Dale also had poor fortune when his engine seized on lap nine; the race was eventually won by Kavanagh on a Norton.

The final 500 cc classic road race of 1953 was the Spanish Grand Prix on the 2.4-mile circuit at Montjuich Park, Barcelona. However, not being fully recovered from my fall at Silverstone, Gilera decided that I should not compete. The race itself was won by Fergus Anderson on a 350 Moto Guzzi—a taste of things to come in this capacity class from Guzzi.

For me, though, my first season with Gilera had drawn to a very satisfactory close with another World Championship title in the bag, in addition to which I had been awarded an OBE. What more could I ask for?

Left *A proud moment after winning the 500 cc* Grand Prix des Nations *at Monza in 1953*

Below left *Dickie Dale leads me into Mere Hairpin at Scarborough in the early stages of the 500 cc final in 1953—I managed to finish in first place, though*

Below *Dickie Dale leads out of Mere Hairpin on the first lap of the 500 cc final at Scarborough in September*

The trouble with brakes . . .

The major redesign which took place in the winter of 1953–54 included some simple modifications that I had suggested. The 1953 Gilera had 1 in. diameter handlebars which, when enlarged by the twist-grip on the right-hand side and a rather thick rubber grip on the opposite side, caused one's hands to ache. This was compounded by the slow action of the twist-grip which needed two twists of the grip to go from closed to full throttle. Handlebars of $\frac{7}{8}$ in. diameter and thin grips cured the ache, and a larger-diameter drum on which the inner throttle cable ran gave a much quicker action from throttle shut to fully open. These were comparatively simple modifications, for which the time and money spent in carrying them out were outweighed by the benefit to the rider in terms of reduced fatigue and increased ability to win.

In addition, the fact that the four carburettors were widely spaced meant that the rear of the fuel tank was wide. This was uncomfortable and pushed the rider's knees out into the airstream, creating yet another projection to increase wind resistance. There was also the possibility that the rider's leathers would restrict the intakes of the two outside carburettors. By machining the inlet ports at an angle, the overall width between the carburettors was reduced considerably without any adverse effect on the power output of the engine, and the width of the tank at the rear was reduced accordingly.

At this point I must pay tribute to Franco Passoni, the man responsible for design after Piero Remor absconded to MV Agusta. The amount of redesigning he achieved during the winter of 1953–54 was almost beyond belief, and the end product was quite the most exciting machine it has ever been my good fortune to ride.

Following this redesign, we arrived in Douglas much better equipped for the bumpy twisty roads on the Island than the previous year. A few laps of practice served to

The weigh-in for the 1954 Senior TT—always of great interest to spectators, but for some unaccountable reason no longer part of the scene. The Regina chain technician is holding my helmet

If only it had been dry! My most disappointing TT, finishing in second place in 1954

convince me that here was my best chance ever, given a trouble-free run, of success in a TT.

Race day dawned wet, and as visibility on the mountain section was down to a few yards the start of the race was postponed, the weather forecast having indicated a later improvement. Then came the announcement that the race was to commence. I remember that while I was sitting on the starting line, after the warming-up period, Mr Gilera came to me, and through Piero Taruffi, who was acting as interpreter, he told me not to take any risks as there would be another day. What a thoughtful and caring man he was.

The race started and under those conditions my race number, 76, was hardly a benefit. However, determined

Left *A huge crowd at the 1954 Dutch TT, Assen, watch as I press ever onwards*

Below *Crossing the finishing line in first place at the 1954 Dutch TT*

to press on I arrived at the full-bore kink in the middle of Crosby Village to have my machine slide, front and rear wheels together, across the road into the right-hand gutter. This in itself made me more careful, but when I arrived on the mountain, visibility was so bad that I was convinced the race would be stopped at the end of that lap. But that was not to be, and I was quite surprised to receive a signal from my pit indicating that I was leading the race.

Things were no better on the second lap, but I was beginning to get the feel of the appalling conditions, whilst taking no risks. Ray Amm at this time was lying second. It was during the second lap, however, that a meeting of the organizers decided to stop the race—not at the end of that lap, but at the end of the fourth! If all fingers were kept 'crossed', the race would then have

On the winner's rostrum at the 1954 Dutch TT with H. Veer, who was the best Dutch rider, finishing eighth, also mounted on a Gilera

covered sufficient miles for World Championship points. What irresponsibility!

To the best of my knowledge, none of the team managers or pit attendants were informed of this decision, which in my case meant that I stopped for fuel at the end of lap three, losing my lead to Ray Amm in the process. The factory Nortons, though, were going through the seven laps non-stop.

By lap four, the visibility on the mountain section was quite acceptable, and when I crossed the finishing line in second place the sun was shining! Needless to say, Gilera were quite convinced that they had been cheated out of victory. There was also an interesting postscript. Julio Carcano, the Moto Guzzi designer, was watching the race from the top of Bray Hill, where at the beginning of lap four (i.e. immediately after my pit stop) he checked the time interval between Ray and me with his stop-watch, and then walked back to the grandstand to compare the time interval as we crossed the finishing line at the end of the lap. From the top of Bray Hill, which discounted the time to slow down, refuel and reach maximum speed again, I had reduced Ray's lead by 26 seconds! But alas, despite the terrific amount of work put into the machine, Commendatore Gilera was disappointed again.

The 1954 Dutch TT at Assen, one week after the Belgian Grand Prix, was then to bring to light an unexpected problem: brake fade. With partial streamlining fitted, the higher maximum speed and additional weight were just too much for the 9.5 in. front brake when called upon to cope with Assen's near-full-stop corners at the end of long, flat-out straights. With the German Grand Prix at Solitude only two weeks away, I expressed my concern to Piero Taruffi, who promised to see what could be done to improve both ventilation and the efficiency of the front brake.

The Gilera transporter was loaded that evening and set off for Arcore. In the meantime, responding to a telephone call from Taruffi, the drawing office at the factory set about designing a new brake, $1\frac{1}{2}$ in. larger in diameter than the existing unit. This involved casting a new magnesium drum, plus brake plate and shoes. Ferodo at Chapel-en-le-Frith were contacted regarding a supply of suitable linings, but they could only provide outdated MZ 41 material within the time available. Nevertheless, the Italians, who are second to none in this sort of situation, designed, cast and machined the new brake, fitted it with a larger, more efficient air scoop, built a new wheel and fitted the complete new assembly into my race machine at Solitude, a mere ten days after its departure from Assen. It was now ready for the first practice session.

Now leading the 500 cc World Championship after winning in both Belgium and Holland, I was looking forward to the German Grand Prix on 25 July. The lower centre of gravity on the 1954 Gilera was bound to pay off,

Warming up the Gilera at Hedemora, Sweden, in 1954

although this was partially offset by the increased gyroscopic effect of the larger-diameter front brake, but I needed the improved handling for I expected, and received, fierce opposition from Ray Amm. His almost fatalistic approach to racing was so far removed from my own that I found it necessary to adapt my pre-race strategy to the ever-changing situation as the race progressed.

Ray was fractionally faster than me in practice and the sun, shining down from a clear blue sky, provided an additional hazard: molten tar. He led from the start of the race, but I closed with him on lap two and went ahead on lap three.

I then set about consolidating my lead, but the concentrated effort I had to put into this made me realize that I could become vulnerable if I tired and failed to maintain my pace towards the end of the race. So at half-distance I eased back slightly, just enough to hold my place. However, Ray sensed this and passed me two

laps later with a 90.42 mph lap record. I regained the lead within a mile or so, but we were then neck and neck with first one and then the other raising the lap record. I was then glad of my mid-race respite, for with two laps to go I knew it was time for me to make a very big effort.

I reckoned that the series of left- and right-hand bends preceding the finish line would favour Amm's Norton; it was more readily thrown from side to side than the Gilera, and I could get caught out if I delayed my effort until the last lap. My penultimate lap was covered at 91.23 mph and then, pulling out all the stops, I set a last-lap record of 91.6 mph, creating a gap over Amm of three seconds, although I had neither the time nor the inclination to look back and check.

Ray came to me after the race, my third win in a row, and said good-humouredly: 'You rotten so-and-so! Why didn't you just clear off earlier?' I didn't bother to enlighten him. . . .

The adverse effect on handling caused by the larger-diameter front brake had been markedly apparent at

Above *A discussion with chief mechanic Giovanni Fumagalli in Sweden in 1954*

Solitude, so, in my pursuit of perfection, and with Taruffi's approval, I visited the Girling Racing Department in Birmingham on my return to the UK, to talk about the possibility of their making me a disc brake. Girling were already involved in the production of disc brakes for racing cars, but at that time, to the best of my knowledge, nobody had then considered the merits of fitting a disc brake to a motorcycle.

After some discussion, I was advised that my idea was feasible, but that the considerable cost of development would require a decision to go ahead from the board of directors. So, I returned home to Southport where I waited rather impatiently for a response to my request. Three weeks later it arrived in the form of a letter, which stated: 'After careful consideration, it is with regret that the directors are unable to offer their assistance, as in their opinion there is no commercial future for disc brakes on motorcycles.'

Today, however, the vast majority of all motorcycles, even trials bikes, do indeed have disc brakes—two at the front and one at the rear. It's nice to have been proved

The Grand Prix des Nations *at Monza in 1954— however, the photographer seems to be more interested in the second-place man!*

right, though, even after some 30 years!

In keeping with the dismal rain-soaked summer of 1954, the Swiss Grand Prix at Berne on 22 August was held almost entirely on wet roads. The 28-lap (126.58 miles) 500 cc race was started on wet roads and the early stages were led by Ken Kavanagh (Guzzi), with team-mate Fergus Anderson holding a good second place; then came Amm, myself, Armstrong and Coleman in close company.

On the second lap, with the road drying slightly, Amm moved up to second place when Anderson's machine had trouble with water in the carburettor. The Norton rider then went into the lead after Kavanagh's machine suffered the same fate as Anderson's. By that time I had settled down in the slippery conditions, but as parts of the circuit dried, so I was able to use more and more power, until on the 21st lap I arrived within a few lengths of Amm's Norton. There I chose to stay, weighing up the situation and content to wait a while for the roads to dry still more before making a break.

Then, at the start of the 25th lap, I drew alongside Amm on the full-bore right-hand curve in front of the pits, taking the lead as we braked for Bethlehem Corner. After that I opened up a 50-yard gap during the final four laps, to gain a win which assured me of retaining the 500 cc world title for the second year running.

Full steamlining was the order of the day at Monza for the _Grand Prix des Nations_ on 12 September. Of all the factory machines, only AJS had exposed front wheels, and even they had fuel tanks which enshrouded the engines and formed, in effect, side panels.

In the 500 cc race, I led from start to finish and won at a record 111.46 mph, with a lap record of 113.04 mph, which was then the fastest-ever performance in a classic motorcycle race. However, with this win, and with the 500 cc world title already sewn up, Gilera decided not to contest the final round of the season, the Spanish Grand Prix, which was won by Dale on an MV Agusta.

A successful season was rounded off with wins at Scarborough, Aintree, and Silverstone—where I was lucky to win; in atrociously wet conditions, John Surtees (Norton) led for five laps in the 500 cc final before he was a victim of engine trouble.

Racing at Silverstone in 1954

The Australian tour

As long ago as 1952 it was to have been my pleasure to visit Australia on behalf of Nortons. Unfortunately, my accident at Schotten, in July of that year, prevented my going. However, the opportunity presented itself again in 1955, when Mr Gilera kindly agreed to lend me two 1954 Grand Prix machines, together with chief mechanic Giovanni Fumagalli, for the occasion.

My decision to make the 12,000-mile journey was, I must admit, partly prompted by the news that Ken Kavanagh and Ray Amm were contemplating having a crack at a season's racing 'Down Under'. But whereas my own arrangements progressed very satisfactorily in the capable hands of George Lynn (editor of the *Victorian and Australian Motor Cycle*), Ray's crash at Aintree caused him to cancel his visit, while Ken apparently decided to wait until another year, leaving me 'high and dry', so to speak. This was, of course, a great disappointment to me, and I think if my arrangements had not been so far advanced I might also have withdrawn.

I had intended to leave for Australia in time to compete at the Mildura races on Boxing Day, but we were unable to make reservations for my machines and mechanic on the ship leaving Genoa in time to make the race. This was a pity, as Mildura was an extremely fast circuit, with a good non-skid surface ideally suited to the Gilera four.

The machines arrived on 2 January 1955 in Fremantle, the port of disembarkation for Perth where I was to contest my first race on Australian soil. There was some amusement among the locals meeting the ship when they learned that, after an unsuccessful attempt to converse with Giovanni regarding the value of the machines for purposes of bond, an exasperated customs official had valued them at £20 each!

I travelled out by plane on the eastern route via Rome, Cairo, Karachi, Singapore, Columbo, Darwin and Sydney, where I transferred to an Australian National Airways plane for the final leg of my trip to Perth, 2500 miles away. Altogether, I covered 14,500 miles in four days. The flight was uneventful, though tiring, but a pleasant surprise awaited me at the only night stop, Singapore, where I was met on arrival by Bill Clough, a

competitor in the Isle of Man in 1954. A resident of Singapore, he kindly took me on a conducted tour of the city and gave me my first introduction to Chinese food.

My arrival in Sydney gave me my first insight into Australian enthusiasm and hospitality when I was greeted by a host of trade people, plus my old friend Harry Hinton, looking not a day older than he did in 1950 and now fully recovered from his crash in the 1951 Junior TT.

Journeying on to Perth, I stepped out of the plane to be almost knocked down by the terrific heat—quite a contrast to the London winter. Giovanni greeted me with his usual big grin, looking more like an African than an Italian after his four weeks at sea. George Lynn was there also, having travelled from Melbourne, 2000 miles away.

I found more sheer enthusiasm in Perth than anywhere else in Australia. Harry Gibson, who up to recently had been the holder of the Australian flying kilometre record at 145 mph on a much-modified Vincent without streamlining, was also there, and had already taken the two Gileras under his wing, having spent hours just looking at and talking about them. Polished and ready to race, they stood alongside the record-breaking Vincent which had now grown a streamlined front and was almost ready for another crack at that record.

My feet had hardly touched the tarmac before I was whisked off to various commercial radio stations, press interviews, film shows, talks, civic receptions, etc, and, in an Australian phrase, 'did I get an "ear-bashing"'! But what a pleasure it was to talk motorcycles and racing with such a keen band of enthusiasts who practically 'lived' motorcycles. From these talks, often going on into the early hours of the morning, I got an initial glimpse of racing 'Down Under', a new and very exciting experience for me.

Generally speaking, I found motorcycling at rather a low ebb in Australia, the aftermath, no doubt, of the boom years since the war plus a period when the accident rate was extremely high, causing general public and official disapproval of the motorcycle as a means of transport. Happily, the work of the National Safety

League Councils, plus a more sane outlook from the riders themselves, had brought about a big reduction in motorcycle accidents, but some indication of the waning popularity of motorcycles was shown in a drop of some 15,000 in new registrations over the past three years up to 1955. This was most surprising when one considers the wonderful, warm climate, which is surely a motorcyclist's paradise. However, the high standard of wages, enabling the family man to purchase the comparatively low-priced small car, could have had a bearing on the matter. In addition, the roads down there were, in the main, rather narrow, with strips of dirt on either side. The two- or three-inch drop off the road edge on to this extremely loose surface was a real hazard for the solo motorcyclist, a state of affairs sometimes aggravated by a lack of appreciation on the part of a minority of car drivers.

Some idea of the official feeling was demonstrated by the enforcement of a general speed limit of 40 mph for motorcycles carrying pillion passengers and 25 mph in all built-up areas. Limits for other vehicles were 50 mph and 30 mph for open and built-up areas respectively. The almost universal use of tram-cars in the cities, with their rather sunken lines which caused even four-wheeled vehicles to kick about, must also have been a problem for the two-wheeled brigade.

Returning to the topic of racing, two things struck me most forcibly on my arrival. First, the universal use of alcohol fuels, even for Clubmans events, and second, the complete lack of trade support for racing which was itself a big factor in restricting the growth of this sport. This was understandable, though, considering the great cost to the rider of travelling as much as 2500 miles to compete. For example, the 1500-mile Melbourne–Perth journey was considered quite commonplace. Nevertheless, racing continued, despite the travelling involved and the lack of trade support. However, I found it difficult to understand the use of alcohol fuels for racing—I am sure this accounted to some extent for the comparatively poor standard of reliability amongst some of the not-so-pukka machines used. It was, in fact, quite surprising to see the number of retirements in some of the comparatively short events of around 30 to 50 miles.

My second day in Perth included a visit to Mooliabeenie, the circuit where I was to ride on the following Sunday, lying about 30 or 40 miles from the city, right out in the wilds. I have to admit to misgivings when the car I was travelling in turned off the excellent bitumen road, about 25 miles out, on to a pure dirt road, running apparently endlessly into the bush. I did not have the heart to enquire if this was the sort of surface I was to ride on, and had all kinds of horrifying thoughts of trying to cope with full-lock slides, brought about by my 60 hp projectile.

However, my fears proved groundless as we shortly arrived at the circuit, which consisted of a wartime airstrip, almost a mile long, leading on to a perimeter road with a good mixture of fast and slow corners, making 2.5 miles in all. The surface, although loose in places, was generally in quite good condition, consisting of bitumen-bound shale. On first observation, this looked rather slippery, but in practice it provided an astonishing amount of grip. A little breaking-up of the surface here and there had been caused by a previous car race, but the course was now under lease to the Ariel Motorcycle Club, who were organizing the event in conjunction with the BSA and Coastal Motor Cycle Clubs.

Race day at Mooliabeenie, a village in the district of Gin Gin, dawned mighty hot, with midday temperatures soaring past the century mark in the shade and rising to 153 degrees Fahrenheit in the sun, that is, the pit area! About 15,000 people turned up to watch in these conditions, such was their enthusiasm. Willing helpers slaved away in the sun, sweeping loose stones off the course just for my benefit, while I sweated in my leathers after practice, flat on my back, in what was probably the only shaded part of the course near the S-bends on the back leg. My first dice was drawing near when I felt the gentle toe of someone's boot in my ribs and heard a loud voice say: 'Righto, maestro, get up and earn your dough—you're on!' The owner of the boot was Harry Gibson's good-humoured brother, Wally—but I was too hot even to think of a suitable retort.

My chief opposition in the 500 cc race was expected to be provided by record-holder Peter Nichol (G45 Matchless) and George Scott (Grand Prix Triumph), who had represented Australia in Europe in 1953. Despite a warning beforehand, I was completely caught off balance at the start when the starter *lifted* his flag as a signal to 'let battle commence' instead of the more usual procedure of dropping it. I had good reason then to thank the shattering acceleration of the Gilera, which took me to the front before the end of the runway was reached. However, Peter Nichol, a promising rider with a nice style who had gone very well in practice, was troubled with a misfire. While investigating this on the move, he took a header into the bush, fortunately without any harm, but the resultant damage to his machine put him out of further racing for the day. George Scott's Triumph eventually stuck in third gear, forcing him to relinquish second place to Jack Lowe (Norton) who rode consistently well throughout the race.

My biggest enemy was the sun, and I began to feel decidedly second-hand about three laps from the end. Had I been pushed at that time, I think I would have had to turn it in. However, a rest in the shade of some trees, a welcome cup of tea and a light breeze, all occurring at about the same time, brought me back to life in time for the Unlimited race.

Australia's wide open spaces, as seen during my tour in 1955

I made a good start this time and made the best of three-quarters of a mile of runway before making a big effort around the twisty part of the course. Imagine my surprise, then, on glancing back at the end of the lap, to find a very determined-looking George Scott hard on my heels with, I hasten to say, his gearbox trouble cured. This state of affairs persisted for several laps in which, try as I might, I was unable to gain more than a few yards per circuit. With no disrespect, it was not often that a Gilera four was pushed by a Grand Prix Triumph, but it did give some idea of the effort put into that race by the local 'champ'. Incidentally, in the process, the lap record was reduced by some six seconds, giving some indication of the effort *I* was putting into the proceedings.

At about three-quarters distance, I was bearing down on one of the backmarkers when a stone was flung from his back wheel like a bullet, hitting my goggles. It completely frosted one lens, cut my face and some of the powdered glass got into my eye, making the final few laps rather painful. However, things worked out in my favour and I was highly satisfied with the day's racing.

We said goodbye to Perth and flew on to Adelaide, South Australia. With such great distances to travel, air fares tended to be cheap—for example, approximately £30 sterling was required to travel by DC-6 from Sydney to Perth, a distance of some 2500 miles. On arriving at Adelaide airport, we were greeted by club officials and several members of the press, one of whom caused us some amusement. After much difficulty in interviewing my mechanic Giovanni Fumagalli, who did not speak a single word of English, the journalist rushed across to George Lynn, who was standing innocently off to one side, and asked: 'And what part of Italy do you come from?'

In South Australia, an Act of Parliament forbade the closing of public roads for racing of any kind, and so I was to try my hand at an event on an airstrip called Gawler, which was, of course, completely flat. The surface was a little loose on the corners and the straight was about an inch deep in loose chippings! The race was run in aid of the Adelaide Children's Hospital, which I was able to visit during my stay. I found that most events were run in

A flying start at Bandiana on my Australian tour

aid of some deserving charity, and in the years since the war, motorcycle racing had provided many thousands of pounds in this way. The hospital governors had been instrumental in obtaining the use of Gawler for the day, and in fairness to the organizers, it was the only circuit available at that time. An anxious eye was also kept on the local weather forecasts, for Gawler was used as an emergency landing strip to the main airport in cases of bad weather.

Race day, though, produced weather just about as hot as Perth, with a gusty north wind blowing the dust in every direction—hardly pleasant for the 15,000-odd spectators. Practice was late in starting but finished on time. As a result, I was only able to complete four legs, which was insufficient to pinpoint braking-points accurately in the wide open spaces of an aerodrome. In addition, it was difficult to gear my machine correctly, as the rev-counter was showing 300–400 revs over the odds, due to wheelspin in top gear down the straight. I was forced to change gear at least 1000 revs down on the normal 10,000 as wheelspin set in very early in the lower gears—the model's progress down the straight was very irregular, to say the least. Maurice Quincey had not arrived to take part in the racing, which was probably fortunate from my point of view, but even so, I had to contend with Keith Campbell, and Roger Barker who, were he to have visited England, would certainly have made an excellent impression. These two had a terrific

scrap in the 350 cc race, finishing first and second respectively.

This time at the *drop* of the flag (one thing about Australia, no rule seems to be the same in any two states!), Keith Campbell shot into the lead, followed by myself and Barker in that order, only for me to be deprived of my second place when braking for the first hairpin. From then onwards it was a struggle to get clear of Barker, who persistently sneaked up on the inside, braking for the slow corners on the loose surface.

Meanwhile, Campbell was rapidly disappearing into the distance. It may, of course, have been my imagination, but it did seem as though Barker was to keep me busy while Keith went off and won the race. Fortunately for me, after a couple of laps I managed to clear off and set about catching Campbell. By this time, visibility at the end of the straight must have been about 30 yards, with the dust hanging heavily in the air. I eventually arrived at Keith's back wheel once more and, with four laps to go, set about working out how I was going to 'do' him. Suddenly he pulled off the circuit—it transpired that his gearchange lever had dropped off! His misfortune left the race wide open for me and I was able to win as I pleased, although not before the dust and small stones entering the two outside carburettors had deprived me of 2000–3000 revs.

From Adelaide, my journey took me to Albury on the New South Wales/Victoria border where I was to try my hand at a road circuit of three miles running through an army camp, Bandiana, which was rather reminiscent of Blandford but with only a little gradient. This proved to be my first experience of an Australian circuit on true European lines, with its granite-chipped surface, some fine full-bore swervery and a fair-sized jump at a cross-road near the end of the back straight, which flung the Gilera four through the air at something approaching 135 mph.

I had completed only four exploratory laps in practice when my motor cut out completely, and as practice time was comparatively short, I pushed my machine the mile back to the pits. In the process I was able to study the neat style and fine judgement of Maurice Quincey on some of the more difficult corners and to observe that Harry Hinton had lost little, if any, of his ability despite the passing years. My trouble turned out to be a detached pivot pin in the magneto contact-breaker assembly which, unfortunately, had rather chewed the rotor. This put an end to my training as it necessitated our return to Albury to carry out repairs at local champion Doug Fuger's excellent workshop.

A very representative entry included the Hintons (father and two sons, Eric and Harry, Jnr), Quincey, Campbell and Fuger—with my practice curtailed, I knew I would be busy. Eric Hinton won the Senior

Well down behind the flyscreen at Bandiana

Clubmans event with plenty in hand, as I found out to my cost later in the day. This rather serious young man had, without a doubt, the makings of a top-flight rider; in spite of his youth, he held himself in check, being extremely safe and at the same time very fast. In fact, he was already way out of the 'Clubmans' class, riding with more finesse than many of Europe's experienced riders. His father, Harry, was no doubt responsible to a large extent for his advanced state, and he hoped to dispatch him off to the Isle of Man and the European Grand Prix races the following year, along with his brother.

In the Senior event at Bandiana, after making a good start, I settled down to learn the course behind Maurice Quincey—and my word, did he keep me busy! With, I imagine, a low bottom gear fitted, plus an outstanding ability on slow corners (not that he was hanging about on the quick ones), he led me for two full laps, to the crowd's delight, until I had learned enough of the course to use the full power of the Gilera. Just after I had taken the lead, a nasty front-wheel slide on some oil curbed my enthusiasm and called for considerable change of line and speed through that particular section. I pressed on to the finish with some 25 seconds to spare, only to be reminded by George Lynn that I had probably cooked my goose with the timekeepers who were busy working out handicaps for the final event of the day!

In this last race, which was reduced to six laps, I conceded 45 seconds to Eric Hinton, on his much-modified 500 cc International Norton, and about 25 seconds to father Harry on his ex-works 350 mount. I

rather think that the handicapper took it for granted that Harry was out on his 500, but this machine had been damaged when he slid off in the Senior race.

As I waited for my turn to move off the grid, I was not really looking forward to my ride, for it entailed overtaking machines as much as 30 mph slower than the four. However, my fears were unfounded, for without exception the other riders gave way to me. 'Chisel', as Harry Hinton was nicknamed, was the first to suffer—on the second lap, he was expecting me and moved over. By now my motor was back in its stride, a long delay before the start having caused it to cool off, thus making it rather sluggish for a while. I pressed on as hard as I could, gradually overtaking the limit men. The record suffered again, but still no sign of Eric Hinton! Then, at the end of the fifth lap, I glimpsed a flying figure in the distance. It was him, but trying all I knew, I just could not catch him,

Tailing Maurice Quincey in Australia

and I was beaten across the line by about 40 yards. I afterwards learned that the estimated top speed of his alcohol Inter was 125 mph!

An enjoyable trip by road to Sydney gave me my first real look at Australia from the ground. There I had the pleasure of meeting some of Australia's Olympic swimming hopes on a commercial radio programme, and also had the privilege of giving a talk and film show to some 1300 enthusiasts in the Town Hall. My visit to New South Wales also included a trip by air into the Blue Mountains to inspect the 'pride of Australia'— the Mount Panorama Bathurst circuit. I was not disappointed—this four-mile road circuit was everything I had been told it was, with a wide variety of medium, fast and slowish bends, and probably more gradient in $1\frac{1}{2}$ miles than any other circuit I had seen. I was very disappointed that the need to return to Italy, to test machines for the coming season, prevented me from competing at the Easter meeting there.

With no other chance of riding in New South Wales, Eric Hinton and his aides had arranged a meeting at privately-owned Mount Druitt, some 30 miles out of Sydney. A look at the circuit confirmed the view that I would require short-circuit equipment and a very low overall gear ratio for this twisty, slippery and extremely bumpy course, with its 1½-mile straight. The organizers kindly allowed me the use of the circuit the day before official practice commenced, as they realized that the Gilera would have to be just right if I were to stand a chance against the joint lap record holders, Harry Hinton and Jack Ehret (1000 cc Vincent).

At the start of the Senior race, Art Senior (Ariel), who was then the holder of the Australian 500 cc record at some 127 mph, headed me into the first bend. Thereafter, I had a much easier ride than I had anticipated, to finish ahead of Keith Stewart (Matchless); Harry Hinton, unable to find his usual form, finished third. My only excitement came early in the race when I hit a series of bumps while changing direction through the fast S-bend, causing a slight wobble. This was reported in the newspapers the next day as a terrific 80 mph power-slide!

Ehret made a poor start in the Unlimited event, whereas I was first away, and piled on the coals from the beginning. Thereafter I was able to keep an eye on the Vincent rider approaching the hairpin as I accelerated away from it. Although he was unable to make up for his bad start, Ehret rode to such good purpose that he equalled my fastest lap, and we shared the honour of being lap record holders, one second inside the previous figure.

The Unlimited sidecar handicap was won from scratch by Ehret in fine style, while Bobbie Brown, one of the Australian TT representatives for that year, beat Hinton

Hurtling along the straight at Mount Druitt, Sydney. Though it was a specially-built circuit, its surface was very bumpy

into first place in the 350 event on his ex-works Junior Velocette. This young man was a joy to watch, and at that time I predicted that he would do well in the TT and on the Continent—in fact, he finished third in both the Junior and Senior TTs in 1957.

I had hoped to include in my programme a ride at Little River, the circuit used for the Victorian TT, but the sailing dates to get Giovanni and the machines back to Genoa meant that this was not possible. We had to be content, therefore, with a combined car and motorcycle meeting on an airstrip almost in the centre of Melbourne, by the name of Fisherman's Bend. With its highly abrasive surface, more usually found on aerodromes in England, this circuit incorporated one medium-fast corner and, although still restricted to the runways, was certainly an improvement on Gawler.

As my own machine had covered over 400 racing miles, including practice, without any real attention since arriving in Australia, we decided in future to use the spare machine. Practice left me wondering if we had done the right thing, for the engine appeared to have very little power under 9500 rpm, and I found it necessary to buzz the unit up to 10,500 before changing gear to obtain really worthwhile acceleration. I knew that there were some experimental parts in the engine and decided, on rechecking jet sizes, that possibly a different camshaft was the root of my trouble, especially as the power, after

Fisherman's Bend, Melbourne, was a great improvement on Gawler! An ocean liner moves up the river in the background

9500 to the maximum 10,500 rpm, was very good. Nevertheless, we decided to persevere with this machine.

With Keith Campbell already on his way to England, my opposition included Quincey (on his home ground), Fuger and Barker. Quincey, making an excellent start, led the 500 race for several laps, while I struggled to get up with him after a sluggish getaway, conserving the clutch as much as possible by taking a wide sweep around the three hairpin bends. With its lack of flywheel effect, I had always found the four to be a difficult proposition to drive out of a slow corner which needed the use of bottom gear and clutch.

I eventually caught and passed Maurice when he left his braking a shade too late at one hairpin. It was interesting to note his line of approach to the hairpin. He would switch to the extreme inside of the road when braking, make a slow turn close in to the straw bales and then, with the machine almost upright, accelerate violently out of the corner. This system had two advantages. It prevented anyone from pinching his corner by riding up on the inside of his line, thus forcing him to run wide, and was a much safer system to use on the first lap, for when peeling off for a corner from the outside of the circuit, one could easily be knocked for six by an enthusiast coming up on the inside who had left his braking a little too late. The other good point was the use of a slow, small-radius turn, which enabled a rider to accelerate out of the corner at a shallow angle with his machine almost upright, thus reducing the chance of the rear wheel sliding suddenly under power—an unnerving experience I had shortly after taking the lead.

Ouch! Girder forks and a rigid frame were not the last word for comfort in the final. This was the scene just before the engine cried 'enough' at Springvale near Melbourne

There is, however, one very big disadvantage, which Maurice found out to his cost: the drastic use of the clutch three times in two miles is often more than fabric will stand. He was therefore slowed a little towards the end of the Senior race with clutch slip, but still retained his second place. And after again leading me for a while in the Unlimited event, clutch slip set in once more, causing him to pull out. A worthy second place went to Fuger, whose Manx Norton had grown a 'nose' similar to the one in use on Ray Amm's machine in 1954.

Of course, I really went 'Down Under' to road race, but, one week after the Fisherman's Bend event, a 250 championship scramble was held only a few miles from George Lynn's house where I was in residence. I don't really know whether I was talked into competing or whether I talked myself into it! Anyway, there I was, wearing a borrowed two-piece leather suit that was much too big for me, and with a pre-war Empire Star BSA complete with girder forks and rigid frame (for weeks I

had the bruises to prove it!). Actually, springers were not popular for scrambles in Australia, so I was not alone, but I soon found out that I had lost my touch, if I ever had any. The course, rather like an extremely bumpy, twisty grass-track some seven-eighths of a mile around, soon became very loose. In my first heat, after struggling along minus goggles in an atmosphere rather like a London smog, I finished fourth, so qualifying for the semi-final. In between times, they ran a sidecar event in the reverse direction of the course. This was really worth seeing; the eventual winner, George Murphy, riding a 650 Ariel twin, gave a terrific and unequalled performance, but the sight of a one-armed competitor (nicknamed 'the One-armed Bandit') rushing around at high velocity on a big

Clad in borrowed riding gear, here I am chatting to Brian Warner before the final motocross race

side-valve twin in third place was probably the most incredible feature of the day. How he controlled that leaping outfit, I shall never know.

With a borrowed pair of anti-gas eye shields I had a much more enjoyable time in the semi-final, footing furiously into third place, not two yards behind the second man. By this time, not used to such hard work, I had scraped a fairly decent-sized area of skin off the inside of my left thumb, and my wrists and forearms felt like jelly. Nine men and one almost-riderless BSA then lined up for the start of the final. A starting device on the lines of a small venetian blind (which dropped suddenly when released by some mysterious electrical system) was used, and I was out in front—but not for long. Two of the giants passed me—round the second corner we went and down went the man in front of me. Not fancying the idea of running over the poor soul, I had to take drastic avoiding action which almost unseated me. Two or three more whistled by. I pressed on with less vigour and then, with one-and-a-bit laps still to go, and lying fifth, the engine ceased to fire and gave forth ominous sounds. Maybe I did hang on to second gear a little too long, or perhaps it was that missed gearchange? Anyway, the game was up. The gallant little engine would stand no more—I needed more practice!

My final dice was to be the Tasmanian TT, a two-day meeting at Longford, near Launceston. We travelled from Melbourne by air, the machine going by air freight service. After giving the usual talk and film show in Launceston the night we arrived, I journeyed by road to Hobart the next day to give a further show. I was at once impressed by the beauty of Tasmania, with its ranges of hills and the pretty harbour at Hobart. Our visit also included a trip to the top of Mount Wellington, which overlooked the city and was well over 4000 ft high. The view of the bay and the surrounding countryside from the summit was truly magnificent, and we stopped at a small hotel on the way down for a real Devonshire-style tea with scones and thick, freshly-made clotted cream.

Longford, the setting for the Tasmanian title race, was the longest circuit I was to ride on in Australia. It had $4\frac{1}{2}$ miles of public roads, with a $1\frac{1}{4}$-mile straight and about a dozen bends of varying character, and was well suited to my machine. Shortly after the start, though, there was a rough section of rather narrow road which led downhill over some corrugations, through a slow S-bend under a railway bridge surfaced with wooden planks running in the direction of travel and with some fairly wide gaps between the planks. With a slight curve approaching and leaving the bridge, I hated to think what would happen if it rained!

A little farther on, the road ran over a railway level-crossing, with races being timed not to coincide with the coming and going of the rolling stock! However, I was told on good authority that, in the past, someone did miscalculate and a race was started when a train was due.

On the first lap, the leader arrived at the crossing just before the train. He made it, and proceeded on down the road at undiminished velocity, occasionally having a look back for the opposition, while the remainder of the field formed a queue at the crossing! However, the race was stopped and restarted later, much to the disgust of the man who had beaten the train.

Maurice Quincey was unable to get his machine ready in time for the race, so I looked like having a comfortable run even though the Gilera's lack of power low down remained an unsolved mystery. I don't think I realized just how much power was missing until I was passed accelerating out of the hairpin in bottom gear by one of the long-stroke Manx Nortons, and it was not until I was well into my stride that I was able to catch up again.

The high maximum speed of my machine saved the day, though, and by half-distance my lead had increased to 25 seconds. Then panic . . . a further fall-off in power, getting worse and worse, forced me to hang on to second

Anxiously awaiting the fall of the starter's flag at Longford, Tasmania

gear on the short straight against the wind. I started leaving my braking later and later until I might as well have been on a 250, all the time wondering if the engine was due to seize and with my hand resting on the clutch lever. Hanging on to my ever-diminishing lead, we went into the last lap; on the final straight, the maximum rpm in top gear with a strong following wind was only 9000 rpm—1600 revs down! What a relief it was to see the chequered flag at last. The second man home, Max Stevens, from Hobart, riding like a man possessed, brought in the ex-Kavanagh, ex-Quincey Norton a mere six seconds behind. My fastest lap was one second outside the two-year-old record of 87 mph.

Back at Launceston for the big investigation, we thanked our lucky stars for the day's grace before the Unlimited event. Seeing badly-blued exhaust pipes and with ignition timing suspected, Giovanni Fumagalli got out his timing disc: full advance only 15 degrees. The trouble appeared to be in the magneto itself; some movement, originally erratic, now permanent, had set the sparks back many degrees, so the lack of power low down now had a possible explanation. The movement inside

the magneto could be giving the effect of an automatic advance and retard, only taking up its fully-advanced position at high rpm, and then finally sticking in a retarded position. There then ensued frantic telephone calls to Melbourne for the spare magneto, attached to the other machine already prepared for the journey back to Italy. The magneto duly arrived by plane late the following afternoon.

The organizers had hoped to start the Unlimited race by 2 pm as we were booked to return to Melbourne by plane at 3.45. However, time went on and the race eventually started at 2.35 pm. The engine fired the moment the clutch went home and I wasted no time getting aboard and down to it. From there I piled on the pressure with the motor as sweet as a nut. I now found that I was slightly undergeared on the long straight, which called for a slight roll-off on the throttle. No snags this time, right through to the flag, with four out of the eight laps at a record 93.4 mph, some 8 mph up on my fastest lap in the Senior race. Then, a quick change out of my leathers and down to the airport before the next race

started, only to find, on dashing into the air terminal, that my plane was over an hour late!

This was really the start of my long journey home. One more night in Melbourne, then a 'cheerio' and thanks to George Lynn and his wife. A day in Sydney to collect my visa for flying back through the United States, plus my income tax clearance . . . and that was that! I said goodbye to Jack Crawford, who had travelled round Europe with the Norton team in 1951 and who had looked after me like a father in Sydney, and to Eric McPherson and a host of others, then climbed aboard the Super Constellation bound for home.

It is quite impossible to describe the friendliness and hospitality which I experienced, no matter where I went, in Australia. Travelling 36,000 miles right around the world in exactly ten weeks, visiting every state in Australia, was a wonderful experience indeed!

Looking bronzed, Giovanni Fumagalli arrives back in Italy with the two Gileras which won ten out of ten scratch races in Australia

The 250 BSA racer

In his book *Whatever Happened To The British Motorcycle Industry*, Bert Hopwood, then chief designer at BSA, stated that I, Geoff Duke, heard of the MCI project over the grapevine and that he, Hopwood, agreed for me to try out the machine at Oulton Park—and that I was so impressed with it, that I 'chanced my arm' and 'without so much as a by your leave' entered the machine as a GDS (Geoff Duke Special) in the 1955 Lightweight TT.

Hopwood continued, stating that although the technical press preserved a tactful silence, the national dailies and even the BBC gave BSA an embarrassing time for a while. He (Hopwood) was called into the managing director's office to have his knuckles rapped, even though he had had no previous knowledge of this somewhat irresponsible action, and it was partly the publicity accruing from the tentative TT entry that killed off the racer project, or so he claimed.

What a sad reflection on the British motorcycle industry, that the leading manufacturer should be even partly put off from developing a promising design, on which a great deal of money had already been spent, by a little unwanted publicity. But Mr Hopwood revealed only part of the story, and his account is somewhat lacking in accuracy.

It was during the early part of 1953 that rumours of the 250 cc BSA racing machine were confirmed, and although I was later to become contracted to ride for Gilera, the prospect of a British 250 appearing on the Grand Prix scene filled me with hope and enthusiasm. So, anxious to do all I could to assist this forward-looking policy, I went to see Bert Hopwood at the BSA factory, telling him of my interest and offering my support. He gave me a brief rundown of the engine's development, and this was the first of many such visits as I tried to keep him up to date with Grand Prix activity, particularly with the progress of NSU and other competitors in the 250 cc class. However, although Hopwood was a good listener, I had the feeling that my words were bouncing off a wall.

Despite this, slow progress was made and in December 1954 I rode the machine at Oulton Park, covering 30 laps in far from ideal conditions. The 33 bhp engine was exceptionally smooth and revved to 10,000 rpm without missing a beat. With no streamlining, the maximum revs in top gear were 9800, indicating slight overgearing, but, even so, I got to within two seconds of Cecil Sandford's lap record achieved on a fully-streamlined 250 cc Mondial—I also lapped faster than I ever had before on a 350 Norton. The BSA handled well, but the full-width single-leading-shoe front brake left a lot to be desired and the separate four-speed gearbox (the original design called for five speeds in unit with the engine) was quite a handicap with the need for high revs.

Doug Hele, Hopwood's brilliant and phlegmatic deputy, was responsible for the design and development of the machine, and after the Oulton Park session he was quietly pleased. I, myself, was convinced that with a little more development, five gears and better brakes, this 250 BSA had excellent potential in Grand Prix road racing and it could have formed the basis of a production sports machine that would have sold like the proverbial hot cakes.

It was soon after this that Bert Perrigo, BSA's competitions manager, became involved, and at a meeting, attended by Bert Hopwood, it was agreed that I could enter the machine for an early-season meeting at Silverstone, using the 'Rudge' title which BSA then owned. I was also keen to ride the machine in the TT, and as the closing date for entries was approaching and a decision had to be made one way or the other, I visited Bert Perrigo at his home. It was agreed that I could submit my TT entry personally, describing the machine as a GDS (Geoff Duke Special) purely to avoid premature disclosure of BSA's involvement. Judging by Hopwood's statement in his book, I can only presume that he was unaware of this agreement, although I do find that difficult to accept. But perhaps it was a case of the left hand not knowing what the right hand was doing.

Meanwhile, having reached this advanced stage, I was instrumental in approaching Charlie Edwards, of Norton fame, and he agreed to join BSA as the mechanic responsible for preparing the machine. Full streamlining was also produced and the machine was made ready for its first race. However, the day before we were due to

leave for Silverstone, Doug Hele telephoned to tell me, totally unexpectedly, that the BSA board of directors had decided that the machine should not be raced!

I was later told that Bert Hopwood had been called to the managing director's office and been asked: 'Can you guarantee that the machine will win?' What a ridiculous question! But it would appear that Hopwood was far from confident or forceful in his support of 'racing to improve the breed', and he quietly succumbed to the board's wishes.

This certainly convinced me that my personal effort had been pointless and I gave up the struggle to concentrate my efforts with Gilera. I know, too, that the

The 250 BSA which showed great promise, but was never allowed to race! It can now be seen at Sammy Miller's Museum in Hampshire

guarantee-to-win demand led to the departure of BSA's trials and scrambles ace Bill Nicholson, who went to Jaguar instead—for it was Bill who had made the frame for the 250 racer. 'Whatever *did* happen to the British motorcycle industry?'

By the way, the 250 race at Silverstone in which the BSA should have made its first appearance was won by a then-youthful John Surtees on a 28 bhp NSU Sportmax.

The 1955 IOM TT

The end of the 1954 season had seen us laying our plans for even better machines, with a tank capacity to enable them to cover the seven TT laps without a pit stop. This would mean carrying approximately ten gallons of fuel; the existing seven-gallon tanks, in the normal position, already had a detrimental effect on handling, when full, so it was decided to fit pannier tanks with $4\frac{1}{2}$ gallons of fuel on each side with a header-tank in the normal position to hold the remaining one gallon. Provision was made for a mechanical pump which would transfer the fuel to the header-tank as the race progressed. The full-front type of streamlining was also to be used, to blend with the pannier tanks. As this would mean using a much higher overall gearing, with its proportionate effect on bottom gear, it was also decided—although these engines were very tractable—to design a five-speed gearbox.

All this effort solely for the TT, and by a manufacturer with no commercial interests in Britain and no state subsidy! One snag occurred in this well-laid scheme, though—a comparatively new class of racing in Italy called for a further effort, namely the design of a completely new 175 cc sports machine. This machine had to be given special priority as the Italian manufacturers sold most of their machines on their home market. This delayed the start of the work on the Grand Prix models until one week after Easter 1955.

It was hoped to race them on the Continent prior to the TT but this was not possible in the time available, and although two machines were, in fact, finished on schedule, it was decided not to risk using them in the Isle of Man. Instead, engineer Roberto Persi, with one mechanic, Reg Armstrong and myself, appeared at the North-West 200 with a pair of the normal racers which were later made available for practice in the Isle of Man.

Withdrawing from the first day's practice after my machine developed sticking throttle slides, the second morning of practice saw my troubles now cured. In fine, cold weather, I completed two reasonably quick laps without any bother. Then, following a request from the factory for the immediate return of the two North-West 200 machines to be prepared for a race in Italy, four replacement machines arrived, accompanied by chief mechanic Giovanni Fumagalli, in time for practice on Monday morning.

The rest of the training, so far as I was concerned, passed uneventfully, and after taking pot-luck in the choice between my two mounts, which were both showing the same rpm in the same places, I took the opportunity to try the spare, which was fully streamlined. It handled very well under the prevailing conditions and recorded the fastest lap in practice—23 min 19 sec from a standing start, only four seconds outside the record. Most of the lap was completed sitting up, but in actual fact this had very little effect on performance when using streamlining. On the same morning, a lap on my race machine, fitted with a small nose fairing, produced a 20-second slower lap with just about the same amount of effort, but keeping fairly well down to it wherever possible. I managed to resist the temptation to use the 'dustbin', with its high bottom gear, in the race, for I considered the weather in the Island to be a little too temperamental, and full streamlining could turn out to be more of a liability than an asset under windy and wet conditions. In the conditions prevailing on the day, however, I think an improvement of about 15 seconds could have been achieved over my best lap time, in spite of the four-speed gearbox.

Reg Armstrong, my team-mate, ran into minor troubles in practice and eventually used my spare machine in the race. Both our machines were pulling a half-a-tooth higher gear than the previous year, although this left them just a shade overgeared under practice conditions. The question of the first 100 mph lap reached new heights in the days before the race, making me wonder which was the more important, the 'lap' or the 'race'.

One last twist occurred on the evening before the race—a news agency report that I had fainted during the day and would not be riding in the race necessitated eight telephone calls to deny this. I could only presume that there had been some mix-up with Des Wright who, due to an unfortunate spill in the Lightweight event, was unable to start on my BSA in the Senior—the entry was in the name of Geoff Duke (Racing) Ltd.

The evening before the race, arrangements were made as usual for a second signalling point, a little beyond the halfway mark on Sulby Straight. Here we had a private telephone connected direct to a point immediately behind our pit. As was our custom, no arrangement existed between Reg and myself; it was a case of every man for himself. However, Reg had agreed to refuel at the end of the third lap while I was to stop at the end of the fourth, which would cut out the possibility of our both being at the pits at the same time.

We both made full use of the warming-up period which, nevertheless, was barely long enough for the Gilera four, with more than a gallon of oil to heat up. My personal plan of campaign was to pile on the coals from the drop of the flag until halfway round on the second lap,

Giovanni Fumagalli puts the finishing touches to my 1955 Senior TT winner before the start of the race

Right *Both wheels are slightly off the ground in this 1955 Senior TT shot*

when I would receive my first accurate signal from the Sulby station. I managed to make a fairly quick start and set off down Bray Hill, though not *too* quickly on the first lap, remembering the brim-full tank. In fact, I never reckoned to start 'racing' until after Braddan Bridge on the first lap, for apart from the weight of fuel 'up on top', it was very easy to make a mistake and drop the model before one had got the feel of it.

Once clear of Braddan, I used all the fantastic power of the bike without any undue excitement, but much to my consternation, a feeling of tightness on my forearms rapidly developed during my first-lap effort. It soon became clear that the cause of the trouble was a new, separate lining to my leathers that I was wearing for the first time. The sleeves of this had worked up to the widest part of my forearms, thus gripping me like bands of steel. This caused a growing weakness in my grip on the handlebars, making even the operation of the clutch a painful effort and necessitating much more drastic use of my legs and knees in controlling my machine. It was therefore a great relief to receive a signal giving my first-lap advantage over my team-mate as 45 seconds.

All through the second lap I debated whether I could afford to stop at the pits to have the lining sleeves cut. I finally decided to hang on until my pit stop, by which time the tightness had eased a little, due to my perspiration (and how!) stretching the material of the lining. A rapid pit stop, at which I took on over four gallons of fuel and changed my fly-spattered goggles, and I pushed off again, glad of the opportunity for a short rest in which I had been able to stretch my weary limbs. But the muscular effort required from my legs in throwing my machine about again began to tell on me, and an attack of cramp developed in my left thigh. This gradually worsened, until the pain was so acute that my judgement began to suffer to such an extent that I was forced to slow considerably. Fortunately, my signals still showed that I was retaining my lead.

Two frights occurred at this stage. On the fifth lap, as I was coming out of the last of the three lefts before Windy Corner, something appeared suddenly to shoot across the road ahead of me. I automatically grabbed everything but realized a split-second later that what I had seen was only the shadow of a seagull flying across the road out of sight above my head. My only really narrow squeak came on the sixth lap at the full-bore right-hander coming out of Bishop's Court. The model unaccountably went into a full-lock slide at about 10,000 rpm in top gear—136 mph! Shades of 1953 again! An investigation after the race

Right *A warm sunny day at Quarter Bridge in the 1955 Senior TT. The Avon golf-ball cleaner on the tank top came in useful for removing dead flies from goggles!*

apparent as Reg Armstrong steamed by—it was only then that I realized that I must have passed him when he stopped for fuel. My surprise turned to pleasure on seeing him and I decided to force myself to follow him to the end of the lap. This revived my interest and helped to relieve the agony of that last lap, and we crossed the finishing line a few yards apart. I have never been so relieved to see the chequered flag.

I later learned that, on my third lap, I had been credited with the first-ever 100 mph lap of the circuit, in 22 min 39 sec, only to have the honour revoked by the timekeepers some 40 minutes later. Due to some anomaly in their lap speed charts, it was discovered that 22 min 39 sec worked out at exactly 99.97 mph!

I was asked many times after the race, and since, if I was disappointed at not achieving the 100 mph lap. I was sorry, of course, particularly after getting so near to it on my third lap. However, the main aim was to win the race, at any speed, and I did feel that far too much importance was attached to this 100 mph business.

In any event, it was a case of third time lucky, and the look of sheer joy on Mr Gilera's face as I came into the enclosure was, indeed, ample compensation.

Above *Standing on the footrests over the bumps on Bray Hill—but the Sergeant seems unimpressed!*

revealed a long strip of tar which had been rather soft. If the four had one bad feature, it was that there was no flywheel worth talking about. Consequently, when you did lose traction the revs went up violently; likewise, if you were frightened into suddenly closing the throttle, the engine slowed very rapidly, so that when the back tyre gripped again you were cast off in no uncertain manner. This had happened to me twice before: at Quarter Bridge in 1953, and in practice for the 1953 Silverstone Saturday meeting.

Returning to the Bishop's Court incident, I must admit to being very frightened, but I did remember to ease the throttle, and not shut it, and the slide gradually diminished until, with a shriek of protest, the tyre gripped again. With a slight headshake, the model carried on its way to Ballaugh with a very detuned rider hanging on!

On the seventh lap, at the beginning of the Cronk-y-Voddee straight, I suddenly became conscious of a back-draught and wondered for a moment if the zip in my leathers had come adrift! However, the reason became

Below At Governor's Bridge on my way to completing that lap at 99.97 mph in the Senior TT of 1955!

The Dutch incident

Following victory at the 1955 German Grand Prix, held at the Nürburgring for the first time since 1931, and a retirement due to timing-gear problems in the Belgian at Spa, my next race was at Assen on 16 July, where the Dutch TT would be contested. This venue would also become famous as the scene of a dispute between the race promoters and private riders concerning inadequate levels of starting-money.

Although the race organizers, the KNMV, denied any previous knowledge of dissatisfaction among the private riders, it was apparent from independent evidence that they were aware of the problem, but chose to ignore it. Faced with this uncompromising attitude, the private riders threatened to pull out of the 350 cc race after one lap if no more money was to be paid to them. The organizers, apparently, thought the riders were bluffing, for when 12 riders pulled into the pits after the first lap of the race, panic broke out.

A subsequent meeting between the organizers and the riders' representatives produced an offer of an additional £15. This was totally unacceptable, though, and the offer was raised to £20 which was also rejected, for the riders were demanding £20 per start—which I, personally, felt was rather unreasonable of *them*, since that was to include the 350 cc race in which they had completed only the one 'protest' lap.

Nevertheless, the riders persisted with their demand, which was again rejected by the promoters until Reg Armstrong and I, plus the Italian members of the Gilera team (Alfredo Milani, Umberto Masetti and Giuseppe Colnago), reluctantly gave the riders our support, thus threatening the 500 cc race. Faced with this, and the fear of an unpleasant reaction from the crowd, the promoters then gave way and the 500 cc race went ahead, which I won. But that was by no means the end of the Dutch incident.

As far as Reg Armstrong and I were concerned, it is necessary to go back to the Italian Grand Prix of 1953 to establish the primary reason for our involvement in the 1955 Dutch dispute. The organizers of the 1953 Italian Grand Prix had refused to pay starting-money to British riders of Italian works machines which we considered to be unfair. As a result, Fergus Anderson, then of Moto Guzzi, took it upon himself to start a petition which was signed by all competitors in the Grand Prix. This protest in no way threatened any further action by the riders, but it did bring about a change of attitude by the promoters and we were paid.

Henry's Corner in the May 1955 North-West 200. In winning, the lap record was lifted to 99.98 mph—a near-miss 100 mph which was to be repeated at the TT!

Bearing that in mind, we, the works riders, were sympathetic to the private riders' cause at the 1955 Dutch TT, for the Assen promoters were notoriously tight-fisted at that time. And with more than 100,000 spectators year after year, this did little to soften the financial frustration suffered by the men who were 'putting on the show', yet still finding it difficult to make ends meet—for it must not be overlooked that the members of the 'Continental Circus' were professional racing riders with no other sources of income.

Reg and I were basically against any form of strike action, for whatever reason, and we would not have become so involved in the Dutch incident if it had not been for the support we had received in Italy two years earlier. So, on returning home, I wrote a letter of apology to Mr Burik, secretary of the KNMV, but received no reply.

A great deal was written and said at the time about the rights and wrongs on both sides. It serves no purpose to go into it all now; suffice to say, there were inaccuracies in some of the statements made by both sides. However, what I cannot forgive is that those private riders who had been in Europe, notably the Australians, having since returned home, were not, to the best of my knowledge, given the opportunity to defend themselves. The remainder were summoned to an 'extraordinary meeting' of the CSI (Commission Sportive International) on 24 November 1955, where they were expeditiously interviewed and sentenced in what appeared to be an almost total disregard of accepted judicial practice, the punishment meted out being irrespective of the degree of each rider's involvement. One could not help but gain the impression that all was cut and dried well in advance.

Reg Armstrong, myself and 12 other riders were sentenced to six months' suspension from all motoring sport activity from 1 January 1956; three Italian riders were suspended for four months. Clearly, we were set up as an example to deter any other FIM-licence holders from contemplating similar protest action in the future.

When the news of our punishment reached Italy, the Italian correspondent for *Motor Cycling* cabled: 'The Gilera factory is likely to react with decisions of the greatest importance, but will not be making a statement until it has discussed the matter with Duke.' Indeed, faced with the suspension of his entire team, Commendatore Giuseppe Gilera, incensed by the injustice of our suspension and the CSI's complete disregard for Gilera's commercial interests, was prepared to pull out of racing altogether. It was only in response to pleas from Reg and myself that he relented and decided to continue his racing support.

Mr Gilera, though, did not forget, and I believe that this episode influenced his decision to join Moto Guzzi and Mondial in their subsequent permanent withdrawal from racing at the end of 1957. It was a move which

Right Talking to Ferruccio Gilera (in the glasses) on the starting line for the 1955 Grand Prix des Nations at Monza

probably affected racing and the industry more than anything else in the history of motorcycle activity, for it paved the way to a period of stagnation with world-title road racing dominated by one factory, MV Agusta, and the ultimate supremacy of the Japanese.

For my part—and against my better judgement—I was persuaded to make a public apology for my involvement in the Dutch fiasco. It was done in the hope that my apology would bring leniency and a reduced sentence for both Reg and myself. All that came from it, though, was permission to ride in national events. This was better than nothing, I suppose, for it allowed me to keep in racing trim, and I was successful in early-season events at Aintree and Oulton Park, where I broke John Surtees' lap record. But from that moment on, I was plagued by an unprecedented, for me, series of misfortunes which, by and large, continued throughout my remaining two seasons with Gilera. However, I do feel that the departure of Piero Taruffi in 1956 from Gilera was a major contributory factor, as without his guiding hand the machines were not so well prepared and the general racing organization was not so precise.

The only good thing to come from the Dutch incident was that at the conclusion of the extraordinary meeting of the CSI on Friday 25 November 1955, a draft regulation concerning the stipulation of, and agreement to, the amount of starting-money offered at international road-race meetings was presented to the meeting. Detailed discussion was deferred until the subsequent Spring Congress held in Oslo, but the regulation later became obligatory.

The wind pressure modifies my features at Monza

The 1955 racing season continued after Assen with the Ulster Grand Prix. However, unable to negotiate acceptable start-money, the factory decided to give the 1955 Ulster a miss for the second year in succession, concentrating their efforts instead in preparation for their home Grand Prix at Monza. Following the withdrawal of the unreliable V8 Moto Guzzi, though, it was left to Gilera and MV to fight it out.

In the 35-lap 500 cc race, I was third away at the start, but by lap five I was out in front on my own. Meanwhile, Reg Armstrong was having a terrific duel with Masetti (MV) which continued throughout the race. With ten laps still to go, though, my engine began to lose power, and after 31 laps Masetti was only four seconds behind me. An out-of-balance vibration at the front end of my machine was a further problem—going past the pits with the sun on my left casting a shadow on the road, I could see that my front wheel was really bouncing up and

down! My lead was reduced to two seconds on the following lap, and with two laps to go, Masetti stormed by with Reg in his slipstream. There was nothing I could do. At the finish, Masetti was the victor over Armstrong, while I came third.

On examination after the race, my front tyre was found to be very unevenly worn and completely devoid of tread in one place. In addition, when the Gilera engines were stripped, 16 broken valve springs were revealed! Only one spring on each valve was intact. The cause? A bad batch of material.

Although the individual and Manufacturers' World Championships were already in the bag, Commendatore Gilera, needless to say, was not happy about his machines being beaten at their home ground. At first, the poor tyre manufacturer got the blame, but it seemed to me that there had to be a more logical explanation for such uneven tyre wear. On the bumpy and ultra-fast Curva

Right *Presentation at Arcore to celebrate my third World Championship for Gilera. Commendatore Gilera and Piero Taruffi view the proceedings*

Grande, I had been conscious of the front wheel stepping outwards when I was really trying in the race. Therefore, perhaps the downforce on the fairing, at high speed, was causing the front forks to 'bottom', and the subsequent stepping-out of the front wheel was causing the uneven wear on the tyre.

The following morning, with the broken valve springs replaced, new tyres fitted, and a distance piece on each fork stanchion to increase the spring preload, I completed the full race distance of 35 laps with perfectly even tyre wear! So far as Avons were concerned, all was forgiven. The attention of the race department could now turn to redesigning the streamlined shell, an alteration in weight distribution, and producing alternative fork springs.

The end-of-season events included Scarborough,

Below *A vain attempt to catch John Surtees' 350 cc Norton in the 30-lap solo handicap at Aintree in September 1955*

John Surtees, on his Norton, talking to me on my Gilera at Silverstone Saturday in April 1955

Aintree, Silverstone and Brands Hatch. I always enjoyed the Scarborough meeting and that year was no exception, although my practice times tended to be a little down on 1954, which was rather disconcerting. However, I had a very enjoyable scrap with Jack Brett in my heat, who gave me a perfect demonstration of how to drive quickly out of a slow bend using bottom gear and clutch—quite the best performance I had ever seen on this type of bend.

The fun and games really started in the 500 final, though, when I had to contend with the brilliance of short-circuit star John Surtees on a very rapid works Norton, by now very much improved on its early-season performance. We changed the lead several times—I became worried about the outcome as I had no signalling arrangements and in the heat of the battle had lost count of the number of laps to go! The situation was relieved by Norton mechanic Arthur Edwards who was busy signalling to John—in view of John's ultra-close proximity to me, he could not avoid showing me his signals. Without doubt, this helped save the day for me, and I proceeded to give the last lap all I had, stretching my lead to 50 yards at the finish, with a new lap record approaching 70 mph which was to remain unbroken for several years.

Aintree was easier, apart from the handicap race which John contrived to win on a 350 by a crafty bit of slipstreaming of Bob McIntyre's 500 cc machine. Then,

in September, at Silverstone, the scene of many epic races so far as I was concerned, Surtees made a superb start while I lost ground in the early stages due to considerable pressure from McIntyre, Brett and Hartle. Eventually, I arrived at John's back wheel with about six laps to go. He was riding at terrific speed, and after a frightening slide coming out of Club Corner, followed by a wobble which necessitated my standing on the footrests 'trials fashion' to avoid being cast off, I decided to give John best, on this occasion anyway! A piece of metal from inside the cambox had penetrated the alloy casing, and a considerable amount of oil was finding its way on to my rear tyre.

After this defeat at the hands of John Surtees at Silverstone, my next outing was the following day at Brands Hatch, a circuit on which I had not previously raced. John was then the accepted 'King of Brands' and considered to be virtually unbeatable on the 1.24-mile short course (the extension to the circuit to bring it up to Grand Prix status had not yet been constructed), so at best I was going to have my work cut out.

The problem with my machine at Silverstone could not be cured outside the factory, so Giovanni Fumagalli set about thoroughly checking the timing, etc, on the

Consolation prize from two-year-old Peter Duke after finishing third at Brands Hatch in 1955

machine which Reg Armstrong had ridden at Aintree and on which he had retired due to lack of power. The cause of the problem could not be traced, though. I practised with the lowest available gearing, but on the short straight the rev-counter was only registering a disappointing 9800 rpm, and that in fourth gear! To compound my woes, grid positions, which were drawn for instead of being decided on practice lap times, had John placed on the front row, while I drew the back row.

At the drop of the flag, John was off like a rocket, and after working my way up into fifth place, further progress became increasingly difficult and I was ultimately beaten to second spot by yet another Brands Hatch exponent, Alan Trow.

Shortly after my return home to Southport, however, I was surprised to receive a letter from a Brands Hatch marshal, who wrote of 'something on my conscience', which he felt obliged to tell me. The draw for grid positions at Brands had been 'rigged'! But he assured me that John Surtees was totally unaware of what had taken place. The writer did not explain how the draw had been 'fixed', so that remains a mystery to this day. However, the instigators might have saved themselves the trouble, because it is extremely unlikely that their action had any bearing whatsoever on the result of the race.

Racing through 1956

With the early part of my 1956 racing season being taken up as an involuntary spectator, due to my suspension as a result of the Assen strike, I was able to assess current form in a rather more leisurely way than usual. I was also able to take an interest in a Velocette, ridden by Jack Wood from the Isle of Man, into which I incorporated a few 'special features' of my own. My immediate worry, of course, was to find out how well MV's new signing, John Surtees, was coping with the fearsome MV four. I knew that John had been spending a fair amount of time in Italy, and realized that his natural ability for pointing out the rights and wrongs in machinery would soon cure any minor faults which still remained in the much-improved Agusta product. John was also credited with superhuman feats around the circuits at Modena and Monza, rumours which may have been circulated for Gilera's benefit! However, John then brought the MV over to the UK and proceeded to break most of his own short-circuit records.

By now a resident in the Isle of Man, I watched the practising for the TT with intense interest, but my involvement with the Velocette held me at the pits during both races, much as I would have loved to watch from on the mountain. Unfortunately, a fine effort by Jack Wood in the Junior race came to an end when the front mounting holding the streamlining broke. Although the machine was rideable, the 'nose' occasionally rubbed the front tyre, so, for safety's sake, we called it a day, although Jack had been assured of a place on the leaderboard—not bad, considering the engine was designed about 1936!

The Junior race, which started on wet roads, was certainly not short of excitement. After leading brilliantly for several laps, Bill Lomas' Guzzi finally retired with the now-common valve trouble, leaving the lead temporarily in the capable hands of John Surtees and the extremely reliable MV four. Knowing the thirst of these fours, and considering the speed at which he was travelling, John's actual time for filling up was fantastically short and he paid dearly in the form of retirement while lying second. Ken Kavanagh (Guzzi) then went on to record his first, and well-deserved, TT win.

Senior day dawned fine, but windy, and John Surtees

made up for all his trouble in the Junior on Monday by leading the race from start to finish, recording the fastest lap in the process. His machine was not the one he had originally intended to use, though, as this was damaged in an unfortunate argument with a cow during practice! How much the performance of this actual race engine was down on his special unit, I don't know, and of course conditions were not ideal, but I took heart from his fastest lap time, which was only 12 or 13 seconds faster than Ray Amm's 1953 record and on a circuit which had since been 'quickened' by some 15 to 20 seconds per lap by road alterations.

Parole from the injustice of suspension allowed Gilera to provide me with a training machine to take to the early-

Cecil Sandford on the 350 DKW in the 1956 Junior race on the Island

Above left *Ken Kavanagh, the winner, riding his Moto Guzzi at Governor's Bridge in the 1956 Junior TT*

Above *The location is Oulton Park in August 1956 where I came first on my 500 Gilera*

season Aintree and Oulton Park meetings. Aintree did not prove to be a serious worry as other works support was noticeable by its absence, although winning was by no means easy. The superior speed of the four on this fast circuit, though, made for a comfortable ride which, incidentally, I appreciated in view of my distinct lack of practice!

Two days later we journeyed to Oulton Park for my first race at this wonderful little course. In the main race of the day, I had a wonderful set-to with Bob McIntyre before winning, and what a joy it was to ride within a few feet of his back wheel, without a care in the world!

Left *Frank Perris on a G45 Matchless passing through Parliament Square, Ramsey, in the 1956 Senior TT*

Reg Armstrong and I then had a short spell at Monza before setting out for our first Grand Prix of 1956 at Francorchamps where, contrary to all rumours, the course was unchanged, apart from a slight easing of the fast right-hander at Malmedy. Our models were really flying, utilizing some new streamlining which gave us another 100 revs or so, although we were troubled with a fair amount of vibration which had been unheard of previously. John Surtees, who had not been to Spa before, soon showed his adaptability by lapping in practice at a speed high enough to put him on the front row of the grid. He obviously meant business, as he completed more laps during training than anyone else in the whole entry.

Race day was very hot, and this for me was the first

test, on a circuit I had always liked. The green light came up, but almost before I had bumped on the seat, John had his MV under way. My own start was a reasonable one and I was soon able to set about trying to cut down the distance between us. It quickly became apparent to me that my machine had slightly better top-end acceleration; all the same, I made little, if any, impression down the hill from Malmedy, though on the rise out of the fast fourth-gear corner, Stavelot, I slowly pulled him back. This may, of course, have been due to our use of unusual indirect gear ratios, with fourth and fifth very close together, allowing a high top gear for the downhill 'flat-out' section. With this arrangement there was no danger of over-revving, and we could then get into our fourth gear up the hill, which allowed the use of maximum revs.

I was within striking distance of John as we entered the extremely fast left-hand bend now known as Artie Bell's Corner, which keeps on going round and is completely blind. Here, I think, my previous knowledge of the course helped, and I was able to close right up behind the MV. Coming immediately after was a second-gear left-hander, and thanks to my acceleration out of this corner I was able to take over the lead. At the end of the lap I had a slight advantage and from then onwards the gap widened.

Signals apart, at Spa it was comparatively easy to keep tag on the opposition as, on leaving the Francorchamps hairpin, one had a perfect view back down the road for some 400 yards. Within three or four laps the road was clear and I was able to use a little less than full throttle down the Masta Straight while still increasing my lead. All went well until, with a little over one lap to go, a piston disintegrated, making a shocking noise in the process! I coasted to a standstill almost within sight of the hairpin and became a spectator once again. Piero Taruffi later told me that they had fitted some lighter pistons in my engine as an experiment! John Surtees, riding a well-judged race, finished a worthy winner but with a now rather sick MV—apparently the mice were beginning to nibble away at his power unit, too! With three outright wins to his credit and not even one point in my championship kitty, it began to look like a Surtees year. Still, I thought, given no further trouble, I might be able to force a draw. . . .

Practice at Solitude for the German Grand Prix which followed was uneventful but promising, and speeds were already in excess of previous records. However, my eagerly-awaited renewal of the Spa battle with John Surtees was nipped in the bud during the 350 cc race when John, in a desperate effort to close with Bill Lomas, threw the MV away on the treacherous Mahtental section, suffering a broken arm in the process which put paid to his racing for the rest of the year. This occurrence lowered the tone of the 500 cc race, or so I thought; but I had reckoned without Bill Lomas and his V8 Guzzi. As the flag fell, Reg Armstrong moved into the lead and

Almost ready for the off at the German GP at Solitude in 1956

entered the first corner with me on his tail, while at the same time, unknown to me, Mr Lomas was already breathing down my neck! Reg was obviously feeling his way and on two or three occasions during the first few miles I could have moved ahead, but decided instead to bide my time. I eventually took the lead as we dived out of the downhill, third-gear, left-hand bend into the main flat-out section.

So far so good! At the end of this section, there was a first-gear S-bend which required heavy braking on the approach, and although I would not say I braked early, I did treat the problem with a little respect first time round; at 300 metres, I sat up and quite happily started to brake when suddenly there was a 'whoosh' . . . and the Guzzi fairly flew by. Bill led at the completion of one lap, and for a further half-lap I was able to take the measure of the bike's performance from the rear, and it was really something! However, braking for the downhill hairpin at

Above *Great while it lasted! Bill Lomas (V8 Guzzi)
and I fight it out in the early stages of the German GP
at Solitude in 1956*

the far end of the circuit, Bill overdid things somewhat,
running wide, so allowing me to slip in on the nearside.

We continued dicing for the lead, when suddenly,
while heading him by 50 yards, my engine started to
misfire badly; I sat up, pulled over and waved Bill on, but
after some delay he arrived alongside, looking down
anxiously as clouds of steam poured out from *his*
machine. Bill was obviously in more trouble than I, and
as no one else was in sight, I stuttered along to the pits for
the mechanic to swap a few plugs. I set sail again in fourth
place, but the trouble was a more serious electrical fault
and I eventually had to retire. There followed an exciting
battle for the lead between Armstrong, Monneret and
Masetti. Yet another unfortunate, Walter Zeller had

Right *Just before the magneto called it a day at the
German GP at Solitude in 1956*

retired with piston trouble when lying third behind Bill and myself and lapping at about the same speed—this retirement meant that John Surtees' 500 cc World Championship was virtually assured.

A last-minute decision by Gilera to enter two machines for Armstrong and myself in the Ulster rather complicated my own arrangements, as I had already taken the plunge and entered a Velocette for the Junior class, a machine similar to the one Jack Wood had been riding. As this machine could only be completed at the last minute, we decided to forego the first practice period and duly arrived, complete with Velocette, on the Tuesday afternoon.

The 500 practice came first, giving me the opportunity to renew my acquaintance with a circuit I had not raced over since Ken Kavanagh beat me there in 1953. I soon discovered that the passage of time had not made it any smoother, but at least the five-speed gearbox we now used made the rather ridiculous hairpin a possibility! I only did a couple of laps in the 350 training period, though, as there had been no time previously to check over the machine. The next day then saw frantic work by many people on the Velo, including the fitting of a reliable chain oiler by the Renolds folk, and we arrived at Dundrod just in time to do a further two laps before the Junior practice period ended! But this was sufficient to show that the fibreglass streamlining was grounding very badly, so in view of the lack of time and facilities to carry out modifications, I decided not to run the machine. This was a bitter disappointment to me as the model was, in almost every other respect, showing great promise.

My 'race' Gilera had arrived with streamlining as well

Astride my 350 cc Velocette which I tried only in practice for the 1956 Ulster GP

as pannier and normal tanks, giving ten gallons total capacity to enable me to go through non-stop. But again lack of time was against us and a few laps on the streamliner with full tanks showed that I was barely able to get within five seconds of my time on the unstreamlined Oulton Park machine. A decision, therefore, had to be made after the last practice, and for me, bearing in mind the usually foul Dundrod weather conditions, it was to ride with just a small frontal fairing; Reg decided to risk the elements and use the 'full front', but to his cost. Fuel consumption tests during practice proved to my surprise that with a normal tankful of fuel we could just make the full distance of the race non-stop. This was a little secret which we kept to ourselves until after the race—not that it did us much good!

One further problem was what gear ratio to use. As I had not tried my race machine without streamlining, I assumed that the race engine would be better than the Oulton Park device and settled for a raising of the gear by fitting a rear-wheel sprocket with one tooth less, equalling 200 rpm; Reg was one tooth higher still with the streamliner.

Race day was windy and the result for me was a steady 9800 rpm down the straight instead of 10,400–10,500. In terms of speed, my time over the flying kilometre was 126 mph, which was slightly slower than the fastest 350—Bill Lomas' Guzzi, which had benefited from the good conditions under which the Junior race had been run—whilst Reg was credited with the kilo at 140 mph. But maximum speed isn't everything when a breeze is ablowing!

Hartle, Murphy and Brett, in that order, made the pace on the first lap while I tailed along behind. The Gilera was steering beautifully and, apart from the lack of revs down the main straight, was just about right for the job in hand. Lap two saw me in front of Murphy and Brett, and just behind John Hartle; this suited me for two reasons. For one thing, the Ulster is a long race and it is more interesting to mix it with somebody reliable for a while—at least when one knows that the necessary urge is there when required. And then, it was always a joy to sit behind a rider like Hartle, knowing that it was most unlikely that he would make a mistake, and conscious of the fact that he was taking pretty well every corner at the maximum speed possible and on a line that was perfection itself. I was quite surprised, though, at the speed of Hartle's Norton, which was visibly quicker than Jack Brett's. It would seem that the advent of 100 octane fuel had given the single yet another lease of life. Gilera were, as yet, using normal premium fuel but, in any case, we would have gained little by the use of better fuel, for a variety of reasons.

At about lap four, I took over the lead down the main straight, but a shade too much throttle coming out of the second-gear right-hander at Leathemstown Bridge produced a slide which terminated on the grass in the

form of a disconcerting (to say the least) wobble. Fortunately, one or two unhappy experiences with the 'beast' had taught me not to turn the power off too much on an occasion such as this, otherwise one was liable to get cast over the nearest hedge! During my struggle, though, I was just conscious of a Norton sneaking past on the inside.

I eventually regained the lead, this time to hold it for a while—up over the top of the rise above Leathemstown Bridge and down the famous Deer's Leap, leaving my braking a shade late for the third-gear bend at the bottom of the hill. Then—oh, calamity! Or very nearly, anyhow. I found myself braking very hard indeed on wet roads—a shower of rain had fallen, terminating in an almost clear-cut straight line across the road just about on my braking point. Luckily, I just made the corner, but proceeded in a slightly detuned state of mind!

My immediate worry was, of course, Hartle, whose almost legendary fame on wet roads I now expected to see demonstrated. I could almost see him rubbing his hands

Above The ignominious end to a wet Ulster GP at Dundrod in 1956

Inset Not so cheerful after dropping the Gilera in the Ulster GP

together as my back wheel spun on acceleration, but, to my surprise, a quick glance back up the road revealed an empty void. Although I had only a suspicion of what might have happened to him, I later learned that he had been unlucky at the Deer's Leap, being forced to do a quick trip down the slip-road at the bottom of the hill. I carried on with the utmost care, on roads which were wet at different places on succeeding laps, until finally the whole course was soaked. Slowly, I settled down and even began to enjoy myself. Riding the four on wet roads was rather like riding a trials bike on surface mud and called for quite a spot of throttle control—thank you, Sgt. Viney!

With a useful lead of over two minutes and the race less

than half over, I banked into Leathemstown Bridge once more, but this time I was just a shade late in peeling off. In view of the adverse camber on the left side of the road coming out, this forced me to heel the machine over that little bit too far on the rather smooth and slippery apex of the bend—and *bang!* I was literally dumped in the middle of the road when my front tyre decided that I was expecting too much of it. Winded, with an extremely painful shoulder and thankful for a good crash hat, I had to call it a day, although the total damage to the machine was merely a slightly-bent footrest. John Hartle went on to record his first Grand Prix win of 1956.

X-ray examination confirmed the doctor's opinion that nothing was broken in my shoulder, the pain coming from bad bruising. Fortunately, there was ample time for my IOM masseur Jack Griffiths to massage my shoulder back to normal again before I had to leave for Monza and the last Championship race of the year—and the last chance for Gilera's luck to turn.

Practice for the Grand Prix began, as usual, about a week before the event. The three foremost Italian marques sent their machines churning round for lap after lap, and then, when all official practice was over, MV still found some reason to do more until night fell! Monza featured the usual one-off Gilera sidecar outfit, at the express wish of the Italian Federation, and that year it swept all before it to receive the chequered flag. How nice it must have been for Milani, on a circuit like Monza, to have a full five seconds per lap in hand, even in practice, over the nearest opposition! In addition, the now-famous

Gilera 350 made its first appearance. With a maximum speed of approximately 147 mph, it blew everything else off the road to such good purpose that one or two people, who should have known better, thought it was a 500 in disguise!

Liberati won the 350 race at a canter, and although the 2 min 52 sec lap he was officially credited with was some three seconds optimistic, he was still quick enough to disappear smartly into the middle distance. For my part, my joy with the other 350 was short-lived. A broken clutch plate resulted in some very jerky gearchanges, and in some places it was a little exciting, especially when it was necessary to change up with the machine banked over at a violent angle. After nearly collecting Bartl's DKW which was close behind me on one occasion, I decided to make room for the folk who could race.

The 500 event promised to be interesting with the better of the two Guzzi eights now in the hands of new-boy Keith Campbell. I don't think he quite realized the responsibility, his chance having come as a result of Bill Lomas' unfortunate prang in the 350 race. We did not anticipate too much trouble from MV, but, as we were not riding to orders, there were always my four team-mates to worry about!

Keith Campbell was unable to get the Guzzi to fire at

The 350 push-start at Monza in 1956. Libero Liberati (number 4), the very comfortable winner, is partly out of picture. Bill Lomas, who crashed, is number 12, whereas I am number 2

the drop of the flag and the story spread around that he had forgotten to switch on the fuel taps. However, I can vouch for the inaccuracy of this as, next to Keith on the starting grid, I saw his mechanic do the necessary for him and remember being fascinated as I watched the fuel flow through the transparent plastic pipes. In fact, Keith had been given strict orders not to flood the carburettors before starting, but after nearly running himself to a standstill, a touch of the 'tickler' did the trick and he was eventually lapping at about the speed of the leaders, until a broken crankshaft brought him to a halt.

This, along with an injector-intake adrift on Walter Zeller's BMW, made it an all-Gilera battle with, at first, Liberati leading, with Monneret on his tail and myself working hard to make up lost time due to a lazy start. I managed, after a while, to dispose of Monneret, who was riding remarkably well on a machine fitted with the new Gilera frame which the rest of us had been loathe to use for the first time in such an important race.

More sweat and toil found me on Liberati's tail, and there, weighing up the pros and cons, I soon realized that any attempt to pass and make a break would be doomed to failure as, for one thing, Liberati was riding extremely well, and, for another, my machine was snaking rather badly for some unaccountable reason—a fault which had not shown up at practice speeds. I decided that the only thing to do was to worry about the 'opposition'. For a while Liberati pressed on, having an occasional look behind him, usually at the same place (coming out of the second Lesmo corner), so I made a point of being particularly close to his megaphones whenever he turned his head! Eventually, I noticed the tempo slowing, with his right wrist a shade less bent, down the straight. He

On the rostrum, feeling particularly pleased with myself after managing to beat Libero Liberati (also standing on the rostrum) across the finishing line at Monza in 1956

apparently wanted me to pass, but I decided I wasn't having any of it; meanwhile, our lead over the rest of the field had steadily increased.

Eventually, with some ten laps still to go, he eased off so much that I was forced to make the pace, though taking care to give nothing away. Previously, I had noticed that when he was trying, he braked at 300 metres for the bend at the end of the long straight—I had experimented and found that I could leave my braking to about 280 metres, but when he forced me to take the lead, I made a point of braking a little before the 300-metre mark, just for his benefit. Having been presented with the lead, I soon realized that it would pay me not to lose it again, if this was at all possible.

Monza is a very difficult circuit on which to pass at the best of times, so with five laps to go I gradually began to increase the pace, but not too much, hoping that my 'shadow' might be tempted to leave his final effort until the last lap, which would suit me best. The important factor was that I had to have a fair lead entering the last corner, as this long, gradually-easing turn was the place where I was having most difficulty with my snaking machine—I knew that Liberati would be able to accelerate much harder round this section than I could and would therefore beat me across the line, unless I could have at least a few yards to play with.

Up popped the signal—one lap to go—and it was every man for himself, with Liberati breathing down my neck. I held my lead into the straight and rushed into the Curva

Grande, almost a shade too quickly for my 'Jelly Baby', braking as late as possible for the first Lesmo, coming out of the second Lesmo showing a couple of hundred more revs than usual, still in the lead, down the long, flat-out section with its first full-bore left-hander, this time with my head a shade below the level of the screen instead of above, and, at the end of the straight, braking at my 280-metre mark, or even a shade later. Into the corner, and turning on the power as much as my writhing back wheel would permit, I scratched across the line, first, by a few lengths—whew! My first major win of 1956, and did I have to work for it!

Peace at last and only two more races to go—and these for the sheer fun of it. Scarborough came first, where riding the Gilera was the nearest I got to motocross in those days! I usually arrived at Oliver's Mount with a machine organized as near as possible to suit the occasion, but with the ultra-fast Kristianstad race in Sweden to follow, and, of necessity, only one machine for both events, I was forced to 'make do' for Scarborough. As things turned out, I just made it, but my last and fastest lap was a full three seconds outside my own 1955 record, and I could not have gone any faster. The close-ratio five-speed gearbox made me think I was playing an organ, rather than riding a motorcycle, and no fewer than 30 gearchanges were necessary during each under-three-mile lap, which played havoc with my left hand and wrist. All in all, if Bob McIntyre had not missed a gearchange during the 500 cc final coming out of Mount Hairpin, I would have been hard pressed indeed to find the opening necessary to win.

The final gallop of the year at Kristianstad was always a pleasure to me as, although the circuit was hardly my ideal, the organizers were of the highest calibre as far as continental races were concerned. Their treatment of both private and works riders was beyond reproach in every respect and was an object lesson to some other countries' organizers.

Competition in the 500 class did not appear to be too serious, but at the last minute Reg Armstrong, who had won the race at the Avus track in Berlin the previous week using my Monza machine, decided that Kristianstad was too good to miss and arrived upon the scene. Practice caused a stir in the Gilera camp when the previously calm, warm weather took a turn for the worse, becoming both cold and windy. It was then, right at the end of the season, that we discovered that our new streamlining was a dead loss in very strong cross-winds. In short, both machines were virtually unmanageable. An alteration to the front underside of the cowling, in an attempt to ease the loading on the front wheel, was producing a most undesirable feature in the form of front-wheel lift. Down the main straight, on my machine, it was impossible to ride at more than half-throttle. As the weather forecast for race day was similar, a decision was taken there and then to use only the small front fairing, and Reg, who had only the full fairing with him, had a small shield made up overnight.

Our team manager was rather keen that we make a race of it only for the last five laps as there was no other works opposition, but Reg, apparently feeling full of the joys of Sweden, wanted to race all the way. And he did! He departed like a scalded cat at the flag drop, while I sat behind, and soon the rest of the field were out of sight. Reg, after his initial attempt to clear off, eased back slightly and we continued to circulate in close formation, but at a more sedate pace. I had one spot of excitement, when Reg lapped a BMW—the rider of the BMW, seeing the Gilera go by, decided that a tow would help and attempted to move into the machine-length gap between Reg's back wheel and my front, with almost disastrous results for himself as well as me!

The circuit consisted of long straights and sharp, first-gear corners and Reg was pulling a lower gear than me, obviously treating the whole business very seriously. I soon realized that his lower gear was helping him considerably out of the slow corners, and as there was a slow corner 200 yards or so before the finishing line, I knew I would have to work for my living. With a lap and a bit still to go, I attempted to 'take' Reg when he was braking for a slow corner, but just to make matters more difficult, he overtook two more riders just before his braking point. The second rider—again on a BMW—apparently deciding he would repass Reg, moved over to the centre of the road just as I was coming through. I was forced to release my brakes and swerve to the outside of the road to avoid a pile-up, by which time, having left my braking late anyway, I was getting mighty near the corner while still travelling at fairly high speed. I trod on everything and flew past Reg with my rear wheel locked, almost taking a trip down the slip-road, but my luck held!

From there onwards, I really got my head under the handlebars and only once, about a quarter-mile further on, did Reg nearly come alongside as we almost reached maximum speed over the short straight past the pits. I think he might have made it, but the sun cast the warning shadow of his machine coming up rapidly on my right, and as we were fast approaching a second-gear corner, I left my braking much later than usual and he was forced to drop back. Keeping up the effort for the remainder of the lap produced a 100-yard lead, with a fair slice off my own lap record thrown in.

A satisfactory end to a rather unsatisfactory year!

The South African tour

I have always believed in accepting every opportunity for world travel arising out of my motorcycling activities. It was therefore with great interest that I learned of a movement afoot to invite me to compete in a series of races in South Africa and Southern Rhodesia at the start of 1957. A telephone chat between Johannesburg and Italy with a man by the name of Bud Fuller—who, incidentally, I never met during the whole of my visit—more or less clinched the matter, and final arrangements were confirmed by letter at the beginning of November 1956 for a two-month tour, during which I would compete in five events. Furthermore, during a conversation with Joy Foster, wife of ex-350 World Champion Bob Foster, at the Motorcycle Show in London, I learned that Bob was contemplating spending the winter out of England for health reasons. This led me to suggest that perhaps Bob would like to accompany me on my tour, to which Bob enthusiastically agreed. Meanwhile, the Gilera factory was preparing two unstreamlined 500s for the trip. I did toy with the idea of taking one of the new 350s, but as these were only in the development stage, the factory people were not too keen.

The two machines, in the care of Carlo Cazzaniga, one of the many excellent Gilera racing mechanics, left Venice for Cape Town on 5 December, while Bob and I arranged to fly to Johannesburg on 27 December. On arrival, we were welcomed by representatives of the organizers of the tour, the Grand Central Race Committee, the Castrol folk, and members of the press. Unfortunately, contrary to what I had said in my interview with the press, the next morning's story was headlined: 'Duke says he will break record' (i.e. at the first race, the Port Elizabeth 200), and described me as World *Speedway* Champion! This, I felt, was a rather doubtful start; and sure enough, there was more trouble coming. . . .

The following morning we flew to Port Elizabeth via East London, to learn on arrival that the mechanic and machines had, unfortunately, evaded the outstretched arms of the people in Cape Town and journeyed blissfully on to Durban, some 650 miles north of their correct destination! There, fortunately for me, the bright secretary of the Natal Motorcycle and Car Club grabbed the équipe before it moved onwards to Australia! I was also to learn that Carlo had left the whole of my riding kit behind in Italy, where I had deposited it to save excess baggage on the plane. Fortunately, these problems were brought under control: a £500 customs bond was paid on the machines and they returned to Port Elizabeth by road, and a cable was sent to Arcore requesting the immediate dispatch of my leathers and other gear.

On the way to Uitenhage, about 20 miles out from Port Elizabeth, we came to the famous nine-mile circuit and paused for a quick look. I had not really known what to expect, but I was very agreeably surprised. The circuit, originally part of the main road to Uitenhage, had been bypassed by a new road. This had left the fortunate organizers with the basis of a really wonderful road circuit running through comparatively open country, with a fair amount of gradient and some fine, fast, sweeping corners. The only two slow corners on the circuit could be negotiated quite easily without any use of the clutch, even bearing in mind the comparatively high overall gear it would be necessary to use.

Only one thing prevented me listing this course as equal to some of the best in Europe—bumps! The old Uitenhage road section, in particular, was deadly in this respect. Although this section was, in fact, almost straight for the most part and would normally be negotiated at maximum speed, even by a fully-streamlined 500, I was to find it almost impossible to ride my machine at the maximum, an experience which was new to me. Other problems included practice on open roads, starting at 5 am, where one had to watch out for such animals as turtles, dogs and even donkeys crossing the road, not to mention the odd native, a fair number of whom lived alongside the Uitenhage old road.

It rapidly became evident that I should spend as much time as possible, outside official practice, in studying the layout of the circuit. With this in mind, I spent a whole day motoring round the circuit, and also walking at each corner, piloted by the obliging Castrol representative. After this, I was at least sure of the sequence of the bends, and had a rough idea of what line to take (sometimes dictated by the bumps) and what gear to use on individual corners.

Official practice at 5 o'clock on Monday morning found me far from happy, though. Fortunately, my guess at the required gear ratio proved to be right first time, so I was able to concentrate immediately on choosing the right line. The rising sun, however, soon put paid to any fireworks on the section of course after the start, and although I was forced to creep along with my hands shielding my eyes, I was soon passed by a flying Norton, which rapidly disappeared into the distance. This sun-bound figure was none other than the South African idol Borro Castellani—apparently proceeding by radar! Concentrating as I was on finding the least bumpy line along the Uitenhage road, I was mildly surprised to meet a double-decker bus picking up early-morning workers—and travelling in the opposite direction to me!

A short stop at the pits to enable Carlo to check carburettor settings produced a worried expression when the removal of four plugs revealed a distinctly 'cooked' appearance; a larger set of jets reduced my maximum by about 500 rpm. By now, there was a fair amount of traffic on the road—all, it seemed, travelling against the run of the circuit, erecting a fine old dust blanket—so I decided to call it a day.

Race day was warm and sunny, with a fair amount of wind blowing, and some 25,000 people turned out to watch the fun. Riders were allowed two pushers to assist in starting on the uphill gradient of a by-road joining the circuit at a point on the right-hand side of a fast, sweeping, third-gear, left-hand corner, some 100 yards before the pit area. This meant, of course, that any rider well back on handicap was liable to be collected in no uncertain manner by riders who had already completed a lap or more if they happened to drift out as they came around the bend. In fact, although I was on tenter-hooks throughout the 30-odd minutes when riders were being started, the only incident occurred when the stronger of two pushers pushed to such effect that the unfortunate, and protesting, rider of an AJS 7R was thrust off the road and down a bank, long before he could drop the clutch! Unhurt, the party finally completed the operation and he roared off on his way.

Eventually, I made my getaway and concentrated hard on learning my way around. I soon came across Dave Chadwick (350 Norton)—in South Africa on a working holiday—who had started a little over one lap in front of me. Shortly afterwards, on the third lap, I came in for a spot of excitement. By that time, I was carving lumps off my old braking distances, but I overdid the carving as I approached one of the slower corners on the circuit. I might just have made it, but for some wet tar on the approach which prevented me from braking any harder than usual. As a result, I had to make a quick dash down the convenient slip-road, losing about six seconds in the process.

From the fifth lap onwards, I began to feel more at home, with the model handling superbly on the bumpy going. I had arranged with Bob to give me a signal when I had completed ten of the 16 laps, with my position shown on the top of the signalling board and the number of laps still to do on the bottom. This I eagerly awaited, only to be shown the number of laps and a big question mark. This I put down to the complication of working out the times of some 65 runners at that stage in the race. It was at about this time, sweeping round the bend into the straight, that I noticed a rider leaving the pit area at high velocity after refuelling. To my consternation, as I approached, travelling at about maximum speed and in fourth gear, the rider swerved towards the tarmac road and went on to the dirt strip bordering the road on each side, disappearing in a huge cloud of dust. I was quite sure he had fallen as he caught the edge of the road and was probably even now sliding across the road into my path. It was too late to brake—I could only shut off as I dived into the dust-cloud and hope that I would miss him. To my surprise and relief, the rider, Castellani, appeared out of the murk still on his machine and going like a bomb! I was able to slip by before the next corner, though, so that was one of the opposition accounted for.

With three laps to go, my signal was once again a large question mark. I began to wonder whether Bob was indicating: 'Why are you going so slowly?' I found out afterwards that, due to the handicap system, I was lying 25th at the first signal, so Bob decided not to dishearten me too much by letting me know! I was lapping at about 106 mph at the time. With two laps to go, my position had improved to 12th, but Bob still thought it best not to let me in on the secret. I decided, however, to pile on the coals, in spite of a deterioration in the handling of my machine—due, no doubt, to overworked shock absorbers and the heat of the day. My lap speed rose to 108 mph, where the previous record had stood at about 98 mph to the credit of Vic Proctor on his 1000 cc Vincent. I crossed the finishing line to learn that I had finished second to Stander on handicap—and no wonder, for this remarkable young man on his home-brewed MOV Velocette had, during his record-breaking ride, actually lapped at almost 91 mph.

The next several days were spent being royally entertained in East London and Durban, where we were able to see much of the beautiful countryside and made many new friends. Then, it was back to racing, this time in Pietermaritzburg. Originally intended to measure three miles, the circuit was shortened to 1.6 miles due to lack of funds—not, I hasten to add, lack of enthusiasm. Here there were a good variety of left- and right-hand bends, both fast and slow, with a straight that was long enough, thanks partly to gradient, to let even a Grand Prix 500 loose on!

On the day, a rather better-than-usual start in the 500 scratch race gave me a lead of six seconds in no time, but

soon the outstanding Castellani, making ground after a poor start, put in some laps which made my lead practically static for some 15 of the 28 laps. Then the gap widened again—the South African champion was having clutch trouble—so that my lead had increased to about 28 seconds at the fall of the finishing flag.

That was just the amount I had to make up on Borro in the general handicap race over the same distance. This did not look so good. True, I had a little bit in hand, but with so many slower machines to overtake, the odds (providing that a slipping clutch could be fixed) seemed to be in Castellani's favour. In addition, Dave Chadwick, who had had a wonderful dice with Cas to win the 350 scratch race (Cas fell off), had broken the 350 lap record, and his consistent lappery at near-record time had caught the handicapper off balance. I decided to have no signals, except the number of laps to do, and waited impatiently for the 'off'. Once under way, I piled on the pressure and

Before the start at the Roy Hesketh Circuit,
Pietermaritzburg, during my 1957 tour of South Africa

found myself overtaking the slower folk without the frequent baulks which I had experienced in the scratch race. Taking no chances, but attempting to keep my lappery as regular as possible, I was surprised at how quickly Chadwick came and went, although I still had to overtake him twice more.

At something like half-distance, I spied the now-familiar figure of Castellani. The slowly-closing gap was further reduced when Cas had a brief spell in the dirt off the edge of the road on a quickish second-gear right-hander. Next time around, a repeat performance gave me the chance to slip by, but I shall always marvel at the South African's powers of recovery in most impossible-looking situations. Usually, the sight of someone overtaking him was like a red rag to a bull with Castellani, but on this occasion, still suffering from the effects of his fall in the 350 race, he allowed me to ride on in peace. At the finish, though, I was quite sure that Chadwick had won, only to learn that he had also been plagued with clutch trouble, with the resultant stop just putting paid to his chances of third place.

A most enjoyable stay in Pietermaritzburg was rounded off when Bob and I were invited to join a picnic party at a dam some 50 miles out of town. This afforded me the unexpected opportunity of trying my hand with a couple of hydroplanes, which were there on test. The more docile of the two, fitted with a Johnson outboard motor capable of propelling it at speeds in excess of 40 mph, was a real joy to handle—even a novice like me could drift it round the marker-buoys flat out, with steering on full-lock. The second craft, though, was a different cup of tea, rather like a 500 racer as compared with a 250. It was powered by a Mercury four-cylinder two-stroke engine, which let loose a positively ear-shattering yowl on full-bore and pushed the boat through the water at 70 mph plus.

Charlie Young, Clerk of the Course, appears to be holding me back at the Roy Hesketh Circuit

What an experience! To round off the day, but against my better judgement, I was talked into donning a pair of swimming trunks and trying my hand at guiding an aquaplane with a difference. This variety had no stabilizing fins and no grips for the feet. There was much merriment when, on contacting the backwash from the boat, I was dunked a few times at, I suppose, a mere 25 mph—but even at that speed, water is very, very hard! A final desperate effort to stay aboard found me aquaplaning beautifully in what could be likened to a four-wheel drift. This meant that I was travelling at something like twice the speed of the boat, a wonderful sensation, and I was just beginning to congratulate myself when I touched the edge of the wash from the boat and—*bang!* I had a stiff neck for days afterwards!

My wife Pat and three-year-old son Peter now joined me in Johannesburg for the last month of my tour, where my next race was to be held at a circuit called Grand Central. This turned out to be neither grand nor central. Some 15 miles out of the city, the circuit had not been used for three years and was overgrown with grass to some extent, and was bumpy enough to make one's teeth chatter when braking hard. However, three days before the race found me in bed with a septic throat and a

temperature of 101 degrees. Fortunately, drastic treatment by an excellent doctor had me out of bed the day before the race, that is, practice day, with a promise not to ride until 'the day'. A few laps on the morning of the race left me perspiring like a racehorse, so I decided to conserve my energy—what there was of it!

My programme here consisted of three races: a five-lap scratch race, a five-lap handicap and a 12-lap handicap. Overnight rain had left one of the rather better corners with water flowing across it, and this was like ice, although the surface looked fairly non-skid. I made a good start in the scratch race and spent the first couple of laps feeling my way around, always conscious of the familiar beat of a 500 'dope' Norton when negotiating the slow corners. That man again! My purely personal worry was relieved when, after three laps, the opposition disappeared; a broken gearbox mainshaft had locked the works up and hiked Cas off at a fair rate of knots— happily without serious injury, but with sufficient effect to lay him low for the day. Although far from wishing him any ill, I must admit that in my state of health on that day I was glad to be relieved of my shadow!

The five-lap handicap was a pretty hopeless proposition for me, but I had a go and, lifting the lap record a shade, finished fourth, just out of the money. Then, for the 12-lap handicap race, the combination of a cool breeze, together with a longish delay in starting the race (due to some members of the crowd wandering on to the circuit), plus my handicap, caused my engine to be just about stone cold at the drop of the starter's flag. Despite liberal flooding of the carburettors, two of the pots refused to fire. Further flooding produced a three-cylinder Gilera, and after completing one lap I again stopped at the pits. Investigation revealed a badly-fitting plug cover, but with this refitted I departed from the scene on full-song.

Although now completely out of the hunt, I amused myself by trying to full-bore the one really quick bend on the 2.4-mile circuit, a long and rather wavy right-hander, and eventually satisfied myself. I managed in the process to lower my own lap record by a further two seconds, but of course finished well down the field.

Our next venture took us out of the Union into Southern Rhodesia, to Salisbury, 750 miles away. While I travelled with my family by air, Bob kindly agreed to brave the elements and drive a distinctly second-hand van placed at our disposal by Boet Ferreira (who had taken over the initial organization of the visit from Bud Fuller), with Carlo and the two machines therein. Their journey was comparatively uneventful, apart from a five-hour argument with the South African customs over some permit which Carlo had forgotten to obtain before leaving Italy, plus an out-of-adjustment fan belt which cut through a radiator hose when the party was miles away from anywhere!

Our first impression of Salisbury, based on the view from the bedroom of our hotel, was not so good, but further investigation proved the district to be the old part of the town and due for demolition. A short drive revealed a magnificent city in the making. Expansion had been ultra-rapid since the war and, with the population doubled in that short period, a terrific amount of building was taking place with evidence of excellent planning.

I decided to give the unused Gilera an airing on the 2.5-mile Belvedere Aerodrome Circuit, just out of town, as the first machine had already done just over 500 racing and practice miles without any attention, although in fact it seemed to be going better and better. The wide-awake chief organizer, Jimmy de Villiers, had already hit on the excellent idea of handing out handbills with information regarding the races to children as they left school. The children, in turn, dragged their willing or unwilling parents along on the day to help swell the excellent crowd to 20,000. The organizers had one big problem, though— the circuit had never before been used for racing, and they therefore had no yardstick to go by when estimating handicap times. Thus, they decided, rightly or wrongly, to produce a list which was subject to alteration after the results of the practice session and the scratch races were known!

My basic handicap was stiff, and rather against my better judgement, I decided to cruise around behind Castellani in the 500 scratch race until the last lap and then 'do a Masetti' on him. This I was able to manage with comparative ease, as the far superior power of the four could be used to its full advantage on the fast circuit. I had, of course, omitted to appreciate that the resultant gentle treatment, by me, of the few corners on the circuit would hardly impress a crowd of enthusiasts, one of whom was heard to remark: 'This bloke Duke should buy himself a pair of roller-skates to help him round the corners!'—and so forth. I therefore determined to have a real go in the handicap, in the hope that not too many people would ask for their money back!

However, my hopes of a real race in the handicap were completely shattered when, after a dry start for the limit men, a torrential downpour of rain hit us just as I made my getaway. The resultant pools of water, which always ruin the adhesive qualities of aerodrome circuits, not only tended to lift the front wheel of my machine clear of the ground when banked over, but also filled the magneto distributor cap with water in no time at all, reducing the model to a three-cylinder again.

A prolonged stop to dry out the works also produced a halt in the downpour, and after losing a considerable amount of time I resumed my ride, although it was now pointless to stick my neck out. One part of the course in particular, soon after the start, was extremely slippery and any drastic use of the throttle produced quick and quite lurid slides from the Gilera. It was here that Cas met his Waterloo. Taking a fast handful of throttle, he about-turned, smartly ejecting his petrol tank in the process and putting paid to his chances. An excellent ride by D. Henderson, mounted on a 250 BSA, produced the desired result. I was, of course, unplaced, and was left feeling distinctly dissatisfied with my own performance.

With the bikes going on by train to Cape Town, some 1750 miles away, where the final race of the tour was to be held, Bob was to drive the empty van back to Johannesburg. Although concerned about the 'health' of the van, he had an uneventful journey as far as the frontier, where the steering failed completely as he reached the customs post. I hate to think what might have happened had the steering lasted until a mile or two further on, when the road became very hilly and twisty, with sheer drops off the edge. In addition to this, due to some water he drank on the journey, Bob became so ill that he was forced to go to bed on his arrival at Johannesburg and so missed the trip to the prettiest part of the Union, the Cape.

After the enthusiasm of Salisbury, there was a distinct falling-off of interest in Cape Town which was reflected in the comparatively small gate of 8000 who turned up to watch the racing there. The circuit chosen for the event, just over 1.6 miles long, was rather flat but had recently been resurfaced, for which I was grateful. The course covered very few acres, twisting and turning its way back and forth to such an extent that I was forced to fit the lowest possible gear to the Gilera, and even then 10,000 rpm was the absolute maximum on the short flat-out section. This was hardly Grand Prix going, but in small doses such a circuit can be good fun.

After about ten laps' practice the day before the event (official training was on race day), my left hand and wrist in particular were feeling the pinch, and the combined scratch and handicap race was over 42 laps! There were 23 gearchanges per lap, equalling 966 in 75 miles. The point was, would I be able to stick the pace? I was to give one second per lap to Castellani and Joubert, which seemed reasonable enough, but the full entry comprised 30 riders, some on very slow machines, and it was obviously going to be difficult to overtake. A great variety of folk and machines practised on the day before the race, some in open-necked, short-sleeved shirts and slacks, with and without boots and gloves, but mercifully all with helmets. One enthusiast on a 250 Jawa, obviously thoroughly enjoying himself, did about 30 or 40 laps while I was there, and was still motoring when I left!

Race day was warm and sunny. After a preliminary stock-machine handicap, won by a 600 BMW, we lined up for the main event, not at the widest part of the road by the pits as I had anticipated, but on the rather narrow section before them. The riders waiting to start were two and three abreast, apparently completely oblivious to the limit men who came howling by in the six or eight feet of road left to them. One of the limit men was my friend on the Jawa (with a home-made cylinder head, incidentally), still motoring after its hard time the previous day. He set sail with great gusto and bought a terrific box of tacks on the second corner. He instantly remounted and rode round the following corner, which was only a few yards from where we were waiting, in extremely lurid but incredibly fast fashion, and stayed on! By the time I had watched this performance three times with what seemed like a never-ending stream of riders proceeding at high velocity past my right ear, I was practically a nervous wreck!

I was almost glad when the starter indicated that I could proceed. Of necessity, my early laps were gentle ones until some of the 29 had fallen by the wayside. Meanwhile, Joubert and Castellani, who had started together, were 'dicing the piece out', with local man Joubert leading by a short head. This battle terminated when Joubert adjourned to the pits for adjustments. On rejoining the fray, he appeared to wait for me to catch up. Then, being overtaken, he proceeded on three occasions to demonstrate that it was possible to outbrake Duke and the Gilera, successfully pinching my corner as he rushed in, banking over with the brakes still on. However, just as I was beginning to get rather annoyed, he disappeared from the scene.

By the time I came across Castellani, who had made good his escape, more than 30 laps had gone by, and I was beginning to feel quite lonely. Cas, handicapped by a loose swinging-fork pivot bolt and a fractured mega-phone, still gave battle, but the superior acceleration of the four eventually paid dividends.

Of all the riders I was able to study on the whole tour (so many handicap races limited my opportunity of doing this), Borro Castellani was outstanding, especially on the extremely-fast type of circuit. I was quite sure he would perform well in Europe, provided he could alter his tactics a little to allow for the solid obstacles he was liable to encounter coming out of some corners, and make more use of his front brake.

I, personally, met some wonderful people out there— people who went to a great deal of trouble on my behalf, for which I was extremely grateful. By their kindness and hospitality, a trip which I had at first been tempted to terminate, almost before it had begun, finished on a very pleasant note indeed.

Gilera withdrawal

Back in Europe for the 1957 season after my tour in South Africa, one could not help feeling that the bottom had fallen out of the Gilera racing effort when the young—and only—son of the family succumbed to a sudden illness in October 1956, while on a visit with his father to the Gilera factory in Buenos Aires. Ferruccio had been the driving force behind the racing programme for some time, and was rapidly being schooled by his father to take over the command of the highly successful *Moto Gilera Fabrica*. For a while I wondered if Commendatore Gilera would fold up the racing department, and I was both relieved and pleased when, instead, he decided to continue with renewed vigour, although it was soon apparent that his personal interest had faded when he failed to attend any of the classic Grands Prix, other than the Italian at Monza.

Prior to this, after the 1956 season, Reg Armstrong had decided to terminate a fine racing career in the interests of his other business commitments, which led the factory to re-examine the possibility of engaging another British rider. In my opinion, there was only one candidate with all the necessary attributes, natural ability, experience and youthful dash, combined with the right touch of restraint: Bob McIntyre. Bob had previously turned down the offer of a ride in the 1956 TT, but I was allowed to make a further approach to him. This time he weakened and travelled to Arcore with me to meet the Commendatore and Ferruccio, and a contract was signed. Bob soon showed his form by lapping Monza at exceptionally high speed under foul conditions, and all was well. Imola, in April 1957, was to be Bob's first outing, on 350 and 500 machines, along with Milani and Liberati.

The factory had refrained from asking me to compete as they knew I had an aversion to riding in Italian races, other than the Grand Prix, after repeated experiences of spectators walking across the road in front of me during the race. In one instance, I was forced to brake heavily when travelling at full-blast down a straight when a woman decided to push her pram—complete with infant—across the road! In addition, the name Imola did not exactly conjure up happy memories. Nevertheless, I decided to spectate, just to see how my new team-mate was progressing. Arriving at Arcore en route, I sensed a slight case of 'panic stations', prompted, no doubt, by recent defeats in both 350 and 500 classes at the first Italian Championship race. The V8 Guzzi, in the able hands of Colnago (late of Gilera, just to rub it in), had scored an impressive victory in the 500 cc class and it appeared to be going great guns.

Imola, next to the Grand Prix, is the most important race in Italy, and in some mysterious way, without being directly asked to compete, I found myself entered! A pre-practice gallop, while serving to confirm McIntyre's talent, also produced the rather disturbing knowledge that many of the end-of-season suggestions for modifications to brakes and suspension had not been carried out, although engine power appeared to have increased a little. This unusual lack of development I put down to a form of complacency, which so often creeps in when a firm has enjoyed the tremendous run of success which Gilera had had during the years since the war.

Possibly the most important modification called for was a change in weight distribution. This plays a tremendously important part in the handling of a racing motorcycle, and, in particular, it is required to vary when a machine is with or without streamlining. As early as September 1954 it had become apparent that the Gilera, although about right in this respect when unstreamlined, required modification when the 'dustbin' was fitted. This was agreed at the time with the brilliant racing manager and engineer Piero Taruffi, but although a move was made to design a new frame at once, Taruffi soon left the concern; the lack of his guiding hand found us at Imola in 1957 with no two frames alike, as far as the relative position of engine unit to wheel spindles was concerned.

Official practice went quite well in spite of these problems, and collectively we occupied most of the front positions on the grid on race day. I made a bad start in the 350 cc event, a habit I seemed to have recently developed; Bob made great progress and had a comfortable lead when an oiled plug forced him to stop (a trouble which occurred many times afterwards in the 350 model). On rejoining the race, although a lap in arrears, he successfully harried the leader, Liberati, until his deficit became a mere half-lap by the end.

For my part, I believe I was lying fifth early in the race when, on rounding the acute, blind hairpin, I was confronted by a pool of oil left by another competitor. With no chance of avoiding it, I fell heavily. The marshals on the spot had known the oil was there—in fact they even knew when it was dropped—and yet they had taken no action whatsoever—until I persuaded them in no uncertain terms!

As the 500 cc race followed immediately after the 350 cc event, I walked back to the pits, still slightly shaken, in time to line up my unstreamlined 500 for the big event. I had decided to run without a 'shell' as there is very little flat-out going at Imola. This was another bad start for me, but, with a more willing motor beneath me this time, I managed to gobble up a few places until I had Bob and Masetti—who were first and second respectively—in my sights, and the gap was closing. Over-eagerness caused my downfall here; too much throttle coming out of a second-gear bend produced a lurid slide, and then a wobble cast me off the model on to my shoulder, dislocating my collar-bone in a big way. Some laps later, McIntyre, by now leading comfortably, once more had bad fortune when the ignition failed, although there was some consolation for him in the knowledge that he had undoubtedly proved himself. The ultimate Imola winner, Dickie Dale on the Guzzi V8, lapping repeatedly inside record speed towards the end of the race, set the seal on his return to race-winning form.

I soon found myself sharing a room at Imola hospital with Bill Lomas, who had fallen in the 350 race, and after a few X-rays of my head and shoulder (my crash helmet had split when I thumped the deck), I was told that I had a minor shoulder dislocation only, which would be right in 15 days. With the TT only weeks away, what a relief! The subsequent trip back to England was an uncomfortable one, with my arm bandaged against my body, and as I found it necessary to support my left arm with my right hand, for comfort, I soon realized that all was not well. Noble's Hospital in the Isle of Man soon confirmed my worst fears. The dislocation was in fact a major one and the TT was definitely 'out', for the second year in succession! Not that the Gilera team needed to worry, for with Australian Bob Brown to back him up, McIntyre took to the new-found responsibility like the proverbial duck to water. No words of mine can adequately convey the true brilliance of his Senior TT ride; he used his head and ability to the limit—and, I suspect, occasionally chanced his hand—and reaped the reward he justly deserved.

The Dutch followed the TT, and it was here during practice that Bill Lomas, scarcely recovered from his

Biting the dust at Imola in 1957, thus setting the seal on a disastrous last year with Gilera

Left Bill Lomas, mounted on the 350 Guzzi, riding through Governor's Bridge in the 1957 Junior race

Below left Bob McIntyre travelling over Ballaugh Bridge on the Gilera in the Senior race of 1957

fractured shoulder at Imola, churned round at a high rate of knots on the V8 Guzzi, which had rapidly earned a reputation for being a bit of a brute in the handling department. Whether his shoulder gave way under the strain, or whether he made an error of judgement due to lack of practice, we never knew, but, headstrong, Bill chose to ignore Moto Guzzi's pleas to take it easy and crashed with disastrous results. His injuries put him out of racing for the rest of the season.

The early part of the 350 cc race provided plenty of excitement when McIntyre, Campbell, Dale and Liberati went at it hammer and tongs, until Dale, a little off line, was forced to bank his machine a bit more, and down he went. This certainly cooled Liberati's ardour—he was just behind Dale at the time—and he dropped out of the picture, while the other two, seemingly sensing the threatening disaster, took the edge off their 'frenzy'! Ultimately, the superior handling and light weight of the Guzzi, ridden by a very determined Keith Campbell, was too much for McIntyre and the race was lost by a few seconds.

The 500 cc race, after looking like a McIntyre victory in the early stages, found him relinquishing his lead when he pulled into the pits to investigate a misfire. The cause being elusive, he decided to restart, whereupon the misfire disappeared! With more than one minute to make up on the flying Surtees, he soon overhauled Liberati and the others between himself and the leader, but although he was gaining, it soon became apparent that he would not make it before the end; then Surtees started to slow. Due to a comic-shaped petrol tank without internal

The powerhouse of the 1957 500 cc Guzzi V8

baffles, fuel was rushing away from the carburettor feed pipes when he braked hard for slow bends, causing the engine to cut out momentarily, thus slowing him by a second or so per lap.

Bob, by now going faster and faster, could definitely make up the deficit at this rate, with two laps or so to spare, but the effect of a hard 350 cc race and the fantastic effort he was now making, plus the heat of the day, appeared to take their toll, and McIntyre ran off the road for no other apparent reason, leaving John Surtees sitting pretty. This unfortunate accident put paid to an almost certain 500 cc Championship so far as Bob was concerned. His racing at that time was so outstanding that I could not see anybody giving him a run for his money in the remaining Championship events.

Still not fully recovered from my accident at Imola, I was a spectator once again at the Belgian. Practice was uneventful with, in the absence of McIntyre, Liberati and Bob Brown upholding the flag for Gilera. Then, on race day, just before the start of the 500 cc event, Liberati's machine refused to start! There followed a most unpleasant episode. Team manager Roberto Persi decided that Liberati should ride Bob Brown's machine. I was incensed by this unfair action and argued the point with Persi, but to no avail. The race started, and all credit to Liberati riding a strange machine, still bearing Brown's number, because he won by a small margin from Jack Brett (Norton)—but then the fun started. Nortons protested, and as the incident was totally irregular, the protest was upheld and Liberati was disqualified.

My first ride of the season was at Hedemora in Sweden, a non-championship event, where I retired with clutch trouble in the 350 cc race, and finished a poor second to Keith Campbell's Guzzi in the 500 cc race.

At the Ulster Grand Prix, my riding left much to be desired. Bob McIntyre, still far from well, elected to use the unstreamlined model, while Liberati chose a streamliner. Although there was another machine partially dismantled with a fairing fitted, it was quite obvious that it would require a great deal of effort to produce this in unstreamlined form in time for me to ride, so I settled against my better judgement for the fully-streamlined model. However, when my machine started to run on only three cylinders in the 350 cc race, I was forced to retire. Bob's 350 failed to start cleanly and a change of plug had to be effected before he could proceed, way back down the field. After a wonderful attempt to get in the picture, though, his motor finally gave up. An excellent and consistent ride by Keith Campbell, despite a failing engine towards the end, produced its rich reward, while a fine back-up ride by a newcomer to the Guzzi team, Keith Bryen, secured second place.

The timed speeds over a flying kilometre past the start during the 500 cc race told their tale with a 5 mph differential between Liberati's machine and mine, although the biggest single factor was the deplorable state of my riding. In spite of this, my machine seemed to be going quite well, but I found myself making a reasonable job of a corner on one lap only to be incredibly slow on the next and quite unable to work up any enthusiasm, and as I had always placed great store on consistency in racing, I considered that here I had reached my lowest ebb! Once, having overtaken John Hartle towards the end of the straight with a fair amount of speed in hand, he calmly switched to the outside of me and almost literally flew past when we arrived at the fast left-hand corner at the end!

Although he was riding against folk on similar machinery but who were by no means at their best, one must pay due respect to Libero Liberati who, I think, surprised all by his fine effort in winning, at the first attempt, the Ulster Grand Prix over what is undoubtedly one of the world's most difficult circuits. With the dice now loaded heavily in Liberati's favour for the 500 cc World Championship, and only a ride on his home ground to come, we journeyed to Monza for the Italian Grand Prix. Here I could work up little enthusiasm for a 350 which, despite a fair effort on my part, would not get within five seconds per lap of Liberati during practice. The 500 recorded reasonable times, however, and I had a good grid position on race day.

A progressively failing motor soon had me relegated to the pits to watch the fun in the 350 cc race, while Bob McIntyre, in spite of all Liberati's efforts, steadily drew away, but it was interesting to watch Montenari's sterling effort to bring the Guzzi up into second place after a hopeless start. But although he eventually taxed himself to such an extent that he ran off the road with a couple of laps to go, he could make little impression on Bob.

During practice, Bob had had several very near squeaks, which I put down to a lack of ability to concentrate resulting from his accident in Holland. In the break between the races, therefore, I took him back to the hotel for a rest. On returning to the track, it was soon evident that he was in no fit state to race; he was advised not to, and he sensibly accepted the inevitable. Subsequent X-rays revealed a damaged vertebra, previously undiagnosed, which had healed prior to Monza only to come 'unstuck' again during the 350 race. This put paid to further racing for him during what was left of the season.

For me, the 500 cc race was almost a repetition of the season before, except that this time my scrap was with Milani after Liberati and John Surtees had cleared off into the middle distance. At one stage it appeared that Milani had the better of me, and he was certainly riding better than he had done for some time. A determined effort towards the end of the race, however, brought me within striking distance of him once more, for my riding had improved a little by now, and I seized my

opportunity on the last lap at the first Lesmo corner, passing him round the outside. I was then surprised to come up behind John Surtees going at reduced speed, due, I suspect, to a hole in a piston (a not-uncommon MV trouble), and swung wide to pass him, thus finishing in an unexpected, but not unwelcome, second place.

As was my custom after the Italian, I asked about the machines for the four end-of-season races in England, which were covered in my yearly contract with Gilera. Roberto Persi told me he would have to ask Mr Gilera, who had left for the mountains after the race; he would then 'write to me'. I returned home to the Isle of Man and waited. Then, on the Saturday afternoon before Scarborough, a letter arrived. It stated that Gilera had some time ago made a decision not to race any more in 1957 after Monza, so they were not competing in the last Italian Championship race and would be unable to provide machines for my four races. . . . What a blow! Here was a difficult situation—I had contracted to ride in the four events, and I felt bound to put in an appearance on *something*.

Hurried telephone calls to Jimmy Hill of Castrol located Alan Rutherford, who had ridden my 500 Manx Norton in the Manx Grand Prix. He, Alan, was only entered at Silverstone, for which Tom Arter would lend a G45 Matchless, so here was something to ride, anyway. The model had been jumping out of third gear in the Manx and might have touched a valve in the process, so it needed a check-over. I flew to Liverpool on the Sunday and motored to London to the Rutherfords. Another hurried call, this time to Mr Hopwood of Nortons on Sunday morning, and he kindly arranged for me to bring the engine and gearbox up to Bracebridge Street for the attention of the service department.

The engine and gearbox were removed from the frame, placed in the boot of my MG, and late Monday afternoon found me at Nortons. This done, I motored on to Liverpool where I left the car at Speke airport for my wife to collect as transport to take her and our son Peter to Scarborough on the Wednesday. I stayed the night at Speke airport and caught a plane to London early on Wednesday morning. I was now really in trouble, as my own Bedford van, which had been due back from the Continent the previous Friday, with Bob Brown at the wheel, had failed to appear!

Once again, the Rutherford family came to my assistance with the loan of their old Morris commercial van. By the time I arrived at their house in West Ham, Alan had the remnants of the Norton loaded and his kindly and thoughtful mother had made some cheese rolls to sustain me on the journey. I motored to Birmingham, once more arriving in the afternoon; the engine and gearbox were ready and speedily fitted, and I set off for Scarborough. I eventually arrived at 11.30 that night, without even having sat astride my new racer and ready only for bed.

The morning practice found me, fortunately, with help from my old friend Harry Johnson, who used to accompany me to all my short-circuit outings when riding Nortons in the 1949–52 era. But the few things which I still had to sort out, such as number plates, etc, meant that the first practice session was missed. The afternoon practice soon made me realize that, after more than five years, it was infinitely more difficult to go from a 'four' to a 'single' than it had been from a 'single' to a 'four'. In addition, considerable engine vibration foretold serious mechanical trouble developing. To cap it all, on the day, the model proved difficult to start in both heat and final, so I could do no more than indulge in a minor scrap with Brian Purslow, which resulted in his crossing the line in front of me, despite a final effort on my part to overtake on the last bend.

Anxious about signs of impending mechanical failure, I returned to Nortons, where my old friend Bill Stone, the works manager, came to my aid, and once again the model passed through the service department. Next to the Reynolds Tube Company, where I had a new frame and front fork in the making, and here, quite by accident,

The great Mike Hailwood on a 203 cc MV at Oulton Park in August 1957

I discovered Bob Brown and my lost van just one week and three days behind schedule! The frame was progressing in the able hands of Ken Sprayson and development engineer Bill Barnett. So after arranging with Bob Brown, who was on his way to Keith Campbell's wedding to my sister-in-law in the Isle of Man, to leave my van for me at Liverpool airport, I motored the Rutherford vehicle back to its London home, caught a plane back to Liverpool, stayed the night at the airport and caught the morning plane to the Island, arriving a few hours before the wedding, where I was to act as usher. Fortunately, my borrowed morning suit fitted!

And so the battle went on, with a shot of 'flu at Silverstone, and streamlining to be made by Peel Engineering in the Isle of Man before Aintree. Bad start followed bad start, with still only the faintest sign of a return to form. . . . And so to Oulton Park, and the chance of using my experimental frame and forks produced by the co-operative efforts of the Reynolds folk and Woodhead-Monroe. Various modifications were necessary to iron out a few 'bugs', and as if we had not had enough trouble, I very nearly missed qualifying in the single practice session as the magneto had to be changed before I could race. After all this, and a front place on the grid, the flag dropped; I ran, dropped the clutch, and the engine, possibly over-advanced, kicked back, leaving yours truly on the line. . . . I was soon under way, however, and was impressed with the handling of the new model, beginning to work my way up through the field. It had been worth it after all.

From 35th, I moved up to finish a steady seventh. After such a bad start I was quite happy—in fact, I had not enjoyed myself so much for a long time. Towards the end of the race, I was lapping at the same speed as Brett and Hartle on works Nortons. At last the 'touch' was slowly returning. My only regret was that the final result could not have been better, to offer some compensation to all the folk who had worked so hard to get me to the line.

During this time, rumours of an impending withdrawal became reality. Bob and I read in the papers that the Italian factories, with the exception of MV, had withdrawn from racing. We, the riders, received no official notification, but it was obviously true. It seemed to be commonplace then for factory riders to read of their fate in the press! So the future was in the melting pot. Personally, at the time, I believed the Italian factories would see the error of their ways in the form of reduced sales once the following summer arrived, for the Italian public were much more easily influenced by racing successes than either the British or the Germans, but I was wrong. In 1958, Gilera sold more motorcycles than at any time in their long history, although sales did decline year by year from 1959 onwards. Nevertheless, they never officially returned to road racing.

With two years of comparative inactivity on the circuits behind me, the Gilera decision to withdraw from racing presented me with a pretty problem. Careful thought brought forward three basic possibilities: turn to four wheels, retire, or find alternative two-wheeled factory machines to ride. The first proposition was attractive as I had enjoyed driving the Aston Martin, even though the team atmosphere had been lacking, and there was the standing offer to renew my efforts with the David Brown Equipe. The car, one of the finest racing sports cars in the world, left nothing to be desired, and

only the magnetic influence of two wheels prevented me from following this course of action.

The second possibility I quickly put to one side, although in April, with an eye to the future, I bought the Arragon Hotel, Santon, on the Isle of Man. I wanted to develop a hotel on the Island with many of the facilities which were the 'norm' on the Continent, and endeavour to create a standard which, elsewhere, had pleased me.

At about this time also, I was approached by a clever engineer, Bob Dearden, with others, to help finance Ronagency, a company formed to create the first freight service in unit loads to and from the Isle of Man. This was a great step forward for the Island, long overdue, using small coasters converted to carry flats and containers. The company prospered and eventually carried around 60 per cent of the Island's freight.

In addition to this, there was the factoring of motor parts, initially brake linings and tyres, managed by my brother-in-law, Guy Reid. So, to all intents and purposes, my future was assured. However, as I see it, one should only retire when one feels no longer capable of coping with the current opposition, and despite the recent setbacks, I did not yet have that feeling. I always believe in acting upon my own initiative. In addition, to retire from the sport which had given me such a great sense of achievement, sheer joy and exhilaration, plus a wonderful opportunity to see the world, was *quite* unthinkable.

There was yet another consideration. The withdrawal of the leading Italian marques had almost knocked the bottom out of Grand Prix racing. An MV benefit in both 350 and 500 cc classes would be very bad for the sport. So I wrote to an old friend of mine, BMW's publicity manager, Carl Hoepner, and visited Munich early in December where I saw Carl and their sales director, Herr Hensel; it was agreed that I would ride for them in 1958. Later, the *Bayerische Motoren Werke* of Munich announced that it was their intention to enter BMW motorcycles in the solo and sidecar categories of all the 1958 World Championship 'classic' road races. The drivers were to be Geoff Duke in the solo class, and Walter Schneider in the sidecar events. Walter Schneider, with passenger Hans Strauss, would in fact win the Sidecar Championship in both 1958 and 1959, but I found the solo machine unpredictable in its handling, while development was virtually non-existent, probably due to financial constraints.

Norton vs Gilera

I have often been asked which of the two famous marques, Norton and Gilera, I preferred to ride. Both machines had their own individual attributes, and although the 350 Norton, from 1951 onwards, was a peach, I always favoured the 500 because it was more demanding. This also applied to the Gilera.

For me, the original McCandless design, as raced in 1950, was the best-handling Norton, although *all* the featherbed Nortons with their 50/50 weight distribution required a touch of steering damper to prevent the occasional headshake or wobble. The development which took place after 1950, including throwing away the McCandless-designed rear shock absorbers, was, in my opinion, a retrograde step. Although it must be said that, in the handling department, the Norton was streets ahead of any other racing machine, at that time.

The Norton engine, although remarkable for what was basically a pre-war design, vibrated, and in a long race this could be quite tiring. Keeping the engine on the megaphone, especially if the carburation was not quite right, could be a bit of a chore on slow corners where the lack of a five-speed gearbox, with its lower first gear, compounded the problem. All our pleas for more ratios seemed to fall on deaf ears, but whether this was for technical or commerical reasons, I never knew—there was little doubt, though, that financial constrictions prevented many of the more ambitious design modifications, such as fully-enclosed valve gear and an enclosed gear-driven primary drive, from seeing the light of day. The surplus oil that was leaked or flung from these sources was often a problem, and when excessive, resulted in an oil-soaked rear tyre which could be a constant source of anxiety when one was riding on the limit.

The Gilera engine was beautifully engineered; not surprising, when one is aware of the enthusiasm, flair and inventiveness of the Italians, and yet, in such matters as squish technology, they were way behind the Kuzmicki Nortons. Valve angles were such that in order to achieve a high compression ratio, the piston crowns resembled the old steep-sided types used in alcohol-fuelled speedway engines. However, the four-cylinder engine was almost completely free from vibration, had real power from 9000 rpm upwards to its maximum of 10,500 rpm, and

Artie Bell's 1950 Senior TT Norton. Note the alloy megaphone, Rex McCandless-designed shock absorbers, and the tail which was discarded the following year

The 500 cc Gilera as it appeared in the 1963 TT races

carburation was clean from 4500 rpm, which made slipping the clutch a rare necessity.

The weight distribution of the Gilera was approximately 60/40. A bias to the front of the machine enabled me to dispense with the steering damper altogether at all events other than the TT, where, at this most demanding circuit, it was considered prudent to fit a damper, although I never found it necessary to use it! Here, it is interesting to note that in 1963 all three riders in Scuderia Duke insisted on the provision of steering dampers. This I found difficult to understand, although it is possible that the frames allocated by the factory could have been the type modified for use with full streamlining—these had less weight forward to allow for the downforce exerted by that particular streamlining, so with a dolphin fairing, as used in 1963, with more lift than downforce, there would have been insufficient weight on the front wheel.

One feature of the four-cylinder engine, which caught me out on a couple of occasions, was its light flywheel. Tyres, not remarkable for their grip in those days, occasionally lost adhesion. This could happen without much warning, causing a rapid rise in rpm and a pretty lurid slide, much more than was the case with the heavy-flywheeled single-cylinder Norton. Conversely, the instinctive snapping shut of the throttle on the Gilera virtually stopped the engine, producing a sudden return to adhesion which invariably caused a wobble and cast the rider off! The heavy flywheel of the Norton, in contrast, tended to keep going when the throttle was shut.

In retrospect, although my most memorable victories were achieved on Norton machines, I must give pride of place to the Gilera!

ON MY OWN

My lightweight 350

Gilera's withdrawal from racing in 1957, I suppose, in retrospect, should have signalled the end of my racing career, but I still enjoyed racing, and a considerable part of that enjoyment had been in assisting with the development of the machines I rode. Although I lay no claim to engineering expertise, I was nevertheless blessed with the ability to assess the pros and cons of modifications carried out by the racing departments, and had developed an acute sense of feeling for the engine performance and handling of the machines I rode. So it was that I came to embark on a programme of design and development of a lightweight 350 machine, based on the Manx Norton.

After much discussion, Ken Sprayson of Reynolds designed and built the frame, which was in light-gauge Reynolds 531 tubing. The duplex-loop frame had a single front downtube, of 4 in. diameter, which was also the container for engine oil. This saved about 5 lb, as compared with a separate tank, and when combined with a longer rear swinging-arm helped to achieve a more forward weight distribution, thus doing away with the necessity for a steering damper. The absence of an oil tank in the conventional position allowed plenty of breathing space around the carburettor intake. The air was cooler and it was easier to experiment with induction pipe length.

I was never completely happy with telescopic forks, which lacked rigidity and therefore suffered from stiction and the adverse effect under heavy braking of a fixed brake anchor. I favoured a trailing-link front fork, which I had suggested to Joe Craig at Nortons, and had been impressed by an admittedly experimental set of Fred Carno's which I had briefly tried out at MIRA before leaving Nortons—although the more definitive version which, I believe, Ram Amm and Ken Kavanagh tried at the TT in 1954 found little favour with them. However, as time and money were short, I eventually settled for the more conventional leading-link variety.

The hydraulically-damped shock absorbers were concealed for most of their length within the stanchion tubes, which were welded, not clamped, to the upper and lower yokes for rigidity and lightness. Geometry of the bottom links was arranged to maintain a substantially constant wheelbase throughout the full range of fork deflection, and the fork trail (which varies with deflection) was approximately $2\frac{1}{2}$ in., considerably less than the trail required on the featherbed Norton. The small trail affords light steering and is made possible because the trail (which produces the self-steering tendency) is at its maximum when it is most needed, i.e. when the front wheel is lightly loaded and the fork fully extended, and at its minimum on full bump. Rear suspension was by pivoted fork, with Woodhead-Monroe hydraulic units being used, front and rear.

The Norton single-leading-shoe rear brake and the AJS 7R two-leading-shoe front brake were cable-operated and had floating brake plates. Direct anchorage of the plates to the rear fork arm or front fork link causes the rear wheel to hop and the front fork to lock under heavy braking, so a true parallelogram was used at the front, which isolated fork action entirely from brake torque. I was against a front linkage which was not quite a parallelogram, à la Moto Guzzi—although they resist nose dipping under heavy braking, they do so only by stiffening the fork action.

The engine, for which drawings were produced by my old friend Stan Hackett of Nortons, was of 80×69.5 mm bore and stroke, with a one-piece forged crankshaft, an alloy connecting rod with plain-bearing big-end, and an outside flywheel. The cylinder, which Hepworths produced in aluminium alloy, had a bore chrome-plated direct on to the alloy. The Norton cylinder head was converted to take double-coil American Withams valve springs to facilitate the planned enclosure of the valve gear. This would obviate oil leakage from the cambox and permit a freer fit for the tappets in their bushes. On standard engines, an undesirable close-fit was usual in an effort to reduce oil leakage. All the development work on the engine was carried out by that engineering wizard Bill Lacey.

The machine was given its first real airing, with a modified standard Manx engine fitted, during practice for the 1958 German Grand Prix, at the Nürburgring. However, the spring poundage and hydraulic settings of the shock absorbers were found to be too high for a machine weighing only 262 lb (some 50 lb lighter than the production machine). The ratio of sprung-to-unsprung weight was part of the problem. The standard Manx and 7R wheels were relatively heavy, so I acquired a twin-disc assembly for the front and a single-disc assembly for the rear, from America, similar to those used on the Provini Morini, although these were never installed. Nevertheless, the test was most encouraging, especially from the point of view of the steering. Later on, this machine, fitted with the development engine which was showing good potential on Bill Lacey's test-bench, was taken to Oulton Park where, after a few laps, the big-end bearing showed signs of tightening up.

It was at this point that I really started to assess the cost to date, as there was still a long way to go. The cylinder head and cambox required major modification to enclose the valve gear, and there was a five-speed gearbox to consider, quite apart from the expected development problems such as insufficient oil pressure to the plain big-end bearing. The fact that I was having to bear all the development costs personally was crippling. So, reluctantly, I finally decided to cut my losses and call it a day.

My lightweight 350 of 1958

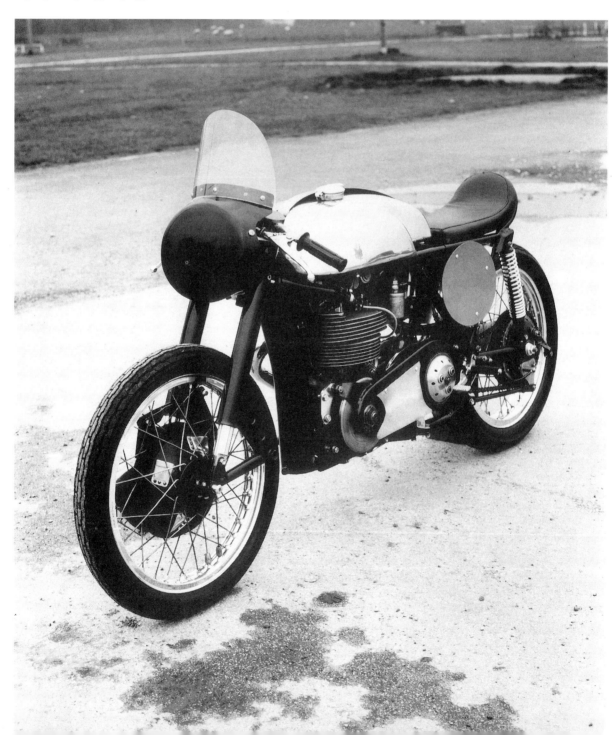

Racing through 1958

After the chaotic end to my 1957 season, my first outing in 1958 was at Silverstone, on one of Reg Dearden's 350 Nortons, which gave me renewed hope of a return to form. Although the engine refused to fire until the rest of the field had departed, once under way it was really flying, and this knowledge had the required therapeutic effect on my riding. By the fifth lap, I had moved up to third, and next time round I was lying second, behind McIntyre. At just over half-distance in the 17-lap race, I caught and passed Bob at Club Corner, pulling away from then on—though, in fairness, McIntyre, who finished second, was finding his Norton difficult to handle.

Silverstone was also my first outing on the BMW which, after the euphoria of my win on Dearden's Norton, served to dampen my ardour. After struggling through practice, trying to come to terms with its peculiarities in the handling department, I was totally uncompetitive in the race.

My first important engagement with the BMW was at Hockenheim in Germany. Hockenheim is not a rider's circuit and machines of very similar performance in the hands of Hiller, Dale, Forest, Hinton and myself soon resulted in a first-class ding-dong scrap. The early part of the race, with the circuit wet in places, demanded a certain amount of caution. However, as the road dried the tempo increased, and Harry Hinton in particular, whose ex-works Norton was quick to respond to a tow, offered a threat of no mean order. Soon, however, the situation clarified itself a little, with first Jack Forest and then Dickie Dale disappearing from the fray. Then, just when it looked like being a three-way struggle for victory, Harry faded a little; he had shed a megaphone.

It was now a matter of assessing when the time would be right to make a break. I decided to risk passing Hiller down the main straight just after the start of the last lap. I left it long enough to allow for a good build-up in speed and pulled out of his slipstream close to the long corner at the end of the straight, so as not to give him the opportunity of slipstreaming me. The first part of my plan worked and I made a big effort to snatch a few more yards round the swerve, then it was 'head under the

handlebars' up the flat-out back section, not daring to look back and hoping against hope that he would not be able to get within striking distance before the fast S-bend. I made it! As I accelerated towards the finishing line, I could almost feel him breathing down my neck—I made it first to the chequered flag by a whisker.

Tailoring the machine's streamlining at the BMW factory in 1958

Above *The BMW at Silverstone in 1958 where I had handling problems in practice*

Left *At Hockenheim in 1958 with BMW's development engineer Herr Falkenhausen—my only success on the Munich twin*

I entered for the 1958 Junior TT on Reg Dearden's potent 350 Norton, the machine on which I had won at Silverstone, and things looked promising for the Island. But that was only until Nortons persuaded Reg to change his engine for one of their experimental units. The Dearden engine was very good. It had propelled me around the Mountain circuit at 94 mph (24 min 0.4 sec) in practice, a speed only bettered by John Surtees (MV four) on race day. It was also faster than John's winning average, although, in fairness, John was never pushed— and the 350 MV four was pretty pathetic by four-cylinder standards.

Right *Note the excessive frontal area of the BMW*

However, the Norton engine change came about towards the end of practice week when Nortons produced their 80-bore engine and five-speed gearbox. Before this engine could be properly tried, though, it was changed yet again for a standard 78-bore unit. With only one practising session remaining, dear old Reg worked all through the night but was unable to complete the work in time, so we had to settle for a brief run at Jurby airport which, at best, was pretty inconclusive.

Race day dawned pleasantly enough, although, with one thing and another, I was hardly brimming with confidence. I had always made it a personal rule never to start in a race unless my machine was 100 per cent plus, from both a safety and a competitive viewpoint. And there I was, about to embark on a race over the second-most-demanding circuit in the world on a virtually untried machine—and there was more to come. . . . On arriving at the tent to collect my race mount prior to the warm-up, I was greeted by feverish activity. At the last minute, the Lucas technicians had expressed doubt about using the earlier type of magneto fitted to my machine. So Reg had applied for, and was granted,

permission to fit a rotating-magnet-type instrument, designed to withstand vibration generated by high-revving single-cylinder engines.

As far as I was concerned, that was very nearly the final straw, but Reg Dearden had worked so long and hard in his effort to provide me with competitive machinery that I did not have the heart to refuse to ride—although I later wished that I had said no, if for no other reason than to save embarrassment for all concerned.

Reg completed the magneto swap just in time for me to push off in the race at my allotted time. The engine fired immediately, but my misgivings were confirmed before I had even reached the top of Bray Hill—the engine refused to exceed 6000 rpm. I continued in the hope of completing one lap, but at Sulby the valve gear decided to call it a day and I was forced to retire.

Switching to the BMW for the Senior race, we settled down to serious work with the race machine after a preliminary canter on the practice BMW. The race bike

At Keppel Gate in the 1958 Senior TT. The BMW was later sidelined with brake problems

was even smoother than the original and was certainly quicker. The extra speed, however, heightened my navigation problems—it was surprising what a devastating effect another 5 mph could have. On two occasions I all but lost the plot on the way down to Brandish Corner from Creg-ny-Baa, and at one place, near the top of Creg Willey's Hill, a wobble developed on almost every lap I did! The limited modifications which could be carried out in the Island made little difference. And yet there was no getting away from the fact that, in previous years, Walter Zeller had put up a superlative performance on virtually the same machine, although the full streamlining he used in 1957 may perhaps have created a downforce which helped to keep the front wheel on the ground. The main problem, however, obviously lay in my inability to adapt myself to the unusual handling characteristics of a machine which had an in-line crankshaft and shaft drive. My admiration for Walter, always high, grew day by day!

At the fall of the flag, I set off with every intention of relaxing and giving the machine its head, but by the time Ballacraine was reached I had started to wrestle with it. This was fatal. My shoulders soon began to ache as I rode with muscles tensed. It was not long, at Ramsey Hairpin to be exact, before I sensed another machine on my tail— Bob McIntyre's Norton! Already 20 seconds down, I moved over before Waterworks to allow him to pass, and then tucked in behind, but to no avail. He was riding like a man possessed on a machine that was astonishingly rapid. We arrived at the Mountain Mile with a fair gap between us, but I fully expected to draw closer again on the full-blast run. To my amazement, though, Bob soon became a rapidly dwindling figure in the distance.

Hard application of the brakes at the end of the Mountain descent now revealed a further problem: brakes. One more lap was enough to leave me almost brakeless, and I pulled into the pits for a conference which concluded with the BMW being wheeled away. How I could ever have believed that the power output and handling of the BMW would match the four-cylinder MV Agusta, I shall never know. I suppose it was just wishful thinking!

After the TT, I wrote a long letter to the factory suggesting many modifications which would, I felt, enable me to do reasonable justice to a basically fine machine. Unfortunately, it was not possible with the facilities available and the financial restraints of the company, which happened to be going through a particularly lean time, to carry out many of the more complex alterations during the season. We therefore journeyed to the Dutch TT with only minor modifications to brakes and riding position. Reg Dearden once again accompanied me with two 350s on a trailer drawn by my Ford Zodiac, while my van, being driven by a BMW mechanic, was used to convey the BMWs. At Assen I chose to try my hand again with Reg's

experimental 78-bore 350 which had been so disappointing in the Island. It seemed to be going quite well in practice, but in the race, after a good start, I was passed by at least eight machines before arriving at the first corner. This sorry business continued, and as I feared that some major trouble was developing, I called it a day. Following this, the 500 race terminated, so far as I was concerned, with a rush down a slip-road after many near visits on the BMW. The Assen circuit was extremely hard on brakes. . . .

The Belgian promised better things—there the BMW would be more at home. The double front brake had been converted to a two-leading-shoe operation and the picturesque circuit in the Ardennes had always been a happy hunting ground of mine. For the 350 event, I elected to revert to the 'Silverstone' Norton, while Reg decided to let Dickie Dale have a gallop on the 78-bore Norton with which, incidentally, Reg was unable to find any fault. The 350 race, once the MVs had disappeared from sight (which took approximately $1\frac{1}{2}$ miles), developed into a four-way scrap between Derek Minter, Keith Campbell, Dave Chadwick and myself for third place.

This went on throughout the race, with first one, then another in front, and little, if anything, to choose between the machinery. I possibly had the advantage downhill as I was a shade higher geared than the others and was therefore able to make better use of a good tow. Invariably, though, the other parties would steam past going up the hill where the high gear became a disadvantage, leaving me in fourth spot by the time we reached Artie Bell's Corner seven-eighths of the way round. This continued until the last lap when I decided to hang back until after Stavelot and then make more use of third gear and delayed slipstreaming, which should hopefully give me the lead just before Artie's Corner.

This worked fairly well, except that I was only just able, with top gear now engaged, to gather enough speed behind Keith after leap-frogging the others to squeeze by. With a bit of a scratch round the remaining corners to the hairpin, I was able to arrive there first, with the others almost breathing down my neck. I was just about to peel off for the hairpin (the last corner) when Derek Minter whistled by and almost flew up the slip-road; apparently, he had been attempting to outbrake us all in one big swoop, but required an anchor—literally—to make it! This excitement rather took the edge off my own effort but, nevertheless, I was able to come out of the corner first—just. This was where my slightly higher gear would again be to my disadvantage, but with a slender lead I was still in there with a chance. However, it was not to be and I descended from third to fifth place before the finishing line, with Dave close behind me.

The 500 race found me a little slow getting off the line with the BMW, but, nevertheless, I was nicely placed by the time the Masta Straight was reached. Here, however,

Keith Campbell came by, out of my slipstream, and to my surprise, although I tucked in behind him immediately, I was unable to hold the flying Norton. Then a most enjoyable battle developed between Dickie Dale on his remarkably-fast RS BMW, Bob Anderson (Norton) and myself. I eventually took fourth place, after John Hartle had gone steaming past.

For the German Grand Prix on the tortuous Nürburgring, I arranged for my own lightweight to be sent over, while Reg produced yet another 'special' out of the bag. However, a short run on the bumpy surface of the 'Ring' soon ruled out my Norton, so I tried my hand with the other 'special'.

It was the same old story regarding the 350 MVs, but once again an inter-Norton battle developed, first between Dickie Dale, Dave Chadwick, Gary Hocking and myself, then Bob Anderson and Mike Hailwood joined in when Dickie and Gary dropped out, and the fun began in earnest. I was hard pressed to stay with the flying trio, and it was quite obvious that Mike Hailwood had plenty of power in hand. For my part, at less than half-distance my machine began to slide about, nearly flying off the road on a number of occasions. A glance back revealed a rear tyre soaked in oil, and as I was now, in my old age, a great believer in the maxim 'live to fight another day', I stopped to watch the fun. However, I could have kicked myself later when I discovered that the breather-pipe had come adrift and was actually resting between the ribs of the tyre, providing a most unnecessary form of lubrication!

I had been shaping up no better than usual in the 500 practice, so when it was discovered that Walter Schneider's engine had wrecked a piston and scored the chrome bore of the cylinder, with no spares to be had, my move was obvious: I had nothing to lose, but for BMW the Championship was at stake. I therefore offered my engine, which was gratefully accepted. A standard RS engine was fitted into my frame, but carburation proved to be too rich on the day—not that I was too sorry, for later in the race the rain came down in torrents.

Just prior to the German had come news that BMW would not be supporting the remaining races in the calendar since these did not include sidecar events. I therefore asked for, and received, permission to use a Norton in the subsequent 500 cc events. The last-minute decision by MV not to compete in the bigger classes in Sweden left these wide open, but at the same time probably robbed John Surtees of a clean sweep of all the World Championship races.

With first place at stake for a change, the 350 race at Hedemora in Sweden soon developed into a battle royal. After several contenders fell by the wayside, it was left to Bob Anderson and myself to fight it out. Bob was riding with such verve that there was no time for last-lap plans—in fact, until the last half-mile, I could see no answer to the problem. Then, as we dived into the last S-

Reg Dearden and myself at Hedemora, Sweden, in 1958

bend with Bob leading, he came up behind Sven Andersson; Bob faltered for a moment, while I took the plunge and went round the outside of him. I quickly switched over to take Sven on the other side as he was almost in the middle of the road, but little realizing that I was there he had drifted out, which almost forced me up the grass bank on the right and caused me to ease the throttle momentarily. This almost let Bob in again, but the flag fell while I still retained a length's advantage.

I made a bad start in the 500 race, but picked up quite a few places on the first lap despite a drop in rpm, managing, eventually, to come up with Bob Anderson who had made good his lead after a fine getaway. I passed him once, only to be repassed, and as my engine had started to vibrate I decided to bide my time until later in the race. Oil had also found its way on to my back tyre, forcing me to ease my pace and allowing Bob to stretch the gap again. Meanwhile, Dickie Dale was slowly closing in on me from behind—my first warning was when the BMW passed me on braking for the town bend! Just then, Bob Anderson began to slow, his poor hard-pressed motor being the victim of big-end failure, and Dickie and I passed him almost abreast.

On the final lap, we came upon three sparring backmarkers, which gave me the opportunity to get past Dickie at last, although I was conscious of the front wheel of his BMW creeping up on my left as we hurtled across the line, inches apart.

It was then over to Belfast with the two Nortons for the Ulster Grand Prix, where Dundrod greeted us with a spate of inclement weather. I made a rather poor start in

Right Such a nice way to go racing! Pictured at Hedemora in 1958

the Junior but managed to pull up quite a few places to fourth by the end of the first lap.

My 350 was a little critical regarding oil, and in making sure of an adequate supply for a long race we had overdone things somewhat, with the result that oil fairly poured out of the breather for two or three laps. The combination of this and a wet road started to produce some excitement towards the end of lap one, so I was soon engaged in an interesting dice with Bob McIntyre, who I had earlier passed.

In the meantime, Terry Shepherd, who was lying third, had disappeared into the blue. Then, at just over half-distance, my engine started to vibrate a little—a big-end cage was starting to go. It was therefore pointless to try anything except attempt to secure fourth place at the finish. So I kept the engine revs down for the rest of the race, rolling off the throttle a little down the straight until the last lap, when I took a chance and gave my model its head, drawing away from Bob's detuned mount.

Feeling rather wet and miserable by now, I made a complete hash of my 500 start, which knocked all the will to have a go out of me. The 500, although normally an excellent starter, had rather a lot of ignition advance, and in my anxiety to get away I dropped the clutch too soon and the engine kicked back, locking the rear wheel and demanding a complete restart, by which time almost the entire entry had disappeared. A hectic first lap in the mist and rain found me in deep trouble on several occasions, and it was not until fairly well into the race that I emerged some 30 seconds behind Minter, the fourth man. I could do no more than reduce this gap by the odd second and soon realized that I was fighting a losing battle on time, although, at my best, I was just lapping at the same speed as John Hartle, which, I suppose, was some consolation.

After my 350 had been rebuilt and bench-tested, showing some heartening figures, I travelled alone to the Italian at Monza, taking also the 93-bore 500 which Alan Holmes had used at Oulton Park. My journey was fairly uneventful, although I nearly 'lost' both machines when they failed to be loaded on to the train— fortunately, I spotted this oversight in time! After a few days, I arrived at the St Eustorgio—the Gilera Hotel, to most people—in time for an evening meal, when a telephone call suddenly came through from the President of the Italian Federation—before I had even finished eating! Would I meet him to discuss an important project? I finished my dinner and dashed off to his hotel by the entrance to the Monza circuit itself.

It transpired that the Italian Federation had a four-cylinder MV at their disposal and Count Agusta would be pleased if I would ride it in the Grand Prix! The reason for the offer was obvious: the organizers were worried about the attendance figures due to lack of manufacturers' support and wanted the publicity value of a pending scrap between riders, if not manufacturers, to boost their event. Although I was sympathetic, there were many considerations from my own point of view, the foremost being my friendship with Gilera and the wonderful way in which they had always treated me. I decided to turn down the ride, but I visited Count Agusta in person at Gallarate in order to put forward my reasons, leaving on friendly terms.

And so to the racing. However, with only three laps completed of the last practice period, the engine of my 350 Norton suddenly lost all compression. Investigation revealed a broken valve-spring retaining collar, while the valve head had touched the piston, bending the stem slightly in the process. A panic rush around Milan to find a collar that might be modified to suit drew a blank, and I had almost given up hope of ever starting in the race when my old friends from Gilera came to my rescue, making not one, but *two* new collars at Arcore that night—one for each valve. In the meantime, Terry Shepherd tapped my valve straight—an operation which he carried out with great skill, borne of long experience, so I was told! Finally, a 6 am start the next morning ensured there was enough time for assembly of the engine and a final check-over of the machine before the race. So, thanks to the generosity and sportsmanship of a wonderful group of people at the Gilera factory, an almost certain non-starter collected, instead, a useful third place in the 350 cc race.

I made rather a poor start in the 500 race, but the 93-bore motor went like a bomb for the next couple of laps, during which time I was able to catch Bob Anderson who, after a good start, had something like a 200-yard advantage over me. Thereafter, though, the maximum rpm and acceleration faded somewhat, and there I stayed, soon to be joined by Dave Chadwick. After a few laps in close company, Bob disappeared, leaving Dave and myself to carry on the good work.

With Dave's nine stone aboard the 500 and its resultant superior acceleration, I knew it would be quite useless to try and make a break, and therefore decided to try and slipstream him out of the final corner, overtaking him on the line. On this occasion, however, I was to be disappointed. With about three laps to go, at full-bore down the straight, I noticed a faint rattle which I was unable to trace until a sharp blow on my right leg heralded the departure of half an inlet-valve spring. There was nothing for it but to tail Dave as closely as possible, and we arrived at the peeling-off point for the final curve in close formation. Unfortunately for me, Dave recovered and accelerated towards the finishing line while I attempted to get back in his slipstream, but any rpm over 6800—below which the 93-bore appeared to be down on power—produced a very marked rattle. Congratulations to Dave on a well-earned sixth place.

On returning to England and my last event of the season at Scarborough, I was most disappointed to learn that the other 93-bore, which Alan Holmes had used at Silverstone and was being prepared for my use at Scarborough, had developed piston trouble, which might well have been the problem with the Monza engine. Nortons, therefore, were not keen to let me use this one, either. Alan had been allocated the only other machine available, so I had little choice but to contact secretary Jack Claxton for permission to use my own 350 in both events.

After a bad start in the 350 heat because of clutch slip which, fortunately, was cured on increasing the already generous slack in the cable, I managed to put in some reasonable lappery to finish second to Mike Hailwood. At first we put our trouble down to old and worn inserts in the clutch sprocket. However, with the facilities available, it was not possible to replace these in time for the final. We therefore replaced the clutch discs, hoping that the better condition of these, plus the added spring pressure, would do the job. I was, however, plagued with intermittent slip throughout the final, which was most annoying for my engine appeared to be on song. Further investigation revealed excessive end-float in the gearbox mainshaft, obviously part of the trouble, but a borrowed clutch sprocket effected a cure.

I made a flying start in my 500 heat and managed to retain the lead for some laps before Gary Hocking took over, and so we remained to the race end. I was surprised and pleased to learn afterwards that I had come within half a second of John Surtees' 350 cc record! The final was, of course, a different kettle of fish. My start was not so good and a more energetic use of the gearbox produced a few missed gearchanges owing, no doubt, to the end-float in the mainshaft. This may have taken the edge off the engine. However, I had to be content with an enjoyable mid-field gallop.

So ended a memorable season which had, in the main, been an enjoyable one. Certainly, some of the battles I would not have missed for all the tea in China!

The final events

An exciting prospect loomed for 1959 when Reg Armstrong announced that he had obtained the loan of a 250 NSU Rennmax, asking me if I would be interested in riding it—sure thing! But, this turned out to be a bit of a damp squib. It was not the high-flying 1954 model which had swept all before it that year, but one of the 1953 variety, and a pretty poor one at that. This was a bitter disappointment to us both, but, nevertheless, the services of Ken Sprayson of Reynolds were called upon to design a lighter, more up-to-date frame and forks.

My first outing with the NSU was at the Austrian Grand Prix, at Salzburg, when, in foul conditions, water in the ignition on the very first lap of the race brought things to a halt. Then, although entered for the North-West 200, the machine could not be made ready in time, and just to compound my embarrassment, the oil return pipe on my lightweight 350 Norton fractured within 300 yards of the start, which did not exactly make me the most popular bloke in Northern Ireland that day! Finally, an entry in the Lightweight TT on the Clypse circuit terminated when the engine seized at Creg-ny-Baa on my first practice lap!

The Isle of Man TT attracted the first official entries from Honda of Japan in the 125 cc class, run on the Clypse circuit, all with Japanese riders who acquitted themselves extremely well and demonstrated the reliability of their machines by winning the manufacturers' team-prize. The writing was on the wall!

So my only ride was to be in the Junior race on my own 350 Norton, with a standard Manx engine fitted in place of my experimental outside-flywheel unit, which, now in the hands of Bill Lacey for development, was making positive, if slow, progress; Bill was stretched to the limit with the demands on his talents by Mike Hailwood, who had priority as a long-standing client, and others.

The Junior was my first 'real' race on the Island since my last appearance on the Gilera in 1955, and for the first time the old system of balloting for starting order had been dropped, in favour of a safer and easier-to-follow grading system—which I had advocated for years, so I was pleased! All those who had ridden in the TT before were graded according to their previous performances,

with the starting order only of the top five being drawn out of the hat. The task of a works rider overtaking less-experienced riders, on much slower machines, had always been fraught with danger, and my personal experience of many a near miss had convinced me that this could be disaster in the making.

I had no illusions regarding my chances of being 'in the hunt', and therefore completed the first lap of the race at a more leisurely pace than usual, to find myself in sixth position behind Alastair King (Norton). At this stage, Surtees was leading comfortably from McIntyre on a works AJS, followed by Hartle and Anderson. Terry Shepherd and Mike Hailwood were neck and neck, eight seconds behind me. On lap two, King, riding like a man possessed, moved ahead of Anderson, while I moved eight seconds nearer Anderson. Then, on lap four, I

At Whitegate Corner on the fourth lap of the 1959 Junior TT

finally caught and passed Anderson, and we then indulged in a wonderful scrap which, so far as I was concerned, livened up the proceedings no end. At the end of that lap I had a one-second advantage, which I was able to stretch to a little over 14 seconds by lap five. Now more into my stride, only 0.6 seconds separated my sixth and fastest lap from my seventh. At the finish John Surtees, as expected, won at a canter, with team-mate John Hartle only ten seconds ahead of Alastair King, while Bob McIntyre retired after a fantastic ride at the end of lap four when a fairing mounting broke.

September 1959 saw me entered in three classes of the non-classic Swiss Grand Prix at Locarno. Benelli had

John Surtees on the 350 MV at Whitegate, Ramsey, in the Junior TT

asked me to ride a single in the 250 cc race along with Silvio Grassetti, and I also entered my 350 lightweight Norton and a standard 500 Manx model. To ride in three different capacity races in one day was unusual for me; I had only done it twice before, and it was strange that it should occur at my last event. Charlie Edwards accompanied me to look after the Nortons, and, always the perfectionist, his work was faultless.

The circuit at Locarno was in the town and consisted mainly of short straights and slow right-angle corners, with only one quickish sweep and some tramlines to cross. This suited my 350 which, due to its light weight, accelerated and stopped better than a standard Manx machine.

Opposition in the 350 and 500 cc races came from a veritable horde of colonial riders who each seemed to be

after my blood. If I completed all three races, it would involve about 170 laps of this very busy little circuit, and after winning the first race, the 350, I realized that with the 250 next, my final gallop on the relatively heavy 500 was going to be very wearing indeed. I therefore asked the Benelli folk if they would release me from my ride, particularly as their contracted rider, Grassetti, should have no difficulty in winning the 250 cc race. They were most upset at my request, however, and when I pressed my point of view, they pleaded with me at least to start in the race and then decide how I felt about continuing. They were such nice people, I did not have the heart to refuse.

In the race, I made a good start, but Grassetti went off like a rocket and straight into the lead. Then, just as I was trying to make up my mind whether or not to stop, Grassetti fell off! He dropped it on the one fast corner of the circuit. Fortunately, he was not hurt, but he was unable to continue . . . and it made my decision for me—from second place, I was now leading the race. So, there was no escape, although I would probably have carried on anyway, rather than retire and disappoint the Benelli people.

It was now two races, two wins. But I knew the 500 was sure to be a tussle against riders of the calibre of Gary Hocking, later to ride works MVs but on this Swiss occasion similarly mounted to myself. In the race, I managed to make a cracking start and soon established an acceptable lead. As the laps rolled by, though, I began to feel the effect of the two previous races. Blisters were developing on my hands from the continual heavy braking and acceleration from the slow corners, and I had no option but to ease my pace and rely on signals from Charlie Edwards to warn me when the opposition came near—hopefully, not before the closing stages when, perhaps, I could make the 'big effort' to stay in front.

This worked quite well and I went into the last lap still leading, aware that someone was close behind, but not realizing just how close. Pulling out all the stops, I eventually arrived at the last-but-one slow corner with only a few hundred more yards to win.

It was strange that, as this was to be my last race, I needed to call upon experience which I had developed in the early days, namely a way of getting through slow corners as rapidly as possible. This involved braking fractionally early, peeling off for the turn a trifle late, but slow enough to arrive at the apex of the corner, then reduce the angle of lean to turn on the power with the machine as upright as possible to minimize the risk of a slide. This enabled power to be turned on sooner with increased acceleration. Sticking your neck out on slow bends, even when successful, gains very little ground when compared to making a first-class job of a fast swoop.

Anyway, to return to that penultimate corner at Locarno, where I arrived just ahead of Gary Hocking—seemingly braking very late, he apparently attempted to

Two single-cylinder Benellis, together with Silvio Grassetti and myself

go round the outside of me, a move of which I was totally unaware. As I accelerated, I unintentionally shut him out, forcing him to take to the pavement. Fortunately, he suffered no mishap but I went on to take the next corner and cross the finishing line a few lengths ahead.

Hocking was livid. Not only had he lost the race which, with only two corners to go, he believed was in the bag, but he was adamant that I had deliberately forced him off the road. Regrettably, some of his compatriots were equally incensed on his behalf and I was unable to convince them otherwise. So, for me, the prize presentation, instead of celebrating my triple success, suddenly became a miserable affair. . . .

In an instant, I decided that motorcycle racing had become a great effort. The exhaust megaphone on the 500 had burnt through the heel of my boot, leaving an enormous blister on my heel; there were painful blisters on both my hands and I was altogether very weary. The following morning I met my late wife Pat at Locarno railway station, prior to our departure for a holiday in Italy, and nobody could have been more surprised than she when I said: 'You will be pleased to know that yesterday I rode in my last race.'

The Japanese tour

My Japanese story commenced early in February 1960, with the voice of Norman Sharp on the telephone asking if I would be interested in an invitation to visit Japan—indeed, yes! There were quite a few problems to be solved, but a letter from Fumito Sakai, president of the Japan Motorcycle Federation and publisher of the Japanese *Motorcyclist*, at the end of February, clarified the position. He also asked me to ship a Manx Norton to Japan on which to give riding demonstrations to Japanese clubmen—a frantic search produced a 500 cc Manx Norton, kindly loaned for the occasion by Bob Dowty, which was duly shipped out.

On 13 April, I took off from London airport on a BOAC Comet 4B, my first experience of jet travel and what an experience! A fabulous rate of climb, to almost 40,000 ft, and we levelled off at a speed in excess of 500 mph in comparatively silent and vibration-free flight. We reached my destination, Tokyo, just 29 hours later, including stops, and 10,000 miles from London.

As we taxied towards the terminal building, I was shattered to see a large banner with the words 'Welcome

Mr Geoff Duke' above the main entrance, and as I stepped from the aircraft, a small crowd of enthusiasts gave voice to their welcome. But there was more to come—after introductions, I was ushered through customs to a private room, packed to the doors, where I was almost buried under bouquets of very beautiful flowers presented by girl members of the Federation and two girls in kimonos, who, I later discovered, were stars from a Tokyo film company! Here also I met Jimmy Matsumiya, who was managing the Suzuki racing team in Europe, and we were immediately great friends. I was then driven to an American-style hotel, The New Japan, to spend my first night in Tokyo, then the largest city in the world with a population of over nine million.

The next morning, prompt at 10 am, I was handed a type-written sheet showing my schedule, literally hour by hour, until 11 May when, according to the schedule,

A group of test riders and mechanics at Suzuki—race manager Jimmy Matsumiya is in the front row on the right-hand side

Sorting the gears out on the neat little twin Suzuki

I was due to leave Tokyo airport once again. This programme called for a daily start ranging from 7 am to 8 am, and often extending to as late as 9 or even 10 pm. Here Jimmy Matsumiya came to my aid, realizing that I would be worn out inside a week, and the schedule was rearranged to provide for rather later starts. In any case, I never was very good at rising at the crack of dawn—and 6 May was the latest I could possibly stay on in Japan!

My first encounter with motor bikes came on 16 April, when we travelled to Fuji-no-miya, at the foot of Mount Fuji, where I was to witness the second all-Japan motocross meeting. Practice was in progress when we arrived at the 3 km course, which turned out to be quite interesting; bumpy, with plenty of gradient, and a surface varying from rough grassland to black peaty soil, where spinning wheels had worn through. In no time at all, I found myself astride a 250 cc twin two-stroke Yamaha scrambler, feeling my way around in an attempt to accustom myself to a left-hand gearchange and right-hand brake, plus reverse operation of the gearbox. I did not even get around to discovering that the machine had five speeds!

The next day found us once again at the Asigiri Highland Motocross course to watch some well-organized racing ranging from 50 cc to an over-250 cc final. The programme ended with a genuine point-to-point event, which consisted of a race to the top of a distant hill and back, where the riders could choose their own route. The point-to-point and the unlimited events were won by S. Itoh, riding a 500 cc BSA Gold Star in a very determined and confident fashion; he would later be found in Europe, road racing an RS BMW which was his true love.

That evening we travelled on to Hamamatsu, where we were to stay for three days. On 18 April I found myself at the Yamaha factory test-course, a piece of road, a little over half a mile in length, where I watched the works

testers put a couple of racing versions of the 250 cc sports machine through their paces. Unfortunately, both machines suffered from partial seizures during the try-out, so I was unable to pass a personal opinion on their performance. But I did have a ride on Yamaha's new 175 cc scooter, with fully-automatic transmission on the torque-converter principle, which really worked, right up to a maximum of 53 mph. Stability left a little to be desired, but this seemed to be a feature of most scooters in those days; the front brake required adjustment, which probably accounted for its lack of efficiency, but the rear brake was powerful. A walk round the factory revealed an extremely modern set-up that was turning out machines of all classes at a rate of 6000 per month.

The Suzuki factory was our next port of call, which turned out to be a highly-efficient organization. They had been manufacturing motorcycles only since after the war, but were now producing machines at the rate of 8500 per month. I soon found myself at their test-track a little way from the factory, and here, lined up for my inspection and trial, were examples of all current models, including their 125 racer. Most of the standard devices were straight off the assembly line, but one, a 250 cc two-stroke twin, had seen a fair amount of use.

The test-track, which was only partially completed, gave little opportunity of reaching maximum speed with the six-speed 125 cc twin two-stroke racing machines, but the works riders took it in turns to hare the two machines available up and down the track. I would estimate their speed as they passed me before their braking point at a little over 80 mph in fifth gear. I was then given the opportunity of a ride myself. Normal maximum rpm, I was told, was 12,000, but I was asked not to exceed 11,000, and also to keep the engine turning at a minimum of 8000 to avoid oiling plugs, due to the exceptionally high petrol/oil ratio of 8:1 (normally 9:1). Unfortunately, the leathers I was wearing, supplied for the occasion, did not fit at all well (my own were en route with the Norton), and also, being a little large for a 125, I was unable to tuck myself away completely. Nevertheless, I was most impressed with the way the engine comfortably ran up to its 11,000 rpm. It was exceptionally smooth throughout its range, and the surge of power from the engine once the 8000 rpm mark was reached was most impressive. The gearchange was both light in operation and very positive, while excellent brakes really retarded progress, and it was still possible to lock either wheel when a low speed was reached. In conclusion, I would say that, within the limits of road available, I had never ridden such a quick, conventional type of two-stroke.

During the whole of my stay at the Suzuki factory, I was showered with questions from every direction regarding the TT, and racing in general. And it was quite apparent that their approach to racing was both enthusiastic and serious, backed up with considerable

The explanation of how it all works!

Our return to Tokyo signalled the long-awaited visit to Japan's largest manufacturer—Honda. This huge concern, which started production in 1948 with 12 workers, now relied upon two Tokyo factories—one for production, the other for research—built seven years earlier. There was also a one-year-old, windowless, air-conditioned unit at Hamamatsu. In 1959, Honda produced 180,000 machines of all types, aiming to raise this figure to 250,000 during 1960. They employed over 4000 people and provided a swimming pool and all sorts of recreational facilities and free instruction to their hands. Not surprisingly, there appeared to be a very happy atmosphere about the place.

Top priority, at that time, went to their three-speed, four-stroke, 50 cc Cub machine, which was pedal-less and equipped with an electric starter. This was being produced at the rate of 1100 per day, and they were also building a factory nearly 300 miles from Tokyo. They had chosen this site because of its suitability for export; the building, seven times the size of the Tokyo factory, was intended only to produce the 50 cc machine.

I was surprised to find that, contrary to other factories I had visited, almost all the technical 'bods' here spoke very good English. And I was in the middle of a conducted tour of the factory with a party of these people, when suddenly I was asked if I would like to meet Mr Honda in person. I looked around, but the only other person I could see close by was a rather non-VIP-looking, slightly-built man in grey slacks, a white coat and a cap with a large peak, rather like that of a baseball player. But Mr Honda it was! A cheerful man of some 53 years, who apparently hated sitting behind a desk and constantly plagued his workers by wandering around the factory—which may be one reason why the standard of production was so high! He was obviously on excellent terms with his staff, who referred to him—behind his back—as 'Dad'. I gathered that Mr Honda had considerable technical knowledge which, from time to time, produced the answer to a vexed engineering problem—much to the disgust of the technical staff!

We then proceeded to Honda's $2\frac{1}{4}$-mile test-course, which had a quickish S-bend in the middle and a hairpin at each end. Here, almost every day, their factory riders galloped the racing machines. This was necessary as there were no road-racing circuits, as we knew them in Europe, available in Japan at that time. I first of all watched the riders warming up twin-cylinder 125s and four-cylinder 250 cc machines. After a little while, 'Dad' Honda arrived, put on a safety-hat and, to the great—but carefully hidden—amusement of all present, disappeared up the road at high velocity on one of the fours!

Later on, I had the opportunity of trying first the 125 and then the 250 for myself. Both machines were, however, without rev-counters, so it was impossible to pass a genuine opinion regarding performance as I had no wish to risk over-revving them. In addition, the 250 four,

technical knowledge. That evening, I was royally entertained by the president of the company and his technical folk, in our Japanese-style hotel. Dinner was followed by a programme of singing and dancing by some very attractive geisha girls!

A visit to yet another factory in the area, Lilac, was rather spoiled by torrential rain, which prevented me from road-testing their interesting 125 and 250 models, with V-twin engines set across the frame and shaft drive. Here, again, there was great enthusiasm, and although, as yet, they had no racing machines, there was some talk of the possibility of a twin- or four-cylinder machine using their V-layout.

Sharing a joke at the Suzuki test-course

after initial acceleration which seemed most promising, began to give symptoms of fuel starvation. It was quite possible, though, that they did not wish me to get too accurate an assessment of the machine's capabilities, as I was not offered one of the alternative fours which by now were buzzing up and down in the hands of the factory boys.

I can say, however, that all the machines were beautifully prepared in all respects. Their twin front brakes were extremely powerful at the speed I was able to achieve, and handling through the S-bend was first-rate. The four, apart from a slight tingle through the handlebars, was quite smooth and altogether felt just like a baby Gilera. Happy memories of some years ago . . . ! Unlike the Gilera, though, both the drive to the gearbox and the drive to the valve-gear were located between the centre cylinders.

After recording an interview with the Japanese magazine _Motorcyclist_, the next few days were taken up with sightseeing. We travelled by air to Kyoto, the capital

of Japan until 100 years before, which was the first stop on the agenda. We certainly managed to see quite a few of the 1600 Buddhist temples and over 600 shrines in and around the city! We also visited many beautiful gardens where peace reigned—the Japanese really excelled in landscape art, in a way that had to be seen to be believed. In addition, although motorcycle sport may have been in its infancy in Japan, wherever I travelled, and by whatever means, there always appeared a small group of followers to bow, shake me by the hand, and demonstrate by some means or other that I was welcome.

There then followed a brief tour of Nara, before travelling on to Nagoya where, on the morning of 29 April, we found ourselves at the largest sparking-plug manufacturer in Japan, the NGK plant, which turned out 75 per cent of the total Japanese production of plugs. Their office block was comparatively new, but the plugs were made in a building that was some 25 years old and

Posing for yet another photograph

had originally been engaged only in the manufacture of ceramics. Up-to-date equipment ensured the production of 1.25 million plugs per month and the previous day's production, I noticed on a blackboard, was a little over 50,000. NGK produced all the 10 mm plugs used by Honda, and they were interested enough in racing to send their chief research engineer over to the TT, the Belgian Grand Prix and Dutch TT that year.

By this time, the Norton had at last arrived, and 2 May was reserved for an attempt to 'clear' the machine through customs at Yokohama. After a couple of hours of hard work by the import manager of Showa Motors, the Norton agents in Tokyo, all seemed in order and we left for Tokyo, well satisfied with our efforts. But that evening, a message from the agent brought the news that the customs people were being difficult again and that a further visit to Yokohama by the Norton agent would be necessary. Somewhat downhearted at this, I was,

however, cheered up a little later by a telephone call from Mr Okumoto of the Honda Export Department, who kindly offered to take me out to dinner at a local German restaurant, which provided the only true European meal I had while in Japan and one which I thoroughly enjoyed. He was accompanied by a Welsh friend, who had spent two years in Tokyo studying judo and teaching English in his spare time—now I knew why so many of the Honda folk spoke our language so well! Incidentally, it was through this friend that I was later approached by Honda to race for them in 1960, with what amounted to a blank cheque signed, of course, on offer. But although this was very tempting, I had already made up my mind to retire and even though an official announcement had not yet been made, I somewhat reluctantly declined— 'comebacks' rarely work.

On the morning of 3 May, we headed off for Utsunomiya by car, where I was to give a demonstration on the Norton on the last day of my trip, during a programme of racing which was to be the first of its kind in Japan. The circuit was situated on a wartime military airfield, but a shock awaited me on arrival. What I had been led to believe was a paved circuit in fair condition was, in fact, a poorly-laid runway plus perimeter, which had failed to withstand the ravages of time. Grass has grown up through the concrete, and even down the main straight there were stretches of track where the hard surface was literally non-existent. All except one of the corners had a loose surface and one short straight was just loose stones and dirt!

However, work to remove the grass was already in progress, and I reminded myself that all things must start somewhere, and once some resurfacing and patching had been carried out, the circuit would in fact be excellent. Needless to say, I was far from happy about riding a road-racing machine under these conditions, but thankful that I would not be involved in a 'race', I decided to do my best to provide what was expected of me.

An early start for the racecourse was logged for 5 May, and after a look over the Norton, which had at last been cleared by customs, we proceeded to the circuit, which by now looked more presentable. Already a few thousand people, many from Tokyo, three hours' ride away, had gathered to see the fun.

After a formal ceremony to open the course, a number of karts were let loose on the circuit, followed by individual classes from 50 cc to unlimited, each being allowed a couple of practice laps. Once the real racing started, things began to warm up quite a bit, although a lack of starters in the 50 cc class rather spoiled the first event. The larger classes were quite exciting, and the way some of the riders handled the larger British machines under the prevailing conditions was truly remarkable.

My turn arrived, and although I had originally been asked to do ten laps of the 1.85-mile circuit, this was reduced to six, for which I was really quite thankful. I started off quietly, gradually working up to a passable speed, and I was immediately glad that I had brought along a 21-tooth engine sprocket, which had been fitted to lower the 'standard' TT ratio. The bend into the start and finish straight called for near-upright treatment, as it was both rutted and bumpy. Of the others, the one with the hard surface was coated with dust, and a few scrape marks, where some of the 'racers' had come to earth, reminded me to treat it with respect. Here, however, I did attempt to take a reasonable road-racing line. The remaining corners, although loose, were reasonably smooth, the main safeguard here being careful throttle control. Towards the end of my run, I settled down reasonably well and put in a lap of 1 min 49 sec—just four seconds quicker than the fastest lap during the racing, so I had managed to keep our Western end up!

It only remained for me to drive back to Tokyo, a pleasant trip in the company of four English-speaking enthusiasts, before returning home to Europe on 6 May by SAS via Copenhagen to London. Although I am

Just waiting for the chance to have a go!

always glad to see home again after a spell away, I was in many ways quite sorry to be saying good-bye to my new-found Japanese friends, who had looked after my interests so patiently and so well during my three-week stay.

On the plane home, I had some time to think and made certain notes which I thought might serve to stir some of our manufacturers out of their complacency. But alas, this was not to be. Edward Turner of Triumph/BSA later visited Japan on a fact-finding tour, but appeared to be unmoved. Perhaps the 'facts' were too shattering! Amazing progress had been made in the Japanese motorcycle industry during the previous few years; this was brought home to me most forcibly by what I saw in the museum kept by Suzuki at Hamamatsu. All the machines there were built by Suzuki, but as this concern and Honda were the two largest producers in Japan and both started to make motorcycles after the war for the first time, I think the exhibits could be taken as typical examples of post-war Japanese machines.

Whereas the 1960 machines, with their sleek razor-edge styling, were bang up-to-date by European standards, the earlier ones were like our own models of the 1930s. The reason for this ultra-rapid rate of progress was not difficult to appreciate when one considered that Honda alone employed 400 people on full-time research work, and were now spending £60,000 per month. Production at the largest Japanese factories was still increasing and in 1959 Honda produced 180,000 machines of all types, with Suzuki falling second at 110,000. The whole industry at that time was producing 62,000 motorcycles per month, made up as follows: 50 cc—30,000; 125 cc—20,000; 250 cc—12,000. Anything of larger capacity was almost non-existent. How long that rate of expansion would last, I did not know, but certainly there were signs of saturation point being reached in Japan, in spite of its 90 million population.

The industry was now looking for export outlets, which was one reason for the sudden interest in road racing as a publicity medium. Honda aimed to export 20 per cent of their total 50 cc production, which then stood at 1100 units per day on a six-day week, and they aimed to increase this to 1700 units. Despite a rising standard of living in Japan, their industry maintained lower wage standards than ours. In 1959, the average wage throughout the Honda factory was £23 per month; this figure included a bonus paid twice yearly to all employees. They had a six-day working week, starting at 8.30 am and finishing at 4.30 pm, with one hour for lunch.

In price, motorcycles in Japan compared fairly closely with ours, but carried a much more reasonable purchase tax of five per cent. The average local price of a 250 cc twin was £170–£180. These machines, however, were all fitted with electric starters and flashers as standard equipment. From enquiries I made, the average life of a Japanese motorcycle was 25,000 to 30,000 miles. One must take into account, though, the fact that most Japanese owners changed their motorcycles at yearly intervals (suffering a normal loss of about 60 per cent in value), and during this period seemed to give them little or no attention.

Road conditions, generally, were atrocious; large potholes appeared, even in the cities, and off the main highway, surfaces were often stony and very dusty, which must have played havoc with cylinder bores, etc, despite efficient air filters. One Japanese engineer voiced the opinion that British machines they had tried lacked suspensions capable of coping with Japanese road conditions. This, I must admit, surprised me, for although Japanese machines generally appeared to have more suspension movement than ours, all the touring machines I tried in Japan seemed to be completely lacking in any form of hydraulic damper control!

I felt very privileged to visit Japan as I did, seeing some beautiful sights and meeting some very nice people, although in my three short weeks there it was hard to do more than just scratch the surface. The Japanese as a nation appeared to enjoy life but work exceedingly hard; emotion played a big part in their lives but they seldom showed it, at least not to strangers.

Some of their customs strike a visitor as very odd. For instance, the Japanese have an entirely different idea of privacy. Staying in a room at a Japanese-style hotel, with its sliding doors without locks or bolts, I often wondered how it happened that the maids, who were always popping in and out, never entered at an awkward moment. That was until I realized that a grille, high in the outside corridor wall, afforded a complete view of the room! If a glance through the grille showed the moment to be untimely, she went away! Shattering, perhaps, but I learned that to the Japanese privacy is not a matter of walls, locks and doors; privacy is a state of mind.

During my stay in Japan, I was constantly on the alert in case, in my ignorance, I should unwittingly commit some unforgivable breach of social code. Even if I had done so, the exquisitely courteous Japanese would never have let on—but I sincerely hope I didn't!

An industrial approach

Criticism of complacency within the British motorcycle industry was strong by the end of the 1950s, even before Japan began its mass exports to America and Europe. But there were people connected with the industry who were seriously concerned and not entirely fooled by the attitude of manufacturers who believed that outdated designs could go on forever. These were the shareholders; it was their money that was at stake.

It was at TT time, in 1960, that I received an unexpected telephone call, followed by a letter, inquiring if I might be interested in accepting a high-level appointment with a major British motorcycle manufacturer. During the initial telephone conversation, I mentioned to the caller that I would be at Mallory Park for the then-very-popular Post-TT meeting, and that it might be possible for us to meet there. Although I did not know the caller personally, he was well known and I knew of him—he was Lt.-Col. W. H. 'Goldie' Gardiner, a highly successful world-record car driver with MG. Gardiner had contacted me from his position as chairman of the shareholders' committee of Associated Motor Cycles Ltd (AMC), manufacturers of AJS, Matchless, Norton, James and Francis-Barnett.

As it happened, the meeting I suggested was not possible, and in his subsequent letter marked 'most confidential', Gardiner wrote guardedly, but most intriguingly, of a likely directorship for me in a boardroom team led by: 'A prospective managing director who is possibly the best for the job in the country. He is responsible for the present most prosperous motorcycle concern in Great Britain and has just made tremendous success in rebuilding a famous car firm.' He continued: 'I am sorry that I cannot be more open at the moment, but from the data I have given, you can deduce a lot.'

Clearly, this was a move aimed by a section of AMC shareholders to gain control of the company. I certainly knew nothing of the matter and simply stated in reply that I would be interested in any offer that might be made to me. Gardiner subsequently prepared an extensive document detailing the failing performance of the AMC company and indicating the vital need to change the entire directorship—and save the shareholders' investment!

As it transpired, this attempt to 'save' AMC came to nought, and in another letter Gardiner informed me: 'The company's bankers, who wield unbelievable power over the "city" and influence completely the views of all the big "institutional" investors, feel that you have not had enough experience to join the board.

'I cannot think what their standards are, since they have backed the present incumbents!

'However, we will get you in some position as technical adviser for the present and when we have control, will review the whole situation.'

The 'situation' never did change in Gardiner's favour, and a profit of £219,000 in 1960 turned into a £350,000 loss in 1961. The company, though, bumbled on until August 1966 when a receiver was appointed, leading to the acquisition of the company by Manganese Bronze, who founded Norton Villiers.

In thoughtful mood after a race

A drive in Sweden

With the decision to retire from motorcycling behind me, my thoughts turned once again to four wheels, so an approach by Graham Warner of Chequered Flag, based in Chiswick, to drive one of their Formula Junior cars in 1960 was eagerly accepted, as it presented the ideal opportunity to gain useful experience in a not-too-powerful car, which, hopefully, would lead to greater things.

However, Chequered Flag were in the process of developing a rear-engined version of their car which, inevitably, was a slow process, so the opportunities to drive were few and far between. On one such occasion, at Monaco, on the first lap of the race, I spun in the centre of the road approaching the Casino, but without touching any barriers. Then, as I was about to rejoin the fray, Tim Parnell ran into the back of my car wrecking the rear suspension!

On another outing, at Silverstone, in torrential rain, I started from the back of the grid and slowly worked my way up from last until I was second, only to strike a pool of water which caused the car to aquaplane and spin off the circuit, from where I was unable to restart.

At the end of that season, however, Graham Warner advised me that Chequered Flag were unable to continue racing due to lack of funds, which was sad because the car showed great promise, and there was no lack of enthusiasm from all concerned. Their withdrawal, though, completely upset my planned intention to start out on the first stage of my new career in motor car racing! I had wanted to work up from the bottom and therefore decided that if I could not do things that way, I would not do it at all—and so I settled back into my business commitments.

Then, quite out of the blue, in June 1961 I received a telephone call from Fred Tuck, an ex-speedway rider and the owner of a Formula 1 Cooper racing car. Fred asked if I would be interested in driving the car at the Nürburgring in Germany and at Karlskoga in Sweden. I had raced my Norton at Karlskoga, a short, bumpy and uninteresting circuit, so that race did not appeal to me very much—but to race at the Nürburgring was something quite different. I had learned my way around

this magnificent circuit in my Gran Tourismo Lancia before riding the Gilera there in 1955, and the prospect of a Formula 1 drive on it was really exciting.

My joy, however, was short-lived. Fred Tuck later advised me that he had been unable to negotiate sufficient starting-money to warrant the cost of competing in such a demanding race. But the Karlskoga race was definitely on if I still wanted to drive. It was a bitter disappointment not to race at the Nürburgring, and my total lack of enthusiasm for Karlskoga should have prompted me to refuse. But I did not want to let Fred down, so, reluctantly, I agreed to race in Sweden.

I flew to Stockholm, where I was met at the airport and taken by car to a hotel near the race circuit. Practice sessions on the day before the race were quite short and I found the rear-engined car a handful to drive. Adding to my problems, the two pinions in the gearbox which determined the overall gear ratio had been put in the wrong way round, thus providing a very high ratio, rather than the lowest one possible. There was insufficient time between practice sessions to correct the gearbox problem, so all practising was carried out using only first and second gear!

Race day was fine, but I was not happy. Due to the slow practice times I was at the back of the grid, and when the race started I had to learn how to drive the car with its now-corrected gear ratios.

After four laps I was beginning to get the hang of things. Then, just as I changed up into third gear coming out of a left-hand bend, the gearbox locked up solid! The car slewed around, hit a grass bank, and then shot high in the air, rolling over and crashing upside down! The last thing I remember was pushing myself free from the cockpit. . . . Roy Salvadori was racing behind me at the time, and he later told me that I dropped to the ground face up—and the car then fell on top of me!

My injuries were extensive: ribs torn from the sternum, a collapsed left lung, damage to my heart muscles, broken collar-bone, cracked pelvis and a burst blood vessel that produced a 'balloon' on my left hip.

After a few days in hospital, but totally unaware of the extent of my injuries, I began to pester the hospital staff to let me go home. Reluctantly, they finally agreed, but a member of the race organizing club had to accompany me, by train and taxi, to Stockholm where I could join a BEA flight to London's Heathrow Airport. It had been arranged for my late wife Pat to meet me there, prior to our flying home to the Isle of Man.

I suppose this arrangement worked fairly well—at least until I reached London. Feeling decidedly poorly, I was duly deposited at Stockholm airport and awaited the flight. On being called, I set off with 50 or so other passengers to walk about 200 yards to the aircraft, but it was a terrible struggle for me and everybody else was seated by the time I reached the Comet aircraft. As I climbed the steps, I remember the worried face of the stewardess as she asked: 'Are you all right, sir?' I was not all right—but I would not have admitted it under any circumstances. I replied: 'Yes, thank you,' and staggered to my seat, never more thankful to sit down.

At Heathrow, I somehow or other missed my wife,

In full flight with the front-engined 'Chequered Flag'
Gemini in August 1960

anxiously waiting outside the customs exit. So, moving very slowly, I made my way downstairs to the domestic check-in area—only to discover that there was no flight to the Isle of Man that evening. At that moment, my wife found me—I was leaning on a barrier for support, because in that same instance my leg locked up!

I was taken to the nearby Ariel Hotel for the night, and while we were waiting to register, I came as near as I ever have to fainting. I felt very ill.

The next morning, BEA provided the necessary transport—wheelchair, etc—and we were soon back home on the Island at our Arragon Hotel. I went straight to bed and Pat called for the doctor. He arrived very smartly, put his stethoscope on my chest, and then immediately called for an ambulance!

Once in Noble's Hospital, X-rays and various tests revealed the full extent of my injuries, and I slowly began to recover from the most physically shattering experience of my life. When I rose to leave after my final clearance from the specialist who had been treating me, he said: 'Just remember that you were very near death!' I got the message. . . .

Scuderia Duke

The agreement between Gilera, Mondial and Moto Guzzi (and initially MV Agusta) to withdraw from Grand Prix racing at the end of 1957 had come as a complete surprise to me, for Gilera had suggested that I might retire from riding at the end of that season with a view to taking over from Roberto Persi as the racing manager for 1958. We had also discussed a major redesign of the four-cylinder 500 cc engine as it was then felt that Remor's ten-year-old design had reached the limit of development; it was going to be necessary to alter the bore and stroke to oversquare dimensions, have four valves per cylinder, and even fuel injection was being considered. I was also keen for a monocoque chassis with trailing-link front forks. Disc brakes were also a must.

However, that ambitious plan was not to be. The Gilera accountants argued that racing the Gilera way was too expensive and that racing success had little effect on selling road machines. The accountants won and for a while it appeared that they were right, for in 1958 Gilera produced and sold more production machines than ever before. But after that, there was an unquestionable decline in sales.

It was during a visit to the factory at Arcore in 1959, and later with Reg Armstrong, that I tried to persuade Commendatore Giuseppe Gilera to provide machines for Bob McIntyre to race. Bob had joined the team in 1957, marking his performance with a double TT victory that included the first-ever 100 mph lap of the Island. He had also regained for Gilera the world one-hour record by covering 141 miles in 60 minutes around the Monza speed-bowl on a 350 cc four. Despite his admiration for McIntyre, however, Mr Gilera refused. But I persisted, and though he did eventually agree, the plan was scuttled when McIntyre signed with Honda for the 1961 season—and Gilera would not consider any other rider at that time.

Bob McIntyre's association with Gilera had begun when Reg Armstrong retired from the Gilera team in 1956 and I suggested that Bob be brought into the team as his replacement. At the time I had forgotten that Bob had done most of his racing in the UK, so I was rather shocked when there was a marked lack of enthusiasm for

my recommendation of him—and more so, when the Gilera team manager, Roberto Persi, asked: 'Who is he?' However, the resistance to McIntyre was soon overcome, and I am happy to say that the subsequent results he achieved gave Gilera no cause for regret and vindicated both Bob and myself.

I had watched Bob's racing progress for some time and had quickly formed the opinion that here was a most tenacious rider, meticulous in his machine preparation and possessing that all-too-rare ability to accurately assess the raceworthiness of his mount and to then successfully pass on that information to development engineers and mechanics.

From memory, I had only one real dice with Bob which was at Scarborough, during the mid-1950s. As I remember, he pushed me hard from start to finish. He was on a comparatively slow Manx Norton, but I had to break the track record to win on my Gilera four. That was proof for me of Bob's tenacity and riding ability.

The 1957 TT, as already mentioned, was unquestionably his most outstanding racing performance. Typical of him, he chose to race with full streamlining, which raised the maximum speed by about 12 mph. Had the weather been unkind, though, it would have been more of a handicap than a help in the strong cross-winds which sometimes affect the Mountain course. Personally, I would not have taken the chance. But Bob did, and thus the first-ever 100 mph TT lap went into the record books, along with brilliant wins in both the Junior and Senior races. Need I say more?

Curiously, Bob McIntyre did play a part in bringing Gilera back to racing, in 1963. Following his tragic death, resulting from a crash at Oulton Park in 1962, a tribute to this fine and most determined rider was held at the circuit, where I was asked to demonstrate the 1957 four-cylinder Gilera. The factory agreed, and provided a most beautifully prepared fully-streamlined 500—identical to McIntyre's 1957 TT mount—and they sent it along with 'my' race mechanic, Giovanni Fumagalli, for the Bob McIntyre Memorial occasion.

Although it had been three years since my retirement from racing in 1959, I thoroughly enjoyed my outing,

On the starting line at the Bob McIntyre Memorial Meeting, Oulton Park, in 1962. This was the demonstration which led to the formation of Scuderia Duke in 1963

which was further enhanced the next day when Avons booked the track for a tyre-testing session. With the machine fitted with the then-revolutionary 'cling' tyre compounds, I could hardly believe the amount of grip I was getting, and after a few laps, I recorded my fastest-ever lap time around Oulton Park.

After this eye-opening experience, and appreciating my lack of race practice—not to mention the advancing years—I could hardly wait to visit Arcore once again in an effort to persuade Gilera that their 'ageing' machine was still competitive. I was convinced that, in the hands of riders of the calibre of Derek Minter and John Hartle, the 500 Gilera four was probably still capable of beating the 500 MV Agusta, which had taken five consecutive World Championships after Count Domenico Agusta

chose to opt out of the no-racing agreement he had originally agreed with Gilera, Mondial and Guzzi in 1957. I emphasized to Commendatore Gilera that this lack of opposition for MV, racing mainly against private-owner singles, probably meant that very little development had gone into the four-cylinder works engines after 1957.

I asked him to lend the 1957 machines to me, but provide works mechanics to maintain them. I agreed to find the necessary finance, thus incurring very little expense to Gilera. Almost, but not totally, convinced, Commendatore Gilera agreed to a test session at Monza where, if lap times appeared competitive, he said the machines would be lent to me for 1963.

It was a historic moment when the old machines, with new fairings to comply with 1963 regulations, the latest Girling rear-suspension struts and Avon racing tyres, were wheeled out for that high-speed testing session at Monza. They were to be ridden by the 'King of Brands', Derek Minter—an exceptionally talented rider regarded

Above Derek Minter (mounted) and John Hartle prepare to test the four-cylinder Gilera at Monza

more as a short-circuit ace, yet overlooked as a TT winner and the first rider to lap the TT at 100 mph on a single-cylinder machine—and also the very experienced John Hartle, for whom I had the greatest respect. Both riders were soon circulating at 115 mph, and towards the end of the session Minter put in a lap of 118 mph, just a touch outside John Surtees' MV lap record.

Thus convinced, Gilera gave me the go-ahead. But unfortunately for the success of the project, most of the anticipated sponsors I approached for financial help did not share my enthusiasm and confidence, and before I started I realized I would have to bear the brunt of the cost myself. I was therefore unable to pay for anything beyond the cost of keeping the machines in race trim. Development work was out of the question, and with so little income, my agreement with Minter and Hartle had to be extremely flexible, allowing them to ride other

Right Minter (Gilera) leads Read (Norton) at Oulton Park in 1963

Below right Hartle in action at Oulton Park in 1963

machines when the Gileras were not available. This decision, though, was forced upon me and was one I was later to regret. Although there was no retainer fee paid to the riders, they were to receive 50 per cent of whatever starting-money I was able to arrange; they also kept all prize money and trade bonuses.

The first outing was at Silverstone in the BMCRC Hutchinson 100. Clearly, the Gileras were the main attraction, for the massive crowd braved a foul day to watch Minter and Hartle take first and second places—so far, so good. The first confrontation with MV should have been at Brands Hatch, but it failed to materialize when Mike Hailwood crashed his 7R AJS in the 350 race, chipping a bone in his left hand. There was great disappointment at Mike's enforced withdrawal from the 500 race, as everyone at the circuit was eager for the personal clash between 'King' Minter and Hailwood. Nevertheless, the crowd rose to a scintillating display by Minter who, in the 1000 cc race, became the first rider to lap the Kentish circuit at more than 90 mph. John Hartle brought his Gilera home in second place.

With Hailwood still sidelined, the following meeting at Oulton Park was a one-two repetition of Silverstone, but with first Minter and then Hartle breaking the lap record, which proved that Hartle, too, was coming to grips with the Arcore four. Then, where better than Imola for the first clash of the Titans. Gilera and MV supporters turned out in their thousands—and what a race it was!

Below The OM race transporter with our logo

Phil Read on the starting line at the 1963 Belgian GP

Hailwood and Silvio Grassetti made superb starts on MV fours, as did Remo Venturi on the Bianchi twin. But Hartle and Minter were particularly slow off the mark. Derek seemed to make a habit of this—perhaps the adrenalin flowed to greater effect when storming through the field, which he was usually able to do. However, in my experience, one cannot afford to sacrifice the advantage of a rapid start when confronted with a rider of Mike Hailwood's extreme ability. But on that Imola occasion, Minter was on the MV rider's rear wheel within five stupendous laps and he soon took the lead. In fairness to Mike, though, I feel sure he must have been feeling the effect of his Brands injury; he seemed unable to sustain his early pace and, before the end, Hartle rubbed salt into the MV wound by taking second place!

It was after this victory at Imola that I came to realize Minter could be a bit of a prima donna. As he was the acknowledged team leader, he always had the engine showing the best power on the test-bed, but quite by chance on this occasion, Hartle was able to out-accelerate

him coming out of slow curves. Derek claimed that to combat this advantage he was forced to outbrake John going into the corners. He seemed upset that Hartle had been given the better engine, but this was unintentional and I was surprised he reacted as he did.

The Grand Prix season now lay ahead of us and, so far, Scuderia Duke had acquitted itself rather well. At the Arcore factory, the Gilera engineers had managed to squeeze six gears into the original five-speed gearbox which, for the Isle of Man TT, should help acceleration. I felt very confident. Hartle was a great road racer and Minter's current form was positively meteoric. Then, during May, disaster struck! While the Gileras were being prepared for the TT, Derek, understandably, I suppose, chose to invoke our agreement and ride his own 500 Manx Norton at Brands Hatch—John Hartle did the same thing and nipped over to the Continent where he scored a win at the Saar Grand Prix.

Minter was not so lucky, however. I was not at Brands, but according to information received later, Minter became involved in a real ding-dong of a scrap with Dave Downer on Paul Dunstall's 650 Norton twin which, if no faster than Derek's 500 single, had better acceleration. During their neck-and-neck race, Derek repeatedly took the lead on the twisty parts of the circuit, only to lose it when Downer used the superior power of his engine coming out of Clearways to overtake Derek on the short straight to the finishing line.

To add to Derek's problems, oil leaking from the cambox of his engine was finding its way on to the rear tyre and his machine began to slide under hard acceleration coming out of corners. It was this lack of adhesion which ultimately caused Derek to crash. Trying really hard towards the end of the race, down he went and poor Dave Downer had no chance of avoiding Minter's fallen machine. Downer was thrown in the 100 mph mêlée and was killed instantly. Minter survived but sustained a broken back.

Of course, it is easy to be wise after the event. Derek, with the prospect of a great Grand Prix season ahead of him and the possibility of the 500 cc world title, should perhaps have been more restrained and settled for second place. But he hated to be beaten, especially at Brands, and in the heat of battle it is sometimes difficult to think logically.

To say that I was shattered when I heard this news would be an understatement. I had pinned my faith on Minter who, at the peak of his racing career, was the only rider capable of beating Mike Hailwood. I had a gut feeling there and then that my plan for a victorious return by Gilera had been dealt a mortal blow. I was reasonably sure that John Hartle could do battle with Hailwood on a road circuit, especially the TT where he was outstanding. But I always had a lingering doubt in my mind about John's ability to sustain the pressure of cut-and-thrust racing in the massed-start Grands Prix. Whether this was due to lack of stamina or some obscure psychological factor is debatable. The fact remains that John was good, but not superb, and could not ride ultra-hard to win.

With Minter injured, I then had to decide whether or not to leave all my eggs in one basket. As things turned out, I mistakenly offered a Gilera to Phil Read. Still young and comparatively inexperienced, Phil Read was even then a rider of exceptional ability. My own observation of him on Snaefell when he won the Senior Manx Grand Prix in 1960 was proof enough of this for me. However, I was totally unprepared for the effect that subsequent success would have on his ego! Read was an individualist, not a team man. Worst of all, though, he seemed incapable of accepting advice from any quarter, no matter how well intentioned or informed.

The 1963 world classic season opened with the West German Grand Prix at Hockenheim on 26 May. The 4.7-mile circuit was then the fastest in the world, with a lap record of 129.57 mph that had been set by Bob McIntyre (Gilera four) in 1957. Curiously, though, in 1963 there was no 500 cc race. The major event was for 350s, and it soon became clear that the resurrected 1957 Gilera was no match for the 1962–63 Honda four ridden by Jim Redman. The essential difference was that the 350 Gilera was a scaled-down version of the 500 cc model, while the 350 Honda was an enlarged 250, being both lighter and more powerful.

Redman won the 20-lap race at a record 121.85 mph, with a lap record of 123.23 mph. Second place went to Remo Venturi on a Bianchi twin, with Phil Read (Gilera), who had been lapped by the winner, placed third.

The first Grand Prix appearance of the 500 cc Scuderia Duke Gilera team was at the Isle of Man TT, where they were raced by John Hartle and Phil Read. Practice was uneventful, except for the ease with which Hailwood reeled off every lap he rode on the 500 MV at over 100 mph! Clearly, this was throwing down the gauntlet to Gilera, but it failed to ruffle Hartle, who went well and remained quietly confident. In the race, though, Mike's performance was sensational. He opened with a lap of 106.3 mph, followed it with another of 106.4 mph, and then eased to win at 104.64 mph. In his pursuit, John Hartle lapped at a magnificent 105.57 mph and third-placed Phil Read also averaged over 100 mph—the fastest-ever Gilera performances at the TT—but still not good enough to win. Hartle was also second to Redman's Honda in the 350 cc race and it began to look as if the 1957 Gilera machines should have remained in honourable retirement. . . .

Team spirit, though, was given a boost at the Dutch TT, where Hartle and Read scored first and second in the 500 cc race, albeit after Hailwood retired with a holed piston on his MV. Mike replied with a vengeance at the Belgian Grand Prix, which he won at 123.99 mph, faster than the previous lap record. Phil Read was a trailing second after Hartle retired with main-bearing trouble.

A brief moment of glory for Scuderia Duke at the Dutch TT at Assen in 1963, with John Hartle on the rostrum

Derek Minter returned for the Ulster Grand Prix where Hailwood was yet again the winner, with Hartle in second place and Minter third, Phil Read having come off. Hailwood then repeated his victory performance at the East German Grand Prix where Minter was second, though five minutes behind, and Hartle retired with a loose front mudguard.

Possible World Championship success had now gone, but after Hartle, the sole Gilera runner at the Finnish Grand Prix, retired, the factory provided Scuderia Duke with three machines for the Italian Grand Prix at Monza, situated just a few miles from the Arcore factory. That made the embarrassment complete. Rather than it becoming a face-saving finale to the season, Hailwood won at a record 118.07 mph, lapping the entire field twice! The Gilera challenge ended with Hartle sidelined by a practice crash, Read retired after ten laps of the race, and Minter went out after completing only three more. It also meant the end for Scuderia Duke.

Racing connections

After the demise of Scuderia Duke, my spirits were raised by an invitation in 1964 from Leo Davenport, winner of the Lightweight TT on a New Imperial in 1932, and then managing director of Royal Enfield, to assist in the design of a 250 cc road-racing machine powered by a single-cylinder two-stroke engine. Although intended primarily as a production racer, Leo was, nevertheless, keen to undertake a limited programme of racing with factory support.

Ken Sprayson of Reynolds was responsible for the frame design which, at my instigation, had a one-piece fibreglass fuel-tank-cum-seat of about six gallons capacity, the fuel being stored throughout the full length of the unit. This helped to reduce the overall height of the tank and distributed the fuel load over approximately

two-thirds of the machine's length. The 'pistol-grip' shape of the well-baffled unit ensured an adequate supply of fuel to the carburettor, down to the last pint.

The front forks were of the leading-link type originally designed for my lightweight Norton. Front and rear brakes had 'floating' brake plates to allow free movement of the suspension, even under hard braking. Alloy inserts in the frame, with a variety of positions for the rear swinging-arm pivot spindle, provided rear chain adjustment, while maintaining accurate wheel alignment and rigidity.

I was instrumental in bringing in Herman Meier, the

The 250 Royal Enfield which I helped to design and develop

Sitting proudly astride the Royal Enfield

brilliant two-stroke engine specialist, to look after engine development, and he was certainly successful in that the horsepower of the engine was increased quite dramatically, although lack of reliability was a constant problem. Some idea of its performance can be gleaned from one appearance at Silverstone when it was ridden by Percy Tait, who led Phil Read and Mike Duff on works Yamahas for three laps, breaking the 250 lap record at 94 mph in the process, although he eventually had to settle for third place due to piston trouble. Conscious of the engine's limitations, Meier proposed the design of an in-line, liquid-cooled, twin-cylinder two-stroke engine, with disc valves, for which he produced a general layout and specification. Funding for the project, though, was not forthcoming.

During my year with Royal Enfield, I suggested a design for a very simple and inexpensive car which I felt sure would be popular at a time when the cost of four-wheeled vehicles was really beginning to take off. The engine I proposed was the Austrian Styr Daimler Puch air-cooled, horizontally-opposed, twin-cylinder,

overhead-valve unit which they fitted into the Fiat Topolino chassis and body, a vehicle which they were licensed by Fiat to sell in Austria. In the Royal Enfield, the engine was to be front-mounted and would drive the front wheels through a simple automatic transmission of the belt and expanding-pulley type, used in the DKW Hobby scooter.

I visited the Styr Daimler factory in Graz later in the year, and after a tour of the production facility we discussed my proposal. A quotation for the supply of engines was made available within two weeks. However, it was soon apparent that this project, too, was beyond the financial scope of Royal Enfield, and so the matter rested.

Then, at the end of 1964, I became involved yet again with a motorcycle event when a meeting of the Isle of Man Tourist Board Race Committee was called to consider a request from the Autocycle Union for the 1965 International Six Days Trial to be held in the Isle of Man. It was agreed that the project was feasible and I later volunteered—or was I conscripted?—to undertake the task of planning routes totalling in excess of 1000 miles as part of the course.

I had no personal experience of the ISDT other than

as a spectator at Varese, Italy, in 1951 when Great Britain won the Trophy, plus an invitation to take part in tests to decide who should be included in the British Vase team in 1949, an invitation which I was unable to accept due to my road-racing commitments. However, I had been Clerk of the Course for several Manx Two Days Trials, so I did have some experience of trials organization plus a good knowledge of the Island's terrain.

My first task was to persuade Jack Quayle to be my assistant. Jack, a great enthusiast who had been an invaluable ally of mine in the Two Days Trial organization, was vital to my plans and I was relieved when he accepted my invitation. My second task, with the aid of an inch-to-a-mile map of the Island, was to plot the theoretical routes of the required length, mainly off-road, split into north, south and central areas of the Island. This large mileage concentrated in a comparatively small area prompted one well-known UK sidecar trials exponent, who had recently taken up residence in the Island, to declare in a letter to the editor of a motorcycle magazine that the project was unattainable, as such mileage would involve the use of everyone's back garden! At this stage, of course, we could not be sure that the previously-unused tracks and sections of moorland, of which there were many, could be traversed by a motorcycle. So the next step was a recce of the ground.

My visit to the Styr Daimler Puch factory in 1964, when I had been very impressed by a demonstration run in a Haflinger cross-country vehicle, prompted me to request the purchase of one of these fantastic little vehicles. Powered by a 600 cc twin-cylinder engine with incredible torque for its capacity, plus a five-speed gearbox, four-wheel drive, and lockable diffs which could be easily engaged whilst on the move, this machine would be invaluable.

My request approved, the Haflinger arrived on the Island and we commenced our recce, much of it involving foot-slogging along paths overgrown with gorse through years of neglect which even the Haflinger could not traverse, and making copious notes as we progressed, always bearing in mind the fickle Manx weather which could dramatically affect ground conditions. Our recce completed, with some route diversions recorded on our map, we then set about checking out the ownership of the land and I personally visited more than 100 private landowners and farmers requesting permission for the trial to cross their land. Some required 'gentle persuasion', but an indication of the general enthusiasm for motorcycle sporting activity on the Island can be gleaned from the fact that there were only two dissenters.

The next move was to enlist the help of members of motorcycle clubs on the Island to clear a way through miles of undergrowth where this was too extensive for Jack and myself to deal with, thus enabling us to establish the continuity of each route. Of course, undergrowth was not the only problem; on two occasions, even the

Haflinger with its four-wheel drive got completely bogged down, needing to be dug out. And sometimes, despite all our efforts, including flat-out attacks on the terrain, the Haflinger ground to a halt. The system we devised to solve this problem involved setting the alternative hand throttle at a fast tick-over with all four wheels spinning, and then we would dismount and push. However, this had its hazardous, though more often hilarious, side when the driving wheels unexpectedly found grip and our unmanned vehicle took off, leaving us flat on our faces in the mud or scrambling to get aboard just in time to prevent it disappearing down a ravine!

The help and co-operation of the Forestry Board, and in particular the Highway Board who built a wooden bridge over the river at Glen Auldyn and dug out a new track on the hillside to bypass an extensive bog, were also invaluable. Thus, months of diligent effort eventually bore fruit.

Detailed schedules covering a wide variety of machines and riders were then submitted to H. P. Baughan, the ACU's expert in this field, who dispatched Jim Whiting, by then appointed joint Assistant Clerk of the Course, to recce the routes and report back when the schedules were fine-tuned and finalized. Early in September, Jack and I started to route-mark the off-road sections of the course in glorious weather. It was during this period that near disaster occurred. I had parked the Haflinger with one wheel against a rock on a one-in-three descent between stone walls, while I placed markers in position. I then suggested to Jack, who was standing by the Haflinger, that he drive the vehicle down the hill to where I was. To date, I had done almost all the driving. Jack climbed aboard, started the engine and had to rev the engine quite hard to surmount the rock obstructing the front wheel. Suddenly, the vehicle leapt forward and Jack trod on the clutch pedal instead of the brake, rocketing down the hill towards me and the near-vertical drop behind me. Helpless, I leapt out of the way just as Jack found the brake pedal. This caused the Haflinger literally to stand on its front-end, within a foot or so of the drop. Fortunately, without performing a somersault!

Also, I shall never forget the look of sheer horror on the face of a shepherd at Glen Auldyn as he watched us leave the track, which still required clearing, to descend diagonally down the steep grass slope into the river. The Haflinger, which was piled high with wooden route markers, had Jack hanging off the side of the vehicle like a trials sidecar passenger to prevent it rolling down the hillside!

It was the evening of the day before the trial commenced when we placed our last marker in position, thoroughly exhausted at the end of 15 days of working 6 am to dusk, thankful that the weather had been kind to us. That night the heavens opened and the rain hardly abated during the following six days, transforming parts of the course into a quagmire. Ironically, one of the best

Above *Jim Sandiford on a 350 BSA (number 258) leads Manxman Dennis Crane (350 Jawa) in the 1965 ISDT held on the Island*

sections in the northern part of the Island had to be cut out—not due to the conditions, but because a timekeeper failed to arrive at his post despite detailed directions.

There was also a protracted argument with H. R. (Harold) Taylor, the Chief Depot Marshal, which at the time was just about the last straw. No doubt the problem was of great consequence to Harold, but neither Jack nor I can even recall the details now. And although the East German team manager complained that the trial was too difficult, in the opinion of many it was one of the best ever (the Trophy was won by Czechoslovakia). There were a number of 'clean sheets', with no marks lost, and as there were 300 riders, many of them international stars, competing from 17 nations in the event, in my opinion it should have been difficult—to sort the wheat from the chaff! And so it did.

Right *British Trophy teamster Arthur Lampkin, mounted on a 440 BSA, during the 1965 ISDT*

Looking back

Nine quite separate incidents spread over a period of 24 years profoundly influenced my racing career. The first was the purchase in 1935, with my friends Alec and Tom Merrick, of that 1923 belt-driven Raleigh motorcycle, originally with the intention of using the engine to drive a four-wheeled vehicle. But, as this proved to be beyond our means, the fun we had with the Raleigh in its original form set in motion the train of events which, ultimately, led to my involvement in motorcycle racing.

The second was the advice of the technical Training Officer in the Royal Corps of Signals in 1943, which indirectly brought about my transfer to dispatch rider training at Catterick, and subsequently my retention there as an instructor.

Then there was the letter from Artie Bell in 1947, which resulted in my joining Norton Motors, while the fourth, my crash in 1952, at Schotten, Germany, signalled the end of my association with Nortons.

The statement by Gilbert Smith, managing director of Norton Motors, which appeared in a Birmingham newspaper in May 1953, was the fifth incident to shape my career, changing as it did my direction from four wheels back to two, and into the arms of Gilera.

Then came the private riders' strike in 1955 at Assen, Holland, which I and others supported, and which led to our suspension for six months—'the beginning of the end'. My crash in the 350 cc race at Imola in 1957 was the seventh event, and its unsettling effect led directly to a second crash, in the 500 cc race, which badly dislocated my collar-bone, thus 'opening the door' to the ascendency of Libero Liberati, who then had first priority so far as Gilera were concerned.

The eighth was the withdrawal of Gilera from motorcycle road racing at the end of the 1957 Grand Prix season, which effectively left me without competitive machinery, at a time when I had barely recovered from the traumas of Imola.

Finally, there was my appearance in September 1959 at Locarno, Switzerland, where the unlikely combination of my success in winning the 250, 350 and 500 races, and

the realization that racing had become an effort, decided me, there and then, to call it a day!

I have often been asked if, with all the benefits of hindsight, I would still have taken up motorcycle racing as a career, and if so, given the opportunity, what changes would I wish to make?

My answer to the first question is an unequivocal 'Yes!' The second is more difficult, but just two important variants spring to mind. As already stated, my enthusiasm for racing included the part I was able to play in the development of the machines I rode, and in this respect, if Nortons had had the financial resources to continue with the development of their four-cylinder engine, I would not have left them.

Then, there was the failure of the directors of BSA, partly, it would seem, because the management lacked the spirit of their own convictions, to appreciate the true potential in their 250 cc 'Mechanical Marvel' which could have been the basis for a production 500 cc V-twin and a 1000 cc V4, which, had the original design been pursued, might *just* have prevented the total demise of the British motorcycle industry!

At the time, I did everything within *my* power to encourage the management of BSA to further develop the machine through racing, but the decision of the directors of that company not to allow me to race such a promising machine because: 'There could be no guarantee that it would win', was almost beyond belief, and a bitter disappointment to me personally.

To conclude on a more cheerful note, fate has been very kind to me, in particular through the opportunity that arose out of my involvement as a dispatch riders' instructor during World War 2, and the incredible timing of the letter I received from Artie Bell—on the very day that I virtually accepted employment at Associated Motor Cycles!—which brought about my move to Norton Motors and set in motion my 'pursuit of perfection' as a racing motorcyclist.

A proud Lap of Honour in the Isle of Man

World Championship Grands Prix

1950
350 cc
2nd   Isle of Man TT
3rd   Belgian GP
2nd   Dutch TT
3rd   Swiss GP
1st   Italian GP

1950
500 cc
1st   Isle of Man TT
Ret.   Belgian GP
Ret.   Dutch TT
4th   Swiss GP
1st   Ulster GP
1st   Italian GP

1951
350 cc
Ret.   Swiss GP
1st   Isle of Man TT
1st   Belgian GP
Ret.   Dutch TT
1st   French GP
1st   Ulster GP
1st   Italian GP

1951
500 cc
Ret.   Swiss GP
1st   Isle of Man TT
1st   Belgian GP
1st   Dutch TT
5th   French GP
1st   Ulster GP
4th   Italian GP

1952
350 cc
1st   Swiss GP
1st   Isle of Man TT
1st   Dutch TT
1st   Belgian GP

1952
500 cc
Ret.   Swiss GP
Ret.   Isle of Man TT
2nd   Dutch TT
2nd   Belgian GP

1953
500 cc
Ret.   Isle of Man TT
1st   Dutch TT
Ret.   Belgian GP
1st   French GP
2nd   Ulster GP
1st   Swiss GP
1st   Italian GP

1954
500 cc
Ret.   French GP
2nd   Isle of Man TT
1st   Belgian GP
1st   Dutch TT
1st   German GP
1st   Swiss GP
1st   Italian GP

1955
500 cc
Ret.   Spanish GP
1st   French GP
1st   Isle of Man TT
1st   German GP
Ret.   Belgian GP
1st   Dutch TT
3rd   Italian GP

1956
350 cc
Ret.   Italian GP

1956
500 cc
Ret.   Belgian GP
Ret.   German GP
Ret.   Ulster GP
1st   Italian GP

1957
350 cc
Ret.   Italian GP

1957
500 cc
3rd   Ulster GP
2nd   Italian GP

1958
350 cc
Ret.   Isle of Man TT
Ret.   Dutch TT
5th   Belgian GP
Ret.   German GP
1st   Swedish GP
4th   Ulster GP
3rd   Italian GP

1958
500 cc
Ret.   Isle of Man TT
Ret.   Dutch TT
4th   Belgian GP
Ret.   German GP
1st   Swedish GP
5th   Ulster GP
7th   Italian GP

1959
250 cc
6th   German GP
3rd   Swedish GP
10th   Italian GP

1959
350 cc
4th   Isle of Man TT
4th   German GP
3rd   Ulster GP
Ret.   Italian GP

1959
500 cc
9th   German GP
3rd   Belgian GP
3rd   Ulster GP
3rd   Italian GP

World Champion 500 cc—4
(1951, 1953, 1954, 1955)
World Champion 350 cc—2
(1951, 1952)

1st   place—33
2nd   place— 7
3rd   place—10
4th   place— 6
5th   place— 3
6th   place— 1
7th   place— 1
9th   place— 1
10th   place— 1
Ret.   —24
         —
        87

Retired when leading 14 times

Isle of Man TT Results
1st   place— 6
     (Senior 500 cc—3;
     Junior 350 cc—2;
     Clubmans 500 cc—1)
2nd   place— 2
4th   place— 1
Ret.   — 4
        —
        13

Retired when leading twice

Gilbert **Delahaye** ◆ Marcel **Marlier**

martine
drôle de chien !

Texte de Jean-Louis Marlier

casterman

Découvre les personnages de cette histoire

Martine

Joyeuse et curieuse, Martine adore s'amuser avec ses amis et son petit chien Patapouf. Ensemble, ils découvrent le monde et vivent de véritables aventures. Une chose est sûre : avec Martine, on ne s'ennuie jamais !

Jean

C'est le petit frère de Martine. Avec Jean, Martine se sent grande, et ça lui plaît beaucoup. En plus, tous deux s'entendent à merveille. Être grande sœur, c'est le bonheur !

Paul

Paul est le petit frère de Martine et Jean. Il est adorable et Martine adore s'occuper de lui… Tous les deux s'amusent comme des fous, surtout quand leurs parents sont absents !

Tante Flo

La tante de Martine vit à la montagne. Elle reçoit souvent sa nièce et ses neveux dans son chalet, entouré de champs et de forêts.

Patapouf

Ce petit chien est un vrai clown !
Il fait parfois des bêtises…
mais il est si mignon que Martine
lui pardonne toujours !

Aujourd'hui, le vent souffle très fort. Un temps idéal pour faire
du cerf-volant !

Paul admire le grand oiseau de toile qui plane au-dessus
des montagnes. Il aimerait bien s'envoler lui aussi…

Soudain, une idée lui passe par la tête et il demande :

– Dis, Martine, est-ce que ça chatouille, un nuage ?

En parlant de nuages…

– Regardez! s'écrie Martine en montrant le ciel qui s'assombrit.

Un orage… Il s'approche à toute vitesse! Il faut rentrer chez tante Flo avant l'averse.

– Attendez-moi! dit Jean en rembobinant la ficelle.

Pas facile avec ces rafales… Le cerf-volant virevolte et se débat!

Et les premières gouttes tombent déjà…

Les enfants filent à travers les champs quand le tonnerre se met
à gronder.

– Trop tard ! crie Jean. On ne peut pas aller plus loin, il faut s'abriter
tout de suite !

– Pas sous un arbre ! s'inquiète Martine. C'est trop dangereux :
imagine que la foudre touche une branche…

Un aboiement retentit à cet instant.

«Ouaf! Ouaf!»

Devant les enfants surgit un chien au poil roux. Il montre les dents, grogne, aboie encore…

Pire : il s'avance comme s'il voulait attaquer Martine et ses frères !

– Filons! décide la fillette en attrapant Jean et Paul par la main.

Ils courent jusqu'au porche
d'une ferme.
– Ouf! souffle Martine après avoir
regardé derrière eux. Le chien ne nous
a pas suivis, et on peut se mettre à l'abri.
Le tonnerre et les éclairs se déchaînent.
Paul tremble comme une feuille.
– Ne t'inquiète pas, dit sa sœur.
Il ne peut rien nous arriver. Et tu
verras, dans quelques minutes,
l'orage sera passé.

Martine a raison. Un quart d'heure plus tard, la pluie s'arrête.

Les roulements du tonnerre semblent déjà loin.

Les enfants s'apprêtent à reprendre la route quand, derrière eux,

une porte s'ouvre.

– Qu'est-ce que vous faites là, mes pauvres petits ? Vous ne seriez pas

les neveux de Flo ? Par un temps pareil, elle doit vous chercher partout !

Entrez donc vous sécher…

Qu'il est bon d'être au chaud !

La fermière donne de grandes serviettes aux enfants, puis elle

téléphone à leur tante.

– Flo saute dans sa voiture pour venir vous chercher, annonce-t-elle

en raccrochant. En attendant, si je vous montrais nos animaux ?

Je parie que vous n'avez jamais vu des agneaux nouveau-nés…

Martine ouvre de grands yeux en entrant dans la bergerie.

– Bonjour, toi, dit-elle doucement en s'approchant d'un agneau.

Oh, comme tu trembles…

– Normal, ils n'ont pas d'habits, s'amuse Paul. Leur maman devrait

leur tricoter un bon pull en laine !

Mais Jean n'a déjà plus la tête à plaisanter…

Les yeux ronds, il pousse un cri :

– Le chien !

Paul se réfugie derrière sa sœur.

– J'ai peur… murmure-t-il. Tu crois

qu'il veut nous mordre ?

– Sors d'ici ! crie Martine. Va-t'en !

Jean brandit un balai pour effrayer

l'animal.

– Aouuh… aouuh… glapit le chien en reculant.

Puis il fait demi-tour et détale !

– Tu le vois ? demande Paul.

Tu le vois encore ?

– Non, assure Jean, il a disparu.

Mais s'il s'attaque aux animaux ?

Filons prévenir la fermière !

– Madame ! Madame ! appelle Martine. Un chien est entré dans votre ferme ! Il a l'air dangereux !

– Il voulait nous mordre tout à l'heure, et nous a suivis jusqu'ici ! ajoute Jean.

– Un chien ? Impossible, notre Rouky aurait forcément aboyé.

– Rouky ? répètent les enfants, étonnés. C'est qui ?

La fermière les conduit vers une niche. Martine et ses frères reconnaissent le chien qui les a tant effrayés !

– C'est lui, Rouky ? Et il n'est pas méchant ?

– Au contraire ! Il est aussi doux que mes agneaux…

– Pardon, Rouky… dit Martine. On n'a pas été très gentils avec toi.

On croyait que tu voulais nous mordre.

– Il boude… constate Jean.

– Je peux te caresser ? demande
Martine au chien.

Contre toute attente… Rouky tend
lui-même le museau !

Les trois enfants caressent l'animal
qui jappe joyeusement.

– Les enfants ! s'exclame tante Flo en sortant de sa voiture. J'étais

tellement inquiète de vous savoir seuls sous l'orage ! Je suis passée

à côté d'un arbre qui a été foudroyé…

– Quel arbre ? demande Martine.

– Celui qui est au tournant du chemin. Venez voir !

Les enfants, inquiets, se précipitent sur les pas de leur tante

et découvrent un tronc complètement fendu !

C'est le même arbre !

Les enfants n'en reviennent pas.

– J'ai compris ! s'écrie alors Martine. Rouky est venu pour nous éloigner de cet endroit ! Pas pour nous attaquer…

– C'est très possible, admet sa tante. Les animaux connaissent mieux que nous la nature, leur instinct est très sûr.

– Vu l'état de cet arbre, Rouky
vous a sauvé la vie… conclut
tante FLo. Vous pouvez le
remercier !

– Merci, Rouky ! s'exclame
Martine. Tu es un super chien !

– Tu mérites une triple ration de caresses ! ajoute Jean en l'enlaçant.

Les enfants et Rouky sont maintenant devenus amis.

Ils passent de longues heures à courir dans les prés, à faire

des roulades dans l'herbe et à jouer à la balle.

Martine lui a même présenté Patapouf.

— Rouky est un héros, a-t-elle expliqué. Il nous a sauvé la vie !

– Et toi, Patapouf, demande Paul. Tu nous aurais secourus ?

« Ouaf ! Ouaf ! » fait le petit chien avec assurance.

– Tu parles… répond Martine avec un clin d'œil. Je le connais, mon

Patapouf : au premier coup de tonnerre, il se serait réfugié sous le lit !

Retrouve **martine** dans d'autres aventures !

martine au parc

martine garde son petit frère

martine fête son anniversaire

martine jardine

martine fait du vélo

martine petit rat de l'opéra

martine à la fête des fleurs

martine fait la cuisine

martine apprend à nager

martine est malade

martine en vacances

martine prend le train

martine fait de la voile

martine et le petit moineau

martine et le petit âne

martine fête maman

martine
en montgolfière

martine
à l'école

martine
découvre la musique

martine
a perdu son chien

martine
dans la forêt

martine
et le cadeau
d'anniversaire

martine
et la sorcière

martine
un mercredi
pas comme les autres

martine
la nuit de Noël

martine
déménage

martine
se déguise

martine
et les chatons

martine
et les lapins
du jardin

martine
à l'hôpital

martine
baby-sitter

martine
en classe de découverte

martine
la leçon de dessin

martine
au pays des contes

martine
et les marmitons

martine
prépare une surprise

martine
l'arche des animaux

martine
princesses et chevaliers

martine
et les fantômes

martine
un amour de poney

martine
la dispute

martine
drôle de chien !

martine
protège la nature

martine
et le prince mystérieux

Casterman
Cantersteen 47
1000 Bruxelles

www.casterman.com

ISBN : 978-2-203-10695-6
N° d'édition : L.10EJCN000507.C002

© Casterman, 2016
D'après les albums de Gilbert Delahaye et Marcel Marlier.
Achevé d'imprimer en septembre 2017, en Italie.
Dépôt légal : juin 2016 ; D.2016/0053/153
Déposé au ministère de la Justice, Paris (loi n°49.956
du 16 juillet 1949 sur les publications destinées à la jeunesse).